Trevor Hu

Turbulent Priest

PIERS McGRANDLE

continuum
LONDON • NEW YORK

CONTINUUM
The Tower Building, 11 York Road, London SE1 7NX
15 East 26th Street, New York NY 10010

www.continuumbooks.com

First published 2004

British Library Cataloguing-in-Publication Data
A catalogue record for this book is available from the British Library.

ISBN: 0-8264-7123-4 (hardback)

Typeset by Kenneth Burnley, Wirral, Cheshire
Printed and bound in Great Britain by MPG Books Ltd, Bodmin, Cornwall

Contents

Contents

Foreword

ARCHBISHOP DESMOND TUTU

When did I first meet Father Trevor Huddleston? Oh, he was father to so many in Sophiatown. I thought it was when I started school in 1944 in what was called Western Native Township. It was a high school started by Father Raymond Raynes when he was priest-in-charge of Christ the King in Sophiatown, a position in which Father Trevor succeeded him. This would have been in 1945, at the end of World War II. Father Huddleston came to our school to speak on VE day and I was always amused at how he pronounced 'Nazi'. I thought he didn't know how to pronounce. But actually that was not the first time I met him.

The very first time was when I was a boy of about eight or nine. My mother was working as a domestic worker/cook in the hostel for black blind women at the Blind Institute called Ezenzeleni, 'place where you do things for yourself', meant to encourage black blind people not to feel sorry for themselves but to know that they could achieve. This institute had been started by a remarkable English couple, Arthur and Florence Blaxall. We were standing with my mother on the balcony of the women's hostel where she was cook when this white man in a big black hat and a white flowing cassock swept past on the way to the residence of the Blaxalls. You could have knocked me down with a feather, young as I was at the time, when this man doffed his hat to my mother; I couldn't understand a white man doffing his hat to a black woman, an uneducated woman. At the time, of course, it was just an incident among many which one thought one has forgotten; but it made, it appeared later, a very deep impression on me and said a great deal about the person who had done this. For it was, as I later discovered, none other than Father Huddleston, who had come to be priest-in-charge of Christ the King Church and prior of Christ the King Priory of the Community of the Resurrection.

I know that he was a man of very deep prayer and that is what sustained him in his campaigns to alleviate the sorry lot of the people that he loved so dearly. He was a spellbinding speaker as he sought to raise the consciousness of South African whites to the plight of blacks, and he was very much in the forefront in the struggle to save Sophiatown when, in 1948, the Nationalist government came to power. Dr Verwoerd was then in charge of what was called Native Affairs and set as his object the destruction of Sophiatown, because it was an anomaly in their policy which regarded all black people as birds of passage, temporary denizens of the white man's town. Sophiatown stuck out as a sore thumb because, there, blacks had what was unacceptable, freehold title to their land.

Father Huddleston helped to galvanize the people in their efforts to resist this, the first move to destroy a stable black community, the first of many such instances. You know that Sophiatown was killed and the white suburb which replaced Sophiatown was called in Afrikaans 'Triomf'. With the subtlety of a bull in a china shop, to rub salt into the wounds of black people who had seen their life's savings going down the drain with the destruction of the homes they had built so painstakingly, many of the street names in Triomf are the street names of the old Sophiatown streets. So many of us who lived in that teeming, bustling place, when we drive through Triomf, drive through Ray Street, Annandale, Meyer Street. I shall never forget what this government did to our people. And Trevor sought to stop that great indignity to people he loved very deeply. He was among those who participated in one of the great political highlights of our country in the 20th century, the signing in 1955 of the Freedom Charter, which set out the ideals for a non-racial democratic South Africa; and Trevor was held in such high regard that he was given the highest award that our people could give: a matted ring worn by great warriors at the back of their heads, a kind of halo.

We just want to thank God so very much for the wonderful, wonderful person who made us blacks realize that not all whites were the same. There were and continue to be many whites who care about justice, about peace, about people, who care about people very much. I was in hospital for twenty months with TB, and if Father Huddleston was in Johannesburg he made it a point to visit me at least once a week during those twenty months. I was just a nonentity, thirteen years old, and yet he paid so much attention to me. He touched my life and I am certain that I owe a very, very great deal to him as I do to so many others. He touched the lives of many others. Hugh Masekala, the jazz trumpeter, got his first trumpet from Father Huddleston, who had got it as a gift from Louis Satchmo Armstrong, as only he could. But there are many, many others that one could name who were probably set on the road to their ultimate vocation by this remarkable man.

And if blacks still talked to white people, an extraordinary miracle in apartheid South Africa, then it would be in large measure due to people like Trevor who made us realize that we too count, we too matter in the sight of God, we too even when we are black are people to whom hats ought to be doffed.

He swore that he would not die before apartheid had collapsed. Well, he attended the inauguration of his friend, Nelson Mandela, as the first democratically elected President of the new and free South Africa. What a glorious vindication for the one who could make a street urchin feel so special.

Preface

Trevor mistrusted biographies. When he became well known in the 1950s, he was pestered by writers keen to write about his life. But he remained wary of their motives, their competence, and – perhaps – what they might find. Writing to one hopeful biographer in 1973, he said:

> My experience with Joe Rogaly [a renowned *Financial Times* journalist] who was going to write such a biography, and who came to Masasi to gather material, was so unfortunate that I deeply regret ever consenting and was only too thankful when he finally gave up the attempt. It meant the creation of a totally false relationship because, although he is highly intelligent and an extremely good journalist, he just could not grasp at all the underlying Christian motivation of my life and therefore he was always making totally false judgements about my actions. It was equally impossible for me to criticize or change these judgements without appearing to be obstructive.

Trevor would later concede that Rogaly was a suitable biographer. But trouble had, apparently, occurred during one of the journalist's visits to Africa. Everything, it seems, went wrong when unsavoury material and conversations appeared; Trevor grew suspicious, was shocked by what he read in the draft pages and the biography never appeared. In a further letter to the same biographer, written a week later, Trevor added: 'It is quite simply that I do not believe a biography ought to be written until the subject is dead . . . It is quite extraordinarily difficult for people who are asked for their views to give them truthfully when the person about whom they are speaking is still alive and will read their views in print.'

Trevor is now dead, and many of his surviving friends have given me frank yet affectionate recollections of a man who was once compared to a kindly English parson armed with a flick knife. These recollections are invaluable, but problems remain when writing a biography of Trevor. Unlike other renowned Anglican clerics, Trevor did not leave behind a mass of material. There are plenty of newspaper articles about him, and a fair number by him; there is also a number of slight books and one masterpiece. There are plenty of personal letters and sermons and rather bland Episcopal missives from thousands of miles overseas. Yet he left behind no spiritual journals, revelatory diaries or gossipy transcripts in the style of Robert Runcie.

This is the second biography of Bishop Huddleston. The first was authorized and written by the Anglican priest Robin Denniston, who published *Naught for Your Comfort* in 1956. It is a shrewd and readable account of his life, though too political for many tastes. Two attempts have been abandoned; one through illness by Canon Eric James, who has handed me his papers and offered all the help he can; the other through frustration by Joe Rogaly. There are many references to Trevor in biographies of twentieth-century Anglican figures, and he appears in any number of theses on the role of the priest in twentieth-century South Africa or the decline of the Western missionary movement.

My book, I hope, will be different. Trevor means nothing to people of my generation; he is as relevant to them as the Campaign for Nuclear Disarmament and the three-day week. I want to show why he matters and why he should be remembered. As the Very Revd Alan Webster noted in Trevor's obituary, published in the *Independent* newspaper a few days after Trevor's death in April 1998, the strength of the Church of England in the 1950s lay in its 'complete inability to control the spiritual powers of Huddleston and his followers, who captivated Christians as did no other religious leader in the second half of the twentieth century'.

So how did Trevor Huddleston show a generation how to be religious? How did a gaunt idealist from a minor public school transform himself into an authoritarian monk? Why did this son of the Empire, a great lover of fly fishing and rugby whose father had commanded the Indian Navy, spend an austere life clashing with authority? What was it that drove this gentle man, who combined the ease of patrician England with the white fury of the agitator?

For, as my book will show, Trevor was angry. He was fuelled by rage, which usually expressed itself in a restless urgency, but could distort itself into a depression and self-laceration which he could not control. His single-minded anger was effective, but ostracized him from many of his colleagues. The Church of England, unlike the Roman Catholic Church, has never been at ease with saints and prophets and martyrs. For all their vaunted catholicity, most moderate Anglicans viewed Trevor as awkward and irritating and a massive bore when it came to South Africa.

There was also a romantic streak in Trevor, which explains why he entered the monastery at such a young age; he was attracted by the heroic strain in the Anglican tradition, and enjoyed the monastic life for its stress on sacrifice and discipline. He was an intense and serious man who needed heroes. It is no surprise that Trevor was 'very greatly attracted' to Frank Weston, the Bishop of Zanzibar at the turn of last century. Like Trevor, Weston, too, had an ambivalent relationship with the Church of England; one lady worker, thinking of converting to Rome, told him: 'I have no longer any faith in the Church of England.' Frank Weston replied: 'I have never had any faith in the Church of England; it is not an article of faith, it is where God has placed me.' Weston exuded urgency and spirit and purpose; so too did Trevor.

But there were differences, too. As a priest, Trevor was largely generous and humble, while Weston was despotic. Trevor's attitude towards himself was biblical ('If any man would come after me . . . deny himself'). He saw himself as a Christian Socialist; he was never content to be just a Christian pastor or a political activist. Or, as the South African author Nadine Gordimer once noted: 'He is a good politician, that churchman.' But he was too worldly to wish his life on other people; equally, he was adept at suppressing his despair, or at least concealing it in public. He exuded warmth and humour, not dullness and gravity. As Archbishop Desmond Tutu said: 'He is so unEnglish in so many ways, being very fond of hugging people, embracing them and in the way he laughs. He does not laugh with his teeth; he laughs with his whole body, his whole being.'

He was also vain. A handsome and striking man, he would exploit his charm and authority when dealing with policemen and politicians.

This vanity could spill over into self-obsession and egoism; he could be flamboyant and behave like a prima donna. We have never taken our bishops terribly seriously, but a certain glamour surrounds those who combine charisma with force of will. Trevor was one of these bishops; he adored the limelight and loved publicity, while remaining aware of the costly nature of leadership. He had a hard life, but it was not just a lonely vocation, spent among the despised.

So there was heroism, generosity, vanity. But was Trevor the depressive missionary priest, who could reduce his chaplains to tears and berate God for not quickening his death? Was he the faithful Man of God, happiest in his prayers or in the company of children? Was he the charismatic self-publicist, who loved the company of journalists and bemoaned that he did not appear on *Any Questions* every day of the week?

What we can say is that Trevor's life cannot be measured against the backcloth of a sleepy diocese or a slum parish or a cathedral close or an academic department; it should be seen, rather, against the changing face of worldwide Anglicanism. Trevor was part of the tail end of a 200-year-old missionary movement from the West to other parts of the world, and it was a movement which transformed the position of Christianity as a world religion. Trevor was a political radical who thrived in this conservative and paternalist tradition; he enjoyed a father-and-son relationship with his flock wherever he served – whether it was South Africa, Masasi, Mauritius or even Swindon.

What is certain, too, is that the dust and filth and open skies of South Africa transformed his life. It was here that he learnt that God 'has made of one blood all nations for me to dwell on the face of the earth'; it was here, too, in the shanty towns and dust tracks of Johannesburg, that he championed those that others condemned. His own life was changed by the simple tasks that furnished his day; sweeping out his tent, checking a boy's homework, dealing with the police, ministering to his flock. It was here that the son of a commander of the Indian Navy, a product of Lancing College and Oxford University, suddenly found the courage to take charge of hundreds of thousands of urban Africans. And it was here that he fought against the Pass Laws, the Bantu Education Act and the Western Areas Removal Scheme, a fight that won him the love of non-white South Africa which the intervening years failed to dispel. Little surprise, then, that back in England he longed for the friendship, excitement and sunshine of South Africa. After an unhappy spell, he went to hold further Episcopal posts – in East Africa, Stepney and Mauritius.

On retirement in England, he lived out of a suitcase in a few rooms on the top floor of a central London vicarage. Here, while prayer remained the centre of his life, he became more involved in the anti-apartheid movement, angrily insisting that a gradual dismemberment of the system was corrupt and self-defeating. Eventually, he retreated to Mirfield, where he endured an angry and often undignified death.

Over his life, his religion, too, changed. He was brought up as a spiky Anglo-Catholic, suspicious of Evangelicals and anything that smacked of ecclesiastical good taste. As a young priest, he was involved in a bitter dispute over the Church of South India, yet by the end of his episcopate he would hold tea parties on his veranda at Mauritius where the great and the good would chew over that week's topic, whether it be 'Whither Hinduism?' or 'The Muslim dilemma'. A theologian might say that his thinking became more Catholic; he left the battles of institutional Christianity behind, and became concerned with universal religion.

In Mauritius, too, he became interested in Eastern spirituality; in a sermon delivered to commemorate the 150th anniversary of the Oxford Movement, he urged the claims of other faiths: such openness attracted him to younger people, who seemed to understand him better than either his Episcopal contemporaries or even his Mirfield brethren. 'If we are truly Catholic, it is interfaith ecumenism – the recognition that dialogue between Hindu and Christian, Muslim and Christian, Buddhist and Christian must have priority – that should be the aim for us all in this moment of history.' At the beginning of his priesthood, he was young and conservative and priggish and he would have hated the idea of women priests; by the end of his life, he battled for their ordination, claiming that there was more than one apartheid in this world, and that women were a lesser breed without the law. 'Women are the great educators, the future. To me it is pathetic not to understand this.'

He received the world's plaudits. In 1991, Trevor, as a white Christian bishop, was asked to open the African National Congress's first conference in freedom. On hearing of his death, Nelson Mandela said that no citizen of Great Britain had done more for the black people of South Africa than Trevor Huddleston. Yet few people under the age of 35 have heard of him, and many of his preoccupations – from his love of *dirigiste* socialism to progressive 'issues' in the Church – seem embarrassingly dated. This book will not attempt to provide a generalized view of South African politics, nor an assessment of how his theological views changed over the years, nor a sweeping perspective on Anglican theology in the latter half of the twentieth century. Instead, I hope to show how a conventional young boy from an educated background became a pale and pious hop picker in Kent and then a laughing, determined and charismatic priest, who performed those essentials of prayer – the rock of his salvation – and righteous action for which Dietrich Bonhoeffer laid down his life. True, Trevor was an angry obsessive with a strong will who contended with depressions brought on by an unhappy personal life, a chronic dependency on insulin and a frustration at his Episcopal role; equally true, too, that through prayer and discipline and courage, his face betrayed – in the writer Nadine Gordimer's phrase – 'the pain of Christ'.

Nadine Gordimer treasures a photograph of Trevor, taken in 1952 at the height of his love affair with South Africa. She describes his face as 'lit only by a tin brazier – a pair of gaunt, tightly clasped hands, the bright white band of a clerical collar . . . the ear cocked intensely, and the eyes concentrated'. And this remarkable vision began in a large Edwardian house in dreary Bedford.

1

A Serious Child

LIKE MANY WHO PROCLAIM their love for the poor, Trevor Huddleston came from a wealthy background. In 1913 the Huddleston family was living at 36, Chaucer Road, a large red brick Edwardian house on the outskirts of Bedford. Trevor was born on 15 June, four years after his sister Barbara, and was baptized when he was five weeks old at the parish church of St Paul. He was given the name Ernest Urban Trevor.

A branch of the Huddleston family was deeply religious. One of Trevor's ancestors was Fr John Huddleston (1608–1698), a Restoration priest and Benedictine monk who helped Charles II escape from Worcester and who received the king into the Roman Catholic Church on his deathbed. There were many generations of Huddleston clergy, spurred on by the family motto *Soli Deo Honor et Gloria* – 'Honour and Glory to God Alone'.

But Trevor did not belong to this branch. He was a descendant of the sailor Huddlestons, who were part of the British Raj in India. In 1890 his Uncle Willoughby, a naval officer, had received a gold medal for rescuing a seaman from shark-infested waters off the Bay of Bengal. Trevor's father, Ernest, the son of an Indian army officer and one of twelve children, had run away from Bedford School at the age of 14 to join the merchant navy. After transferring to the Royal Indian Marine, he ended up commanding the Royal Indian Navy, before returning to England as a nautical adviser to the Indian government. He, too, had received a medal for his courage; in 1897, he was awarded a Silver Medal for gallantry at sea, when a troop ship, with over a thousand men on board, was wrecked on an island off the coast of Mauritius. He was awarded a knighthood in 1937.

Ernest Huddleston had a huge jaw and a deep, gravely voice. He never liked India, despite the presence of his brothers out there; he found the climate hot and the company artificial. Ernest enjoyed fishing and shooting, reading and crosswords. He was too clever and sensitive a man to relish the sheer heartiness of Raj life, which – with its endless games of hockey, billiards, cricket and lawn tennis, played against a backdrop of churches, clubs and fine neo-classical town houses – re-affirmed the English virtues of fair play and honourable behaviour.

But India was no longer enslaved by these very English qualities. Before the First World War, the British could successfully present themselves as the emblem of Mughal power, embodying a style of governance in which precedence and order held sway. Such sweeping self-confidence was displayed when George V visited India in 1911, the only reigning British monarch to visit his Indian empire. The highlight of the visit was an ornate durbar in Delhi, which was attended by Ernest. Here, in the greatest imperial spectacle ever mounted by the Raj, the newly crowned King Emperor and his Queen Empress paraded themselves in front of their fawning Indian subjects.

And many of their Indian subjects were grateful. Under the British, the country had a new system of law and a growing economy, sustained by railway lines, bridges and irrigation systems. There was greater access to higher education, although general education was cursory and slipshod and illiteracy remained widespread.

But unease grew. There had been agitation about British rule before, especially among the aggrieved new class of Indians educated in government colleges and, sometimes, in British universities. Yet before 1914, the Government of India held the initiative; but after the First World War it was seized by the Congress Party. Indian troops, who had fought bravely for the Empire along the Western Front and in Mesopotamia, now felt that they deserved a reward. No longer were the British seen, along with Russia, as one of the two super-powers; their mask of command had slipped and they were now one of many roughly equal forces in the world. Ernest, as Commander of the Royal Indian Navy, would have been aware of just how far war had sapped the mystique of the Empire; by 1919, the British were forcing through a series of constitutional reforms which would surrender a large measure of government to the Indian provinces.

In August 1904, Ernest had married Elsie Barlow-Smith in St Paul's, Bedford. She was gracious and slim, with black hair and dark eyes. She came from a family of affluent bankers in Buenos Aires. The couple had met in Bedford, where Elsie had also attended school, and they had a lengthy engagement while Ernest was a struggling officer in the Royal Indian Marine and then at the Naval College at Greenwich. On his wedding day, Lieutenant Huddleston wore full dress uniform; his wife wore a dress of 'white duchesse satin, trimmed with Brussels appliqué lace and court train of the same satin trimmed with white chiffon and sprays of myrtle and orange blossom'. After the wedding, Elsie followed Ernest back to the naval bases of Madras, Bombay and Calcutta. Unlike her husband, Elsie adored India and its people; she also appreciated the grandiose houses that they lived in, with their ranks of servants, drivers and cooks.

So Trevor and his sister Barbara were products of a privileged background; their parents were upper middle class and Conservative and upholders of the Empire. But they were also creatures of the Raj; their childhoods were defined by their parents' absence. Trevor did not see his father until he was seven years old, and only remembered three occasions when his parents were together in England before his father's permanent return five years later. His mother, too, would divide her time between India and England, spending up to eighteen months in each country. Today, such an abandoned childhood seems bizarre, and would attract nannyish contempt from child experts and welfare agencies. But few of Trevor's peers would have questioned the way he was brought up; for Britain's ruling class, it was the norm. As he said in his own way: 'It was a very happy childhood. It is difficult to express nowadays: people always seem to have deep psychological traumas about neglect, but I never felt that in the least.'

Trevor was obsessed with the Empire, and most particularly India. Letters from India would be eagerly awaited and devoured; timetables for steamers from Asia would be scrutinized. Trevor was a tender boy and missed his parents desperately. He did not accompany his parents to India, and the parting – before the days of aeroplanes or radios or telephones – would have been absolute. Nevertheless, he was always keen to describe his childhood as 'idyllic'. He was surrounded by aunts and uncles and cousins. He was largely raised by his Aunt Lottie (nicknamed 'Potsa') and by a nanny, Ada Pateman.

Aunt Lottie had returned to England after the death of her banker husband Henry Dawson Robinson, and moved into 53, Hampstead Way, a large house overlooking the Heath. There was plenty of money. Aunt Lottie had a cook and a parlour maid who provided excellent food for young Trevor and his sister. Aunt Lottie was a flamboyant character who loved cocktails and dinner parties; Trevor would help do up his aunt's corset and she, in turn, would bring him a little treat from the table of her dinner party. Despite the occasional appearance of his Uncle Jack, Trevor was largely brought up by women, who both spoiled and just occasionally disciplined him.

But, swizzle sticks apart, a boy born in 1913 lived in despondent times. Trevor would have sensed the anxiety of his family, who had friends and relatives at the Front. He also knew of several families who were bereaved. Yet Trevor found the war exciting rather than frightening; along with most Londoners, he huddled in the streets when Zeppelins flew over the city and cheered when they were shot down by the pilots of the Royal Flying Corps. During air raids, he would crouch under the stairs until the bugles shouted the 'All Clear'. One day, a bomb dropped directly outside his Hampstead home.

Trevor was a shy and serious boy; his sister Barbara was a tomboy, good at music and tennis and lacrosse. They both had plenty of friends, and would play games in the garden and have picnics on the Heath. They set up a shop outside Potsa's garden gate and sold bootlaces to passers-by. They devised an amusing game called 'Tug-the-purse' in which they tied a purse to a long string and left it on the pavement. Both brother and sister would then hide on the roof of the garden shed and yank the wallet when a passer-by stooped down to pick it up.

When Trevor was feeling disheartened, he would lie on the bed in his mother's room, which always remained hers, even when she was absent. He had an imaginary friend, who was rather older than him and called Gilkert. Gilkert had a svelte figure and fair, wispy hair. They used to play together and have long conversations, especially at night, when the darkness haunted Trevor. Trevor bore, in Graham Greene's phrase, the 'peculiar burden of childhood' by having this imaginary playmate. Thanks to the compelling presence of Aunt Lottie, Trevor's childhood was marked by a strong pattern of family life; but it was a family without the constant presence of mother and father. Trevor's abiding need for praise and fear of rejection stemmed, at least in part, from his parents' invisibility when he was a young boy.

53, Hampstead Way, was a devout house. Trevor devoured religious nursery books, alongside Kipling's poetry and stories about

Scott's expedition to the Antarctic. In his bedroom, in front of an illustration of Christ, he would pray daily for his aunt, his absent parents and the British soldiers at the Front. He would also curse the 'dirty Germans'. Both Trevor's aunt and mother were strict High Anglicans, and Trevor would go to St Michael's, Golders Green, twice on Sundays, attending catechism classes in the afternoon. Here, Anglo-Catholicism, born out of the nineteenth-century Oxford Movement and headed by John Newman, Canon Edward Pusey and the saintly John Keble, meant the separation of men and women, birettas, Benediction, a daily Mass and the illegal reservation of the Blessed Sacrament on the High Altar. The Anglo-Catholicism of Trevor's youth had nothing in common with its lukewarm and disenchanted successor today. It was expressive, florid and rebellious.

There is no doubt that Trevor would have been a different type of Christian – both more congenial and less certain – had it not been for the fiery Anglo-Catholicism which he encountered in his early years at St Michael's. To the crushing disappointment of many High Anglicans, Trevor's theological views became more fluid as he grew older; yet throughout his life, he was proud of his attachment to the Catholic wing of the Church of England, and at times exhibited all the belligerence associated with that faction.

Every Sunday, from the age of 4, Trevor would dress up in a scarlet cassock and carry the boat of incense at St Michael's. He enjoyed the worship at St Michael's, and admired the parish priest Fr Vincent Keelan, with whose sons he was great friends. He looked up to Fr Keelan, not because of his clothes and status, but because he was clearly a man of God. It was at St Michael's that Trevor was taught that the Mass was at the heart of all worship and that the Church could be a place of beauty and not fear.

Trevor adored religion, and could not remember a time when he did not want to be a priest. For him, as for many clergy, ordination and allegiance to the Church were identical; he would never consider life as a layman. When he was 6 years old, he played 'churches' with Barbara and Bill, one of Fr Keelan's sons. Trevor, covering his shoulders with a red bedspread and using the laundry basket as a pulpit, lit candles and spread a sheet over the nursery table as an altar. He began preaching, leading processions and hearing confessions. He then knocked over a candle, burnt the sheet and ensured that his elder sister was sent to bed early. As usual, Trevor was too angelic to be thought guilty.

In a magazine interview many years later, Trevor recalled his attraction towards ordination: 'I remember feeling when I was six or seven that I wanted to be a priest. I think children are much more open to the deeper spiritual influences than adults. I suppose the priestly life appealed to me because it is to do with worship, which is connected with colour and movement. And the role of the parish priest was a very significant one, that of a rather authoritarian, but also kind, father figure.'

After a short spell at a dame school in a Hampstead Garden suburb, Trevor was sent away at the age of 7 as a weekly boarder to Tenterden Hall in Hendon. The actor David Garrick had once lived opposite. The prep school, which was set in an attractive Georgian house surrounded by a large garden with a vast cedar tree, was a typical product of post-war times – modest, austere and run by a peculiar couple. Jimmy Bacon, the headmaster, was a wiry and authoritative Cambridge hockey blue; he was only 4 feet tall and had to wear children's shoes. His wife was even smaller.

Trevor was a very ordinary boy from a Tory home. He moaned about the school food and occasionally was beaten by the headmaster when he was naughty. Like all his friends, he jeered at the General Strike of 1926 and liked to boast that his father was ADC to two Viceroys in India. His father was his hero, and one day he took to school the flag of the Commodore of the Royal Indian Navy and a telescope that his father had left behind. He was not very interested in books, although he loved Sapper's *Bulldog Drummond* and *The Scarlet Pimpernel*. He enjoyed history and classics, and loathed mathematics and music, failing the Grade One piano exam. He never won any cups in the school's sports competitions, but he played in the First Rugby XV and boxed enthusiastically. He would bring friends home to Hampstead Garden Surburb, where they would play board games and trains and charades with Trevor's sister Barbara.

In 1927, Trevor's last year at Tenterden Hall, his father presented a cup to the school known as the Vox Populi; it was to be awarded each year to the boy who was voted the most popular. Trevor, who could display formidable charm when he wanted to, won the prize. Indeed, Trevor kept some of his friends at Tenterden Hall right through his life. His best friend was Hubert Lamb, the nephew of the artist Charles Lamb who became a professor of climactic research in the University of East Anglia. The pair would accompany each other on trips to Madam Tussaud's, to see the illusionists Maskelyne and Devant at St George's Hall and to Bertram Mills' Circus. He would also play tennis and ping-pong with Yvonne Brown, whose parents lived in a large house in Hendon which was always crammed with children. He would escort Yvonne to the ice rink and cinema, or sometimes they would just walk together and argue earnestly. They were too young to be anything except 'just good friends'.

It was in Aunt Potsa's house that Trevor was first introduced to South Africa. A family from South Africa, refugees from the Russian Revolution, turned up in a neighbouring house. The family showed lantern slides in Potsa's house of their photographs of South Africa, particularly of naked black natives standing outside their houses.

One other childhood incident would haunt Trevor. One evening, when Trevor was home for Christmas and still a pupil at Tenterden Hall, the bell rang and his father answered the door. It was an Indian beggar, asking for money. Trevor's father replied: 'No, there's nothing here for you.' Trevor was shocked, not just at the man's colour but because he was poor. He could not believe that his father, a decent man, could turn away such a person at Christmas.

Trevor viewed the religious life at Tenterden Hall with disgust. He hated divinity and church services. Every week, after Matron brushed down his hair with coconut oil, he would walk in a crocodile line with the other pupils down to Matins at St Mary's Church, Hendon. Inside the church, there was a transept which concealed the clergyman from the school. Wearing his navy-blue suit and Eton collar, Trevor would be forced to sit through a leaden service, followed by a church parade. Trevor was raised in an insolent and vibrant wing of the Church of England; he never learnt to like polite and conventional Anglicanism or, as the noted historian and CR preacher Fr Neville Figgis put it, 'the tepid weak tea of choristers' Anglicanism'.

At the end of his time at Tenterden Hall, Trevor's mother arranged for the Revd Cyril Proctor, who taught Latin and Greek at the school, to coach Trevor for a scholarship to Lancing College, which he did not win. Revd Proctor owed Trevor a favour, as the young boy had ferried love letters to his future wife. 'He was not a scholar,' wrote Proctor, 'just an average, charming, friendly prep school boy. My impression is that he was what is often called a "late developer".'

In December 1925, at the age of 12, Trevor was confirmed at St Mary's, Hendon, into the Church of England along with his good friends Bill Tyndall and Patrick Keelan. His parents, who had just retired to London, were present along with Aunt Potsa, who gave him a leather-bound prayer book. In later years, in a Mission to Oxford University, Trevor described his confirmation dramatically: 'I can remember, then, as clearly as it was yesterday, standing in a suburban church, with my father and mother, on 15 December 1925 and watching the bishop lay his hands upon the heads of boys and girls in the sacrament of confirmation, and awaiting my turn to move to the sanctuary step and kneel before him . . . My confirmation was the beginning of what I can only describe as my real life.'

At this time, Trevor also heard Fr Basil Jellicoe preach at All Saints, Margaret Street, about the slums at Somers Town, near St Pancras. 'Slums are the Devil's Sacrament: the outward and visible sign of an inward and spiritual disgrace. If God became man, it was intolerable that man should live in such filthy conditions.' It was a sermon that Trevor would remember, but not yet.

2

Lancing College

LANCING COLLEGE was an unremarkable English public school set on the Sussex Downs, saved by its lofty, incomplete chapel which remains one of the great monuments of the Oxford Movement and the Gothic Revival. It was the obvious choice for Trevor. His father, who had an Englishman's interest in religion, was keen that his son should attend his *alma mater* Bedford School; his wife, who was more vehement, was certain that Lancing, with its all-male and rather enclosed Anglo-Catholic community, would suit Trevor. She was right.

Trevor arrived at Lancing in September 1927, a few months after his fourteenth birthday. A boy with his deeply religious nature would feel at home there; the school was set up as a clerical foundation, a large number of the boys were the sons of priests and one-tenth of the 400 boys of Trevor's generation were ordained themselves. After the insipid religion of his prep school, the chapel and its services – two every day and three on Sunday – made a profound impression on Trevor.

Lancing College had been founded in 1848 by Nathaniel Woodard. Woodard was a convinced Tractarian clergyman, a combative and secretive man and a poor scholar. His Tractarianism was not the flamboyant ritualism which dominated the second part of the nineteenth century; it owed more to the Prayer Book principles of the Oxford Movement as typified by Keble and Froude. Woodard was a determined man, and he pursued his idea of creating a public school for the middle classes with vigour and panache.

Woodard realized that the ancient public schools – Winchester, Eton, Shrewsbury and Westminster – had once been charitable institutions, but were becoming the preserve of the sons of the governing aristocracy and the richer country gentry. In Lancing, which was the first and principal Woodard School, he wanted to create a school which derived its character from the central teachings of Christianity. 'Education without religion is in itself a pure evil', he would remark. He would try and inspire pupils with his piecemeal aphorisms: 'Never play the hero' and 'Seek to pass through life without attracting the eyes of men'. Most importantly of all: 'Do all to the sole glory of God.'

So Trevor, the son of a naval commander, arrived at Lancing College with the fellow sons of lawyers, doctors, army officers, gin palace keepers and clergymen. But the school was different from its grander rivals in other ways too. Unlike the brutal atmosphere of many post-war schools, it was a small and rather pleasant institution and relationships between boys and masters were relaxed. Trevor's headmaster, Cuthbert Blakiston, was an irascible classics master who was popular with the boys, although after Trevor's time he was forced to leave following a financial scandal. Trevor would refer to him glowingly as 'deeply religious, kind and strong, a man of enormous vision'. A number of other masters influenced Trevor, and most particularly E. B. Gordon ('Gordo') – his form master when Trevor first started at Lancing.

The cheerfully resilient Gordo had been Captain of the School in 1908. Owing to rheumatism, he was invalided out of the First World War and returned to Lancing to teach the Lower School for the next 40 years. He had all the humour and individuality of a good schoolmaster, but none of the dreariness. A dedicated churchman, he was devoid of piety and particularly good with unusual boys, like the explorer Gino Watkins and the writer Evelyn Waugh. He showed teenage boys, who are natural conservatives, how to look at the world differently. He taught his middle-class pupils, most of whom were more sheltered than selfish, how to care for other people. In the holidays, Trevor would pay visits to Gordo, who lived with his brother in a cottage in Sevenoaks. They would often attend stamp collections together. Gordo was Trevor's greatest mentor at Lancing. In return, Gordo would say: 'I have not always agreed with Trevor, but then, perhaps I'm not such a good bloke.'

Years later, when E. B. Gordon had retired from Lancing and was working as a prep school master in Lymington, he gave an interview to *The Sunday Times* magazine. In it, he described Trevor, who was now the Bishop of Stepney, as 'a very attractive chap, nice-looking and simple, not much of an athlete, very friendly, certainly not obtrusively holy, well-behaved . . . I see him in my mind rather as he is now, upstanding, tall, nicely-coloured, a fresh complexion, sensible and humorous.'

Apart from Gordo, there was also the history master Christopher Chamberlain, who had strange mannerisms and was nicknamed 'Monkey' by the boys. He knew the name and the date of birth of every boy in the school. He encouraged Trevor to think for himself and write essays on his two main interests – the Emperor Hadrian and British colonial history. Fifty years later, Chamberlain would write:

> Trevor was at Lancing only four years (1927–31) and so was never one of its leaders, but observed the School closely and quietly; and his friends, men of quality, respected him.
>
> I worked with him in his first year and I thought him very mature; and he was such a good writer that I can quote the last sentence of his 'Welsh protest at Edward I's castles': 'For all their magnificence, I curse those castles.'

His housemaster, Alywn Woodard, was a rather aloof character, but deeply respected by all the house and warmly liked by Trevor. However, he could be petulant; on Trevor's last day at Lancing, he and his friend J. R. C. G. Wheeler decided to walk over the Downs through the night, returning to their house – Sandersons – at dawn. Woodard was furious, and claimed in a letter to Trevor's father that his exploits had ruined his school career. Sir Ernest brushed it off.

Alongside his masters, Trevor also enjoyed deep friendships among the boys. One of his greatest friends was Patrick Cotter, the son of a Lewisham vicar, who was Head of Sandersons when Trevor joined the house. Despite their difference in ages, Trevor grew close to Patrick, who was courteous and amusing and non-conformist. After Trevor's first year, Patrick won an Exhibition to Hertford College, Oxford; their friendship endured until Patrick was killed while serving in the RAF in the Second World War. Patrick was one of 137 former pupils who lost their lives in the Second World War, and Trevor knew many of them. Another great friend was Peter Hadley, who accompanied him to Christ Church, Oxford, and who was a member of the same school societies – the Gramophone Society, the Modern Play Reading

Society, the Shakespeare Society and the Debating Society. Other chums included Peter Burra, who played the violin at Lancing with Peter Pears and was killed in a plane crash in his twenties; John Gough, who became a conscientious objector in the Second World War, and Rupert Godfrey, who ended up as a Canon in the Church of England.

So what kind of pupil was 'Hurdlestone', as the boys in his House called him? In the rather damning words of his housemaster, he was 'steady, solid and sensible'. He was friendly and well behaved and used to dress well. He was made a house prefect after only three years, and staff admired him for his quiet strength and the quality of his friends. He enjoyed playing rugby and the trumpet. He was a drum major in the Officer Training Corps, and loved tossing the mace high in the air ahead of the parade. He edited the College magazine in 1931 and contributed to the literary *Lancing Miscellany*.

His friends found him charming, but often withdrawn – a loner with a capacity for intolerance who was guided by Kipling's poem 'If'. They did not see him as a future priest; he neither sang in the choir nor played a significant role in the Chapel, although he did serve regularly at the altar. Like many of his generation, they imagined that he would join the civil service or run a small engineering firm in the Home Counties.

Yet the signs were there. It was at Lancing that Trevor thought that he might be a Socialist. Trevor wrote excitedly to his father when an Old Boy, Lord Sankey, became Lord Chancellor and a member of the first Labour government. His father was not interested. Trevor had also been influenced by a biography which his mother had given him of Frank Weston, the Bishop of Zanzibar. In a famous challenge in 1923 to 15,000 bishops, priests and laity at the Anglo-Catholic congresses in the Royal Albert Hall, Weston said: 'You have your Mass, you have your altars, you have begun to get your tabernacles. Now go out into the highways and hedges, and look for Jesus in the ragged and naked, in the oppressed and the sweated, in those who have lost hope, and in those who are struggling to make good. Look for Jesus in them; and, when you have found Him, gird yourself with His towel of fellowship and wash His feet in the person of His brethren.'

Most importantly, it was at Lancing that he was introduced to the College Mission. The Mission had been founded by the school in

1909, and from the draughty church of St Michael's, Camberwell, it administered to 10,000 people in the worst slums in South London. Lancing gave the parish money, provided clothes, organized outings to the Sussex Coast for the slum children and encouraged its pupils to visit the parish at first hand. Although the *de haut en bas* style of the missions feels embarrassing today, they certainly showed public schoolboys that Christianity was more about helping the poor than Matins and village fêtes. Sluggish consciences were awakened.

In later life, Trevor would say that the Lancing Mission introduced him to the poor. Trevor saw much of the Mission at the height of the Depression, when undernourished children wandered barefoot around the slums, suffering from rickets. He never forgot their hunger, nor the smell of the 'smoke-'ole', where kippers were cured next to the church. In his holidays, Trevor would wander over to St Michael's, where he loved the ritualistic worship prepared by the ebullient Fr Austen Collyer, whose vicarage always smelt of gas. Fr Collyer, a fat and grey-haired bachelor who later married a much younger and very beautiful girl, showed Trevor what a parish priest could do.

In July 1931, Trevor left Lancing. He wrote, in a perceptive if whimsical last editorial in the *Lancing Magazine*:

> If there is anything that we are really sorry to lose, it is not the friends we have made – them, we feel, are never lost – nor is it the buildings in which we have lived – we shall probably tread their floors again within the year. It is the loss of ourselves that causes us any real sorrow – the dreadful thought that before we can be noticed again, we must compete not with a school of four hundred, but with the world. It is with this egoism on our lips that we would say goodbye.

That year, Trevor also said goodbye to his mother, who died in January after suffering from cancer for three years. His beloved Aunt Potsa had died three years before, in her early fifties. Trevor and Barbara were shocked by their mother's death, but believed that too much grief would undermine the truths of the Resurrection which she had taught them. Their father wanted a full year's mourning, but his children refused. Trevor, however, did carry the coffin at the funeral and wore a black arm-band. Eighteen months after his wife Elsie's death, Sir Ernest married Lorna Box, who was a member of the congregation of St Michael's, Golders Green. Trevor, who had known and liked his father since his return from India in 1925, was the best man.

3

Oxford

TREVOR WENT UP TO CHRIST CHURCH, OXFORD, in Michaelmas Term 1931, to read Modern History rather than Theology, which
he was never very interested in. By his own account, he was a nervous
young man; but then he had every right to be.

More than any other Oxford college, Christ Church would have
been overwhelming for a reticent undergraduate. Although by the
early 1930s nearly half the undergraduates went to Oxford on scholarship or public grant, Christ Church was a wealthy college and
Trevor did not have much money. Tom Quad was the grandest and
largest quadrangle in Oxford, with Wren's tower on the west side and
the cathedral spire on the east. On the college's war memorial there
were two viscounts, three earls, seven lords, four baronets, an Italian
marquis and a French count. Thirteen Prime Ministers had entered
Tom Gate. Many of the fellow undergraduates on his staircase had the
fearless self-assurance that only class and money can bring; they had
nicknames like 'Bimbo' and 'Bobby' and were rumoured to belong to
the 'Bullingdon set'. Trevor, despite his patrician air, was a diffident
and serious boy from North London.

His father accompanied Trevor when he entered Christ Church,
and together they chose crockery and curtains. Trevor had been given
attic rooms in a corner of Peckwater Quad, and would occupy them
until Trinity 1933, when he moved to filthy digs in the Iffley Road and
concentrated on his Finals. For the first time, Trevor was independent and enjoyed living grandly; at Lancing he washed his own dishes,
but now he had a scout who looked after him. He would have been
addressed as 'Mister' by the Warden. Sometimes he had breakfast
brought to him as he lounged in his dressing gown. He could have a

four-course meal, known as a club breakfast, which was carried on the heads of college porters.

Trevor would also have enjoyed the beauty and restlessness of Oxford, away from the regimented life of Lancing with its lessons and chapel and games. With more time on his hands, he would have found the eight-week university term longer than a three-month school term. A certain Edwardian opulence and languor still remained at Oxford; bills were run up at tailors' shops, the term time was for socializing and the holidays for work; those who had money gave breakfast and lunch parties in their own rooms. Even those who could not afford the gilded life of subscriptions to parties, or travel or pub crawling, certainly fell under its spell.

At first, Trevor was lonely, and clung to fellow Lancing under-graduates for friendship. With such friends he joined the Mermaid club, where he wore a white dinner jacket with green lapels and read Shakespeare aloud while drinking rum punch. He also made a con-certed attempt to organize his day, say his prayers and go regularly to church. Slowly, in his self-contained but warm way, he made other friends; his greatest undergraduate friend was an Old Etonian and keen oarsman called A. J. Rickards, who gave him a copy of Kenneth Grahame's *Wind in the Willows* as a twenty-first birthday present.

William Deakin, one of Trevor's fellow historians at Oxford, went on to work with Winston Churchill on his memoirs. He said of Trevor: 'I have a firm impression of a warm-hearted young man of marked integrity and kindness. He mixed easily and simply with his contemporaries. He was not only a dedicated Christian but also quietly self-contained, and, in the best sense, sure of himself. He never held forth, and was always good company.'

Dinner in Hall was a daunting experience. Trevor would have entered the great pre-Victorian sixteenth-century Hall by a fan-vaulted staircase, and once seated would have gazed up at a Reynolds, a Romney or a Gainsborough – portraits of judges and scholars and statesmen. As he drank and gossiped with friends, so the whole sweep of English history lay above him. Soon, he would begin to recognize the members of the High Table who ate at the far end of the Hall. There was Dr Henry Julian White, the Dean of Christ Church, whom Trevor thought reclusive and desiccated; there was Dr N. P. Williams, the Lady Margaret Professor of Divinity, who knew more about sin than any man alive. Others became public figures: the linguistic philosopher A. J. Ayer, future Foreign Secretary Patrick Gordon Walker, the dome-headed Hon. Francis Pakenham and the economist Roy Harrod.

Two tutors shaped Trevor at Oxford – Keith Feiling and J. C. Masterman. Feiling, who had helped Winston Churchill with his *Marlborough* and the first volume of his *History of the English-Speaking Peoples*, was a cultured and liberal man with a stammer. He was deeply loyal to his wife and pupils. As a historian, he was interested in religion and the constitution rather than society and the economy. An English High Tory romantic, he founded the Oxford University Conservative Association in 1924 and established himself as the leading historian of the Tory Party. But he was not politically partisan and Trevor, despite a sentimental bewitchment with socialism, admired him. J. C. Masterman, a double blue who had been a naval cadet at Dartmouth and was imprisoned in Germany throughout the Second World War, was a humorous and loyal tutor to Trevor. Both men taught with a light, humorous touch and an air of self-mockery; a critical lesson in style for the stern-minded Trevor. Both men were disappointed when Trevor obtained a Second in History; but Trevor, though intelligent and industrious, was never an intellectual and his degree reflected this.

Even from the isolated quad of Christ Church, it was the perfect time to be reading Modern History. One month before Trevor went up to Oxford, Ramsey MacDonald had resigned as the Labour Prime Minister and formed a National Government to balance the budget. By 1932, there were nearly three million people without work in Great Britain; in Germany, unemployment was even higher and in July the Nazi Party had won a majority in the Reichstag election. While R. H. Tawney's *Equality* was published, Oswald Mosley had created the Britain Union of Fascists. By December of that year, miners and dockers and hunger marchers had walked from Jarrow and South Wales and to Westminster. They were not violent or bellicose; they were hungry, and on their marches they sought shelter in the town halls of cities like Oxford. By January 1933, Adolf Hitler had been appointed Chancellor of Germany.

And then came the 'ever-shameful resolution', as Winston Churchill described it in *The Gathering Storm*. On 9 February 1933, the Oxford Union Society passed the most important motion in its history: 'that this House will, in no circumstances, fight for its King and Country'. Germans seized on the motion as proof that young Englishmen would not fight. Leader writers bristled and harrumphed, claiming that the young were soft and decadent and had rejected the Great War. In wild fury, the mercurial Randolph Churchill tore pages out of the minute book.

Trevor, meanwhile, was not a member of the Union and not present at the debate. He was the 19-year-old son of a naval captain who was too naïve to understand the realities of European and international politics. When Hitler came to power, he was mildly shocked when his old friend Hubert Lamb sent him a postcard celebrating the arrival of National Socialism and scrawled with the words 'Heil Hitler!' He would have called himself a pacifist, in the way that undergraduates today call themselves vegan or spiritual. But politics bemused then bored him; he was more interested in girls and religion. Fr Marin Jarrett-Kerr, Trevor's contemporary at Oxford, and, later, fellow member of the Community of the Resurrection, remembered him combining 'conscientious membership of the Oxford University Church Union with easy acceptance in the rather well-dressed, suede-shoe, aristocracy'.

As a schoolboy, Trevor had looked tall and distinguished. At Oxford, he was gaunt and rather beautiful, with dark hair and a pinkish complexion. At Lancing, he would have learnt about sex from dormitory whispers and friends' jokes; inevitably, homosexual scandals occurred, and he would have been aware of them. From an early age, he was attractive to girls, and by the age of 15 he used to accompany one particular girl on walks, where they would argue in an adolescent way, and dances, where Trevor would wear a white bow tie and tail coat. He was always an excellent dancer.

In his second year at Oxford, Trevor, who loved cars all his life, bought a fifth-hand Morris Oxford. Now girls found him exciting as well as attractive, and Trevor hammed it up by buying a smart suit in Prince of Wales check, from which he would extract a wooden snuff box and a long cigarette-holder. He would drive girls around in his car, and then make them listen to his collection of 1930s jazz and dance music on his gramophone. He would dance with girls until sunrise, while holding their hands and whispering in their ears. He fell in love frequently, and was infatuated by the young wife of a much older man. Her husband looked on it with tolerance and amusement. For Trevor never slept with any woman. At that time, most Oxford undergraduates – unless they were rakes or libertines – saw sex as something you did when you got married. Indeed, Trevor's attraction to falling in love was heightened by the realization that nothing could come of it. For even at his most debonair and handsome, Trevor knew that he would never marry.

On arrival at Oxford, Trevor had assuaged his terrible solitude by going regularly to church and continuing his schoolboy offerings of prayer. He was one of the more devout undergraduates, and every Sunday would wear a surplice and walk across the Quad to early morning Communion at the Chapel. Like worship at Tenterden Hall, he found religion at Christ Church colourless, and later in the morning would stroll past church walls stacked with bicycles to an ugly Victorian building in the poor, north-west part of the city.

For more than sixty years, since its consecration in 1869, St Barnabas had been an oddity; it was a slum Anglo-Catholic parish which attracted both devout undergraduates and excellent preachers. The parish priest, Fr A. G. Bisdee, was welcoming and unpretentious, and the congregation would cram into his vicarage after Mass. Trevor, naturally, felt comfortable at St Barnabas; for a homesick young man, it offered the same warmth and spirit as St Michael's, Golders Green, and the Lancing College Mission at Camberwell.

And then there was Pusey House, an Anglican centre for Catholic-leaning undergraduates. When the Tractarian theologian Edward Bouverie Pusey died in 1882, his followers bought all his books and a house in St Giles to house them. Attached to the house was a chapel, which had been dedicated in 1914. It had once been an enclosed community for Pusey's admirers; when Canon Freddy Hood joined the staff, it became a point of contact for undergraduates who could stroll in off the street. Canon Hood was friendly and direct; he understood the turmoils of Man, and preached that all those who lapsed could be restored, as long as they were contrite. It was at Pusey House that John Betjeman, three years before Trevor, had attended Mass at Pusey House and learned the Catholic faith.

Another outstanding pastor at Pusey House was Miles Sergeant, a former public school chaplain and lover of steam trains who had a strong social conscience. Fr Sergeant had arranged for food and bedding to be delivered to the hunger marchers. He also formed the Fellowship of the Transfiguration, where Trevor learnt about the disciplines of the Christian faith. Trevor, who had a servant in his rooms and Viscounts for friends, talked about Marx at Pusey House and began to argue that the Church should always serve the poor. Miles decided to test Trevor's polemics by inviting him, and a dozen other undergraduates, to staff a ten-day Mission to the hop pickers at Crowhurst Farm, Kent. Trevor joined in the summer of 1932, and went the following year as well.

The hop pickers were Cockneys who came from London slums, and lived with their families in individual huts with no windows and an earth floor. Whole households would sleep on one mattress on the floor, and in front of each hut was an open fire, with a couple of stakes to support a kettle. There was one tap for the whole farm; all day long, children would cross the fields with buckets of water, spilling half the contents as they straggled back to their huts.

The Missioners wanted to live like the hop pickers, although they had single bunks in their huts and the use of the bathroom of a grand house nearby. Some would be in charge of an open-air cinema; others would organize games for the children and organize a sing-song – 'Knees up, Mother Brown' was a favourite. When they were tired of screaming children, they would join the hop pickers in the local pub. A stable in the farm was transformed into a church, and a statue of St Mary and St Francis would be placed among the straw bales. On Sunday, up to sixty children would roam around the church and a small congregation would overflow outside; hymns sung both in the service and Sunday School would be accompanied by a harmonium.

Miles Sergeant wrote a book about the Mission – *St Francis of the Hop-Fields* – in which he bemoaned the gulf between the educated Missioners and the hop pickers: 'We can never really see life through their eyes, because that can only happen if we ourselves have been bred and brought up as they have.' He then imitated a hop picker:

> See that crahd up by my 'ut this afternoon, Father? It was my son bashin ''is missus. Saucy piece she 'is [*sic*], and 'as been arstin' for it for a long time. Now she's got it – I thort I'd just let yer know it wasn't nothing' to worry abaht, Father.

The book soon went out of print.

In the summer of 1933, Trevor attended a summer school on Marxism and Christianity at Keble College, Oxford. Trevor was introduced to Christian Socialists like Maurice Reckitt, Canon V. A. Demant, Ruth Kenyon and the notorious Conrad Noel, the 'red' vicar who hung the hammer and sickle flag in his church at Thaxted, Essex. T. S. Eliot, whose poetry Trevor would recite until his death, gave the introductory address on 'Christianity and International Order'; Dr Julius Hecker travelled from Moscow to talk about the religious challenge of Communism. Trevor found many of the talks baffling but intoxicating; he learnt what a Christian Socialist was and signed petitions and wrote angry letters to the newspapers.

A month before his final year at Oxford, Trevor was enticed by Miles Sergeant to help with a Mission to Bournemouth. The Mission was not sectarian; it involved all the parishes in Bournemouth, and was run by an Evangelical curate called Max Warren. Trevor had never met Evangelicals before, and was impressed by their holiness and mania. Another Missioner was Fr Andrew Blair, who was a novice in the Community of the Resurrection, a male community in West Yorkshire based on the life of the first Christians. Fr Blair and Trevor stayed with a wealthy widow called Mrs Smythe, who plied the young men with whiskey while they talked about daily offices and living simply and letting the old self die. Fr Blair was moved by Trevor's 'goodness and evident strength of character'. Fr Harold Ellis, a more senior member of the Community, promised to write to Trevor as both men left Bournemouth.

Fr Harold Ellis was a ritualist and very left-wing. He loved aphorisms, like 'Every true Religious has a shaven head' and 'The good novice leaps as it were on fire at the sound of the rising bell.' In his weekly letters to Trevor at Oxford, he would explain what a monk was, and give a strict rule of prayer, daily offices and daily Mass. He would visit Trevor, and intimidate the undergraduate with his overbearing manner. In December 1933 Trevor spent four days in retreat and two days in conference at the Retreat House of the Community at Mirfield, West Yorkshire. As soon as he arrived at the ugly stone building, he knew that God had led him there and that this is where he would stay. By the time he left, he knew that he would be a monk.

At Mirfield, Trevor chatted to Fr Keble Talbot, who was the Superior of the Community. Fr Talbot was the son and brother of Anglican bishops, and determined not to become one. He was warm and devout and adored by everyone. He loved books and pictures and music and, most of all, conversation. But Trevor liked him for what he was and not what he said. He was a consecrated person, and used to utter: 'Religion is saying Yes to God!' One day, the two men were walking in the monastery gardens, when Fr Talbot stopped suddenly, turned to Trevor and said perceptively: 'You know, what will be most demanding for you will be having no children.'

Looking back, Trevor felt that he had wasted much of his time at Oxford, being too immature. Yet, like many of his generation at Lancing, he had made the decision to become a priest. Unlike many of them, though, he knew that he was attracted by the monastic life. His religion, too, nurtured by the Missions he had attended and the priests he had met, taught him that you could not separate Christ from His world. Over thirty years later, at the Mission to Oxford in May 1963, he said: 'It was here, at Oxford, very dimly, very feebly, and very intermittently, that I first began to realize that you cannot love the invisible God unless you find him in "the brother whom you have seen".'

Trevor celebrated his twenty-first birthday in the month he came down from Oxford. His father and stepmother threw a party at their house in St Albans, and Trevor was given a pair of ivory hairbrushes engraved with his initials. Trevor then told his father that he was going to be a monk; his father was confused and angry, and told him to set sail and see the world.

4

From Oxford to Ordination

TREVOR OBEYED HIS FATHER. Although he was certain that he wanted to be ordained, he realized that a Grand Tour of the East might still change his mind. After attending the 1934 Anglo-Catholic School of Sociology, he sold his car and, with the £500 legacy that his Aunt Potsa had left him, set off from Tilbury on a freighter bound for Ceylon. He was very keen to visit India, which he had thought and dreamt about for much of his childhood.

His old Lancing friend Patrick Cotter suggested that he contact John Hardy, a half-Italian priest in his mid-forties, who was now the vicar of St Michael's, Colombo. Trevor arrived in Colombo wearing a white drill suit and Christ Church tie, and travelled by rickshaw to the vicarage of St Michael's. He arrived during the afternoon siesta, and John Hardy, who had forgotten that he was coming, greeted him with the words: 'I suppose you've come to put up your banns of marriage.'

St Michael's was an eclectic church, which attracted English and Sinhalese gentry, Portuguese and Dutch burghers. The Sisters of the Society of St Margaret, from East Grinstead, cleaned the church and visited the poor. John Hardy looked after Trevor, who was nervous on his own; he made sure that the young graduate saw much of Sri Lanka, including Jaffna in the north and Kandy. He saw the Perahera, in which dancers, trumpeters, flame-throwers and decorated elephants processed through the streets in honour of the Sacred Tooth. He visited Trinity College, Kandy, which was run like an English public school and promoted itself as the 'Eton of Ceylon'. After four months in Ceylon, he went on a memorable journey with John Hardy: they travelled by boat across to Burma, up the Irrawaddy River, from Rangoon to the Chinese border, via Mandalay. They travelled through remote Burmese villages, and all the time Trevor was aware that he was visiting the same villages as his father. John Hardy then left Trevor, but provided him with Espramuttu, a Sri Lankan servant, who accompanied Trevor to those places in India where his father had served – Bombay, Poona, Delhi, Agra and Madras.

Trevor then sailed by Japanese steamer to the Holy Land, to spend Holy Week and Easter of 1935 there. He was following in the foot-steps of his hero Charles de Foucauld, the former cavalry officer, explorer and Trappist monk who had made his first pilgrimage to the Holy Land in 1888. De Foucauld had spent two years as a servant at convents in Nazareth and Jerusalem, and it was during these years that the former soldier discerned his vocation. In the Holy Land, de Foucauld had learnt that a disciple needed to be in 'an intimate friend-ship with our Lord, expressing itself more especially in the cult of His words in the Gospel and His presence in the Blessed Sacrament'. Trevor never forgot de Foucauld's injunction to himself: 'Be kind and compassionate; let no distress leave you unmoved.'

After a brief trip to Florence, Trevor returned to England and the-ological college. Sir Ernest Huddleston, who did not understand his son's politics or religion, had hoped for a change of heart. But his son had travelled widely, but narrowly; he had spent much of his Grand Tour among his father's service friends or in the familiar world of Anglican ecclesiology. Understandably, he still wished to be a priest and not a naval captain or businessman.

In the summer of 1935, Trevor began training for ordination at Wells Theological College. The choice of college was bizarre; Trevor loved full-blooded and disturbing religion, and detested a compro-mised, respectable faith, yet he was happy to join a college which produced English Gentlemen in Holy Orders. Mirfield, or another Catholic college, would be a natural home. Perhaps Trevor was encouraged by his friend Patrick Cotter and Walter Frere, the Superior of the Community of the Resurrection, both of whom studied at Wells. He may have tired of 'slum religion', with its extreme Catholicism and aggressive demands, and felt that a 'middle-stump' Anglican college, with its strong reputation for hunting and fishing, would give him a broader sense of his faith. It still seems a strange decision.

Trevor spent a year at Wells, before going up to Mirfield. Religion at Wells, with its cathedral, bishop's palace and close, was often gossipy and social. The bishop, St John Wynne Wilson, was a former headmaster of both Haileybury and Marlborough College. The Dean, R. H. Malden, was a classical scholar and historian who wrote caustic prefaces to Crockfords and went around in a top hat and frock coat. He used to be fetched from the Close by a verger carrying a wand, and was nicknamed 'Pompey' Malden.

All the students at the College lived in houses in the fourteenth-century Vicars' Close. Trevor's neighbours at Wells included Sam Wodehouse, later Archdeacon of London; George Sidebotham, who would also join the Community of the Resurrection; and Spencer Trimingham, who became Professor of Islamic Studies in Beirut. There was much laughter and drinking and partying in the Close.

But Trevor was different. He joined in the life of the College, but it was his vocation that mattered, not his ability to mimic the bishop. He needed to study hard for his General Ordination Examination, for he had not read Theology. Every morning he would be up before anyone else, starting the day with the half-hour of prayer which he had learnt at Mirfield. He read the mystics and studied the lives of contemplative monks, although he did not wish to join their orders. He visited the Benedictine monks at Downside Abbey, a few miles over the Mendip Hills, and considered becoming a Roman Catholic. But he decided that the Church of England was part of the Catholic Church, and therefore there was no need to live outside it. He read *The Cloud of Unknowing*, St Augustine, von Hügel. He waded through religious hagiography, much of it drivel: the lives of St Francis of Assisi, St Francis Xavier, St Dominic and the important Jesuits.

Above all, there was a 'hidden', reserved side to Trevor at Wells; he was trying to make his soul and brought a measure of concentration to all parts of college life – the Daily Offices and Eucharist, the tutorials, the lectures on Old Testament prophecy, the administrative meetings, the Christmas parties. He was not priggish, and happily put up with his housemate playing the radio all day and night. But he was resolute and single-minded; he was learning that the kind of religious life he had chosen would not make him comfortable, but might make him holy. This striking, austere man was not self-conscious, but his spiritual character made cleverer people feel they were learning from him.

Young ordinands at Wells like Trevor would spend time in the small whitewashed cottage of Fr John Briscoe, an Oxford scholar and rector of West Bagborough, at the foot of the Quantock Hills in Somerset. Fr Briscoe lived a secluded, scholarly life, happy with his devotions and his books. He was an exacting and obsessive man, but devoted as a priest. He hated holidays, sat on an upright chair and slept on a plain iron bed, which was often untouched in Lent. Unlike most priests, he hated sin and taught other people to hate it to; he avoided vague platitudes, and was severe with those who deserved it. He told one impenitent woman that she would go to Hell through her own free choice if she did not repent and amend her ways. He would support delinquent priests, who would stay for up to six months in a separate cottage which he owned at the end of the village. He looked after them kindly but firmly, and their stay was their penance. He led Anglican opposition to birth control and the 1928 Prayer Book, and taught that no priest could share his life with both God and a wife. When a curate married, Fr Briscoe wrote 'One gone' in his diary. When a close friend married, he would refuse to speak or write for years, only to send a postcard out of the blue: 'You are now out of quarantine. Come and see me soon.'

Fr Briscoe was a steely influence on Trevor, who would cycle over from Wells on Feast Days to lunch and learn how to become a good priest. This man, who lived a perpetual life of abstinence, told Trevor that a priest ought to be 'holy and clean'. A good priest was God's most glorious creation, because he was an imitation of Christ. No priest should ever accommodate his views to seek high office. 'Don't expect preferment if you're a true Catholic,' he warned young priests like Trevor. He would then add, with a wicked glint in his eye, 'To be a bishop you must be resilient, ambiguous, accommodating, and with a mind so broad that it can accept anything and change at all times to suit modern conditions.' Trevor felt unworthy in his presence.

Trevor recognized that Wells was an important, if uneventful, year in his life. Years later, he said: 'In the Christian life you get a kind of rhythm. There is a period of withdrawal followed by a great deal of outward activity. The one is necessary to the other. Great chunks of one's life can be a withdrawal. Wells was that for me. Oxford and the tour of the East was behind. Wells was like a prolonged retreat. It was the preparation for my whole future life. It helped me to draw closer to God, and it gave me a better understanding of what I must do.'

In Michaelmas 1936, Trevor was ordained a deacon in Bristol Cathedral by Bishop C. S. Woodward. Fr Andrew Blair, with whom he had shared digs in Bournemouth, had worked as a curate at St Mark's, Swindon, and suggested that Trevor do likewise.

5

Swindon

SWINDON WAS A DRAB TOWN of 66,000 inhabitants, set among the green plains of the Wiltshire Downs. The old town was a prosperous village of West Country stone, solid and well proportioned and coloured to blend in with the countryside around. The new town was red brick and working class.

In the mid-nineteenth century, the Great Western Railway (GWR) decided that Swindon would be a good place to change their trains' engines as they approached the steeper climb to Bristol. The GWR also needed to establish a large repair shop for their locomotives, which meant that cottages would have to be built for the GWR workers. Old Swindon and the surrounding villages could not absorb such a workforce, so a plot of three hundred houses made out of Bath stone was built near the factory. The new village looked like a French boulevard with trees.

Generations of railway workers were employed by GWR, and sons saw such employment as a vocation. Railwaymen would only leave their cottages if they were dismissed from the company, or if their wives behaved scandalously. They would be woken for work by the sound of a hooter, and went for their two-week holidays when the company told them to. One-sixth of Swindon's population worked for the railways; others worked in the schools or Wills cigarette factory.

To one side of the village was the 'pattern-book Gothic' church of St Mark's, which was uncompromisingly Catholic. The church was designed by Gilbert Scott and opened in 1845, when the directors and shareholders of GWR realized they needed a church in the new town they were creating. It was in a dreadful position close to the railway line: sermons would be interrupted by whistles and passing trains;

diesel fumes would blacken the leaves and tombstones and eat into the steeple.

St Mark's was a thriving working-class parish. Many of the congregation worked for the railways and would meet at work and worship. The assistant general manager of the GWR sang in the choir along with fitters and tuners from the workshop. Apart from laying on Bible classes and Sunday Schools, the church organized reading rooms, five cricket and football clubs, two Temperance Societies and a cycling club for children to roam the countryside. In front of the church was a large recreation ground – the Park. John Betjeman, who loved both the GWR and St Mark's, once described Swindon's churches as the New Jerusalem; he claimed that their priests taught a simple and definite faith which was neither Sabbatarian nor smug. Swindon restored his faith in the Church of England.

Anglo-Catholic clergy were particularly effective in 'slum' parishes like Swindon, as they worked relentless hours and saw themselves as uniformed priests on active service. Unlike many of their drearier colleagues in 'middle-stump' parishes, a good Anglo-Catholic priest was interested in people and understood them. He had the rare ability of identifying himself with them, and he knew what he wanted to do with them – which was to bring them to the Mass. He was often eccentric and had a subversive sense of humour, which mean that parishioners did not have to appear pious when they were visited by their priest or curates. An afternoon's visit by a slum priest could often be lively, purposeful and argumentative. Confirmation classes would produce good and fervent communicants, even if they were unclear about the finer details of the Christian life. Wearing their cassocks and birettas, they would tramp up and down the streets of provincial towns like Swindon, fulfilling the idea of a priestly ministry offered by our Lord: 'I know my sheep, and am known of mine.'

The priest of St Mark's was Canon Alexander Ross, a wealthy Old Etonian who paid Trevor's stipend out of his own pocket. Canon Ross, who had served in Swindon since his ordination in 1891, was a generous but shy man, who had a stutter and did not enjoy chatting to strangers. But he could leave his staff to sip tea with the workers and teach Scripture in the schools; when Trevor arrived in Swindon as a 23-year-old at St Mark's, there were four other curates and a handful of Sisters from the Community of St Mary the Virgin, Wantage. They all lived together in the Mission House, and served

St Mark's and her daughter churches, which had been built as the town grew.

Canon Ross lived alone and treated his cavernous vicarage like a London town house. It was run by two elderly maids, and every night they would haul an old tin bath and buckets of water up the stairs for the vicar to use. On Sunday nights after Evensong, all the curates would be summoned to dinner at the Vicarage, where they would be served hock and claret by the maids, who wore their best caps and aprons. After dinner, each curate would be asked to give a précis of the sermon he had preached that day. It had to be very short, and Canon Ross would listen assiduously and write down notes in a big book before delivering some acerbic comments. Trevor was rarely praised. An often tetchy staff meeting would be held the following morning, and Trevor would be outwitted by Fr Ross, who was an excellent chess player and understood his opponent's weaknesses.

Trevor would begin his day with prayer, followed by Matins, Mass and breakfast. He kept his religious rule, and devoted the mornings of his first year at Swindon to study for his diaconal examinations. It was the height of the Depression in 1936, and many of the workers were without jobs and tried to hide their poverty. In the afternoons, he would visit them in their stone cottages and talk about church outings to Marlborough Forest and Cirencester Park, or the timings of cate-chism classes for their children. At St Mark's, Canon Ross had asked Trevor to be in charge of the 'little catechism' class, which was held on Sunday afternoons for children between the ages of 10 and 13. The first time Trevor entered the class, the children mimicked the young curate and made revolting noises, but Canon Ross punished the troublemakers and Trevor was soon popular.

A few workers were suspicious of this lanky and handsome man with large feet who cycled around Swindon wearing his dark cassock and biretta; they would slam the door in his face and mutter abuse about clerics. Most parishioners, though, would have him in and give him a cup of tea. He was known to be humble, but had presence and could fill a room. They liked the way he was at ease with people – although shy, he loved to talk and tell funny stories while smoking Churchman's cigarettes. He was also forceful in conversation with people, and rarely lost his nerve. Trevor worked hard, and watched how Fr Ross conducted services at St Mark's. He was fond of Fr Ross, who would sometimes appear for Mass with coal on his dog collar, having stoked the boiler in the vicarage.

In 1937, Canon Ross was succeeded by Fr Ronald Royle, a gruff and forceful man who had been awarded an MC in the First World War. Fr Royle worked the curates hard, and kept them in order by demanding they all lived with him in the Vicarage. Trevor soon became disenchanted with Fr Royle, who had a Northern bluntness and lacked his predecessor's charm. Nevertheless, he could have remained for many years in Swindon, where he had learnt how to teach the faith and visit the poor.

But his thoughts were leading him elsewhere, to the Community of the Resurrection. Before he set off for Mirfield in the spring of 1937, he gave a dance for his girlfriends. Most of them cried.

6

The Community of the Resurrection

To reach the Community of the Resurrection's House, you pass through the old mining town of Mirfield in West Yorkshire. You stroll pass some stone cottages, once black with soot, and make your way up a steep road. To your left are the mill chimneys of the valley of the river Calder, scarred by railway tracks and power lines. The road slopes into the gate of a large neo-Gothic house. You walk up the drive, past shrubs and a well-tended lawn. A crucifix faces out across the valley. It often rains.

Once inside, you wait silently in a wide hall with a large panelled staircase to your right. It could be the entrance to a headmaster's house. It is always peaceful, although there are distant noises of cutlery being washed up and doors being opened and slammed. In front of you is a table, upon which are placed messages for members of the Community. Close by is the portrait of a startling figure with a red beard and translucent eyes. This is Charles Gore, who founded the Community over a century ago.

Charles Gore was an Old Harrovian aristocrat with an anguished conscience who, by his early thirties, had been a fellow of Trinity, a Vice-Principal of Cuddesdon Theological College and Principal of Pusey House, where Trevor first discussed Marx. He was a restless scholar, who in 1899 had contributed to a volume of essays – *Lux Mundi* – which explained the Christian faith in the light of new historical and scientific knowledge. His own chapter, entitled 'The Holy Spirit and Inspiration', caused particular offence, as he claimed that Jonah and David were mythical creatures rather than historical figures. Myth, he added, was not a falsehood, but simply the means by which a child or a simple person made sense of his faith. Gore was a liberal Catholic, who rebelled against the dogmatic certainties of Pusey and Keble.

He was also a shy man, and would make startling comments to end conversations. Once, when he was offered tea by the ferociously teetotal wife of a bishop, he replied: 'I never drink anything but alcoholic beverages'. He was an Anglo-Catholic celibate, and a socialist, although he was suspicious of the word, because it was confused with free love and atheism.

When he was at Pusey House, Gore decided to set up his own religious order in the Church of England. With five friends, he made his profession at Pusey House in July 1892. Religious communities emerge when people believe that their Church has strayed. Gore abhorred the contentment of the Established Church, and would write 'I hate the Church of England' (he didn't) and 'The Church of England is an ingeniously devised instrumentality for defeating the objects it is supposed to promote.' He would describe bishops as 'useless creatures', even when he wore a mitre. He loved youthful fervour, and had an intense dislike for clergy who were middle-aged and respectable.

Gore wanted to establish an all-male community like the first Christians in the Acts of the Apostles who 'continued steadfastly in the Apostles' teaching and fellowship, in the breaking of bread and the prayers'. His community would live together simply, dedicated to God; members were not withdrawing from the world, but they were spurning its standards.

The Community of the Resurrection was not the first men's community in the Church of England. The Society of St John the Evangelist, at Cowley in Oxford, was established in 1866 by Fr Benson. Fr Benson was an ascetic man, who wanted to create a diligent and unobtrusive order. With four other priests, he vowed to live 'in celibacy, poverty and obedience, as one of the Mission Priests of St John the Evangelist, unto my life's end'. First, they were to sanctify themselves 'in conformity with the will of God'; second, they would serve the Church by preaching to missions around the country and by showing the presence of Christ through their lives. They were an intellectual order.

Both communities had emerged from the Catholic Revival of the later nineteenth century. They believed that through lives of individual holiness they could resuscitate a flabby Church by linking it with the One Catholic and Apostolic Church of its past. Yet Charles Gore was different from Fr Benson; his order would dedicate itself to Christ by teaching and helping the poor. He was disgusted with the Church of England for 'having failed so long and on so wide a scale to behave as the champion of the oppressed and the weak'.

Gore was a loner who needed community, and the Rule of his Order reflected this ambivalence. The Rule was new and not based on Benedictine or Dominican patterns, although it borrowed from both. Brethren only made vows of obedience for thirteen months, rather than life; they renewed their vows yearly, and only need show the 'intention' of remaining permanently. They should be obedient to their Superior, but could appeal to the General Chapter if they were disgruntled with any order. They were to obey their conscience, and do nothing which violated it. They should be free to leave at the end of each year.

Having made a vow of poverty, they were to hand over all their material possessions and income to a common fund, but were allowed to keep capital. They were to intend to remain celibate, but need not promise it for life. They were to dress as ordinary priests, wearing cassocks with neither sandals nor girdles. Those entering the Community were called 'probationers' rather than 'novices', the 'refectory' would be known as the 'dining room', Gore was to be known as 'Senior' rather than 'Superior'. It was a very Anglican arrangement, for the Community was struggling to reconcile two opposites – personal liberty and corporate authority.

After making their professions, Gore and his five friends left Pusey House and moved to the Vicarage of Radley, Oxon, where Gore was the vicar. They would carry out normal parish duties while living a communal life of fellowship and prayer. They would write books and take retreats, in accordance with – in the words of the Rule – 'the special gifts which God has given to them'. But it was a silly move; Radley was a village set in the Oxfordshire countryside; the farmers and labourers were bemused by the sudden presence of six highly educated clergymen, and dozed through their sermons on socialism and corrupt bishops. Gore grew depressed, and ill, and looked for a new home in the North. In 1897, the Bishop of Wakefield suggested they move to Hall Croft, near Mirfield; an unpleasant but large house which had belonged to a wealthy mill owner. The brethren, who now numbered eleven, moved to Hall Croft the following year.

The appearance of a monastery in an industrial heartland close to Leeds and Huddersfield made Yorkshiremen shudder. The Protestant Truth Society distributed pamphlets: 'Christians! Churchmen! Englishmen! Beware of the Mirfield Monks! The Community seeks to entrap our wives into the hateful confessional!' As tensions rose, a member of the Community was summoned to defend his faith to a crowd gathered outside the Black Bull, in the middle of Mirfield. A lot of beer was drunk, and the matter was forgotten.

Gore, who soon tired of the Community he established, left and became a Canon at Westminster. His successor, Walter Frere, was shocked at the temperamental Gore's behaviour, and wrote: 'Poverty and obscurity is what we want, and really Westminster is enough to stifle anyone's religion.' Frere, a calm and diligent man, was an outstanding Superior from 1902 to 1922. Under his leadership, the Community emerged as a large worshipping, teaching and missionary organization. He made two vital moves; in 1902 he founded the College of the Resurrection, which offered a five-year training course to ordinands unable to afford university. The same year he sent three brothers to South Africa, after the Bishop of Pretoria asked if the Superior could spare some brethren to work with the 200,000 Africans in the gold mine.

Back home in Yorkshire, the Community House was enlarged, a retreat house was built and work began on the Community church. A Fraternity of the Resurrection was formed, in which lay and clerical friends observed a rule of life and supported the Community. The Community turned a local quarry into an open-air theatre, and persuaded Keir Hardie and other Labour politicians to talk with clergy about factory conditions and low wages. Mrs Pankhurst spoke once, for far too long. A Community House was opened in London before the First World War. Religious tracts and academic literature poured out of Mirfield. In 1923, Frere left Mirfield and became the Bishop of Truro, although unlike Gore he remained a member of the Community.

Frere's successor was Fr Talbot, who had strolled around the monastery gardens with Trevor on his first visit to Mirfield. Talbot was an effective and genial leader, yet reflected the pre-War temper of the Church – he was happy to discuss socialism and the Church, but did not share the younger generation's distrust of nationalism and the old order. While Talbot would preach about the conditions of the poor, younger priests argued that a new understanding of God was needed in a post-war society; more money was not enough. A new generation of restless priests would soon join the Community, and they sought a more dogmatic and fevered religious response to society's ills. The Young Turks were led by the startling Fr Raymond Raynes, who as a 24-year-old curate in Bury was already expressing the need for deeper commitment and obedience:

> The world is redeemed through suffering – it is a great mystery but it is true. Christ died for us and we have got to die for Christ. Sacrifice and suffering are the heart of the Christian faith and it is from this sacrifice and suffering that comes the calmness and union with God that is the lot of every true Christian. Men will not face this truth – they have never really seen that at the heart of our faith there is suffering – that to be a real Christian takes far more physical and moral courage than anything else in the world.

When Trevor, and other members of this generation, joined the Community in the 1930s, their passion could exist with the phlegm of an older generation. This was down to Gore, who left a Rule which combined the needs of his own generation with the ideals of a younger one. Fr Talbot, too, had been astute; in Fr Harold Ellis, he had appointed a Novice Guardian who would teach discipline and austerity to his young charges. He was ideal for Trevor.

7

The Young Novice

IN THE SPRING OF 1939 Trevor arrived at Mirfield to test his
vocation. Trevor always had an overwhelming sense of being 'called'.
At Lancing, he could have followed his father into the navy or become
a solicitor, but he chose to spend part of his holidays helping Fr
Collyer's Mission at Camberwell. At Oxford, he might have married
one of his pretty dancing companions and become a historian, but
instead he entertained the hop pickers in Kent and listened to Marxist
philosophers at summer conferences. After Wells, he could have
settled as a cultivated country parson, yet worked as an austere curate
in a working-class parish at the height of the Depression. Even at
Swindon, he could have become an eccentric yet dedicated priest,
adored by the railway workers. But here he was, at the age of 26, in a
dark monastery next to a smog-filled town with a poisoned river.

Not only did Trevor have a sense of being called, but he was
responding to a call which required one particular step of faith. In
faith, he entered the novitiate at Mirfield. The monastic vocation
requires the most naked act of faith; as the author of the Epistle to the
Hebrews writes: 'He that cometh to God must believe that He is, and
that He is a rewarder of them that diligently seek him.' This is true of
any novice in a religious community.

The idea of monasticism seems strange, but it does make sense. For
the deeply religious, and especially for those whose vocation demands
celibacy, it is very straightforward; one's attachment to God takes
precedence over attachments to people. Although such people may
succeed in loving their neighbours as themselves, the injunction
'Thou shalt love the Lord thy God with all thy heart and with all thy
soul and with all thy mind' is truly 'the first and great commandment'.

Within the walls of a monastery, intimate attachments, or the desires for such attachments, are not unknown, but they are regarded as distractions and frowned upon. This is why the best monks are a little separate and unknown, even to their fellow brethren.

Indeed, many monks believe that human relationships are an obstacle to communion with God. They follow a path of European thought, which assumed until recently that happiness could not be expected from human relationships, but from Man's relationship with God. The founders of the monastic movement were the hermits of the Egyptian desert, who believed that perfection could only be achieved through renouncing the world, mortifying the flesh and leading a solitary life of contemplation and hard discipline. It was soon recognized that the life of the anchorite was not possible for everyone, so the 'coenobitic' tradition arose in which monks no longer lived alone but shared the life of dedication to God in communities.

It would also be wrong to assume that all those who have put their relation with God before their relations with their fellows are abnormal or neurotic. Of course, monasteries have their misfits; some of those who choose the monastic or celibate life do so for the wrong reasons, perhaps because they are scared of responsibility, or their human relationships have failed, or they want to retreat from the world. But this is not true of all; and even if it were so, it would not imply that a life in which close attachments to other human beings played little part was necessarily incomplete.

Trevor was not scared of life and he was not fleeing from a broken love affair. He was, however, attracted by the heroic strand in religious life, and the constancy and mettle required of a novice would have appealed to him. But Trevor found his novitiate difficult – a quiet but forceful character, he was confined to Mirfield while friends from school and university were being called up and slaughtered to defend their country. As he chopped trees in the quarry and listened to Fr Talbot's anecdotes, his friends were being summoned to fight, leaving their wives and families behind. Through the months of the gathering storm before the Second World War; then the months of the phoney War; then the fall of France, then Britain's darkest hour; then the Battle of Britain and the Blitz; then the years when events turned in Britain's favour – all this time, for four years in the prime of his life, Trevor remained in West Yorkshire and had to go on believing that he was called by God.

He himself wrote:

One Sunday morning – September 3rd 1939 – we were all in the garden after Mass. The outbreak of the War was announced. I was young, fit and strong enough to join up. It was announced that the Community would choose who would go as army chaplains and who would not. I was not under the lifetime vow of obedience, but only under the novices' vow. I could have pulled out of the novitiate and was sorely tempted to do so. I could not help feeling that it was a terrible waste of time to hang about at Mirfield while there was a war on. But if I was to remain a novice, I had to obey. In the end, I became even more surrendered to God. Millions were going through hell, and Christians had no business to be soft and sit back. But it was a terrific withdrawal. With all the other people out fighting, it was very hard not to be with them. It required a very difficult discipline. I am certain that this withdrawal, very much into monastic seclusion, coiled the spring tighter and tighter, and when I got to South Africa it gave me whatever punch I had.

For a novice like Trevor, the old self has to die. A novice will be confronted starkly with the resistance of the old self to the new life of Christ which he is trying to embrace in a monastery; the purpose of a monastery is not to break the will, but to form a will to seek God and to love Him. He must realize that his own wishes and talents no longer matter. Something more is demanded, and it is the Community that makes that response possible. Trevor's two years as a novice were the most inward-looking of his life; once again he flirted with Roman Catholicism and considered becoming a contemplative monk – one who never leaves the monastery, but devotes his life to prayer, study and labour.

Trevor would not have been allowed to leave the house, except for a couple of hours in the afternoon. He would have been given a small amount of pocket money, and would need to ask permission if he wanted to buy a stamp. He would only be allowed to smoke at certain times; all activity would be curtailed at the ringing of a bell. Such discipline taught the novice to depend on the Community. Trevor was learning to detach himself from his own cast of mind and to find God's will in the life of the Community. Now he would live according to the Rule, which stated: 'Every brother shall consider it of the highest importance to fulfil his whole duty to each of the other members of the fraternity. He shall examine himself in respect of those virtues which make communal life healthy and spiritual: Industry, Gravity of Speech, Punctuality, Openness, Cheerfulness, Patience.'

Trevor, though inflexible, was an excellent novice who remained thoughtful and silent when fellow brothers irritated him. He did not seem a leader and was never a rebel; he was the last person to stand up to authority. One day, Trevor was serving lunch to a priest who was on retreat. When he had left the room, the priest turned to his companion and said: 'Who is that young man with the face of an angel who would gladly go to the fires of Smithfield?'

Prayer was at the centre of the novice's life. Trevor would need to be taught how to pray, in the same way that a child needs games teachers to be taught how to use his limbs. Trevor would be in the Community's church seven times a day, apart from Mass. He would rise before six o'clock, and meditate silently in his room. At 6.45 he would enter the church for Matins, where one brother would intone prayers and sentences while Trevor knelt in the stalls. Mass was at 7.45, followed by a simple breakfast – often porridge and bread. After breakfast, he would be given a job in the Community – perhaps cleaning the church. He would have to set aside three hours a day for study. At nine o'clock there was the service of Terce, after which talking was allowed. At one o'clock there was Sext, then lunch. A couple of hours in the afternoon would be set aside for recreation, and Trevor might dig for potatoes or wander around the monastery gardens. Tea would follow at four, followed by None and then time for study. Evensong, when hymns would be sung and guests would read the lessons, took place at seven. The brethren would meet in the Community Room between supper (7.30 p.m.) and Compline (9.45 p.m.), where they might chat or remain silent depending on their mood. After Compline there would be complete silence until Terce the next day; the corridors were always silent. Trevor would rarely leave Mirfield; it was now his home.

Trevor's Novice Guardian, Fr Harold Ellis, had met and liked Trevor in Bournemouth. Fr Ellis was similar to Trevor; they both had a theatrical streak and were prone to bold statements. Fr Ellis would talk about 'my novices'; but he was not possessive and encouraged

Trevor to pursue his interests. Fr Ellis introduced Trevor to Counter-Reformation thought, including St Theresa of Avila ('Think great thoughts of God, and serve him with a quiet mind') and St Vincent de Paul ('It is only by the love you bear them that the poor will forgive you your "charity"'). Trevor devoted himself to the life and writings of St William of Saint Thierry, the abbot who met Bernard of Clairvaux in around 1120 and rekindled the spirituality of the Desert of centuries earlier.

St William attracted Trevor, for he spelt out how a disciplined will could be the vehicle of love. One of William's sayings fascinated Trevor: 'The love of truth drives us from the world to God: and the truth of love drives us from God to the world.' Trevor, who loved words, was struck by how William expressed deep truths clearly. More importantly, William taught Trevor that the person of God lay in the image of every person, and that Man could behave like a barbarian, but was not an animal.

The night before he was professed on St Mark's Day in April 1941, Trevor sat with two other novices – Mark Tweedy and Douglas Edwards – and waited for dawn in the Chapel of the Resurrection in the Community's neo-Romanesque church. Throughout the long night, other brethren came in silently, to sit with the three young men. Owing to the war, Trevor's father was unable to make the ceremony; besides, he was disturbed by the life his son had chosen.

But Trevor had no doubts. At Mass the next morning, the three young men were taken to the Sanctuary. Each man was asked whether he would live by the Rule of the Community until he died. The Superior asked:

Q: Dost thou desire to be professed as a brother in this Community?

A: I do.

Q: Hast thou considered the difficulties and trials that await thee if thou wilt live worthily the Religious Life, and the still greater evils that will ensue if thou live therein unworthily?

A: I have duly weighed them: yet, God helping me, I cannot but go forward.

Q: Dost thou intend, if God give thee grace, to abide therein till thy life's end?

A: I do so intend, by the help of God.

Trevor was then led round a semicircle of his brethren to hold each other's hand in turn. Trevor was presented with his Community cross, which was the sign of his brotherhood. After the Mass, all the brethren ate a slice of his profession cake.

The four years that Trevor spent at Mirfield – two years as a novice and two years as a professed monk – were during the war, and therefore unusual. Food was scarce, and the growing of it essential – novices would 'dig for victory' under the eye of the lofty Fr Ralph Bell. Several members of the Community were absent, being chaplains to the Armed Forces. Parishes had closed down many of the activities which involved the monks. However, the Community continued visiting the poor at local parishes; Trevor helped a parish mission at nearby Heckmondwike and would hear the confessions of priests and laity. He was a gentle and understanding confessor. He would also read the letters from members serving in one of the Community's five houses in South Africa and Southern Rhodesia, and listen to old stories from the older brethren who had served there.

One brother was now returning from South Africa, to become the Superior of the Community. He was Fr Raymond Raynes, who had been in South Africa since December 1932, first as a housemaster at St John's College and then as prior and parish priest of the college. He was the only nomination for Superior, to replace the kind but ageing Fr Bernard Horner, and was elected in January 1943.

Raynes arrived back unannounced, having spent Holy Week and Easter as a chaplain at sea. He walked up the drive from the bus stop and Trevor, who was on kitchen duty that day, answered the door. The two men had not met before. Trevor said: 'There was Fr Raynes, looking like death. I knew who it was from the photographs. He did not, of course, know me. He announced himself. "Well, I'm Trevor," I said.' Raymond went to bed with flu and Trevor was told to look after him. Raynes was sick, but only 39 and bursting with unusual ideas. 'I was immediately captivated by him,' wrote Trevor. 'He was a very attractive person. From then on, I loved him dearly and got to know him well. I kindled to all he said.'

Fr Christopher Millington, another member of the Community, was supposed to succeed Raymond Raynes, but he had withdrawn on personal grounds. After two weeks of chatting to him by his bedside, Raymond decided that Trevor should take over from him as Prior of Christ the King, in Sophiatown, a suburb of Johannesburg. Trevor was nervous, and told Raymond that the Novice Guardian would say that he was too quiet and immature for the job. Other brethren thought that Raynes was acting rashly, but he brushed their complaints aside; he was perceptive about Trevor's potential and knew that Trevor was his first appointment as Superior, so people would grumble but not object. Raymond wrote to the acting Provincial in South Africa: 'Trevor is really the goods and I am sure our beloved Sophiatown and Orlando will be greatly blessed by his goodness and efficiency.'

Trevor knew nothing about South Africa. Fr Raynes, and other brethren who had served in South Africa, recommended books that he should read about the Boer War, the Dutch Reformed Church, segregation, the political constitution. He knew that he had to learn about the history of South Africa, for once he arrived in Sophiatown, he would need to argue with facts and not emotion. He was now a 30-year-old white priest, a product of Lancing College and Oxford, who had spent a three-year curacy in a working-class parish and four years in a monastery in West Yorkshire. He had never spoken into a microphone, printed a poster or separated a fight. Now he would be sent out to be in charge of a parish of 60,000 Africans in Sophiatown and another 40,000 six miles away in Orlando. But he could not fight the move; he was a member of a community of faith and prayer, and had prayed for God's support – 'O thou that has prepared a place for my soul, prepare my soul for that place.' The place was Orlando and Sophiatown; Trevor felt inadequate, but he knew that he must go.

On 29 July 1943 he embarked on board the SS *Themistocles*, which was sailing in convoy from Liverpool to Cape Town. As soon as he got on board ship and left England behind, he tossed his gas mask over the side. He then dug into his pocket and grasped a letter from his Superior:

I hope I have told you all that I can that is of any use about Sophiatown. Of course I cannot explain everything. There is much you will learn only by experience about Africa and about Sophiatown in particular. I know that in time you will probably want to change things and do new things. That is all as it should be – that is what you are going for. The only advice I dare to give you is this. Don't change things too quickly (even times of services!) as the natives are slow moving in these things. Above all things try to be unendingly patient with the people – and you will be rewarded with their love and their confidence; and try to be meticulously just – for that is what they look for in the Church and in her priests. They get little of it in the world, poor dears. Be fearless and outspoken when and where necessary on their behalf with government and municipal officials, etc. I just venture to say these bits of advice for what they are worth. But I am entrusting to you with a glad heart what is very important work of the CR and one dearest to my heart. I am quite happy that all will be well. Life in a small house is different and some-times rather trying, but stick to your prayers and all will be well. Give Africa my love – my heart is still there – and my greetings to all the people and the mission staff. Tell them I am well and looking forward to seeing them again one day. God bless you, dear Trevor; may His cross be your refuge; His resurrection your strength; His spirit your guide. May Mary and the Saints pray for you and the angels guard you.

Your affectionate Superior,

Raymond CR

Trevor spent seven weeks at sea; his convoy was bombed frequently, and he was sick throughout the voyage.

8

Sophiatown

AFRICA CHANGED TREVOR UTTERLY. He sailed into Cape Town on 6 September 1943; it was bright and hot, and he went to a club and ate an enormous lunch. The drizzle and austerity of England seemed a lifetime away. He then took the train to Johannesburg, where he was met by Fr Eric Goodall, the Provincial of the Community, and Fr Stephen Carter. The two men, who told Trevor that Mussolini had fallen, wanted to take him to Rossetenville, the Community's house in the centre of Johannesburg. Trevor, however, had different ideas: he needed to see Sophiatown.

It was a Thursday morning, and there was a school Mass. The young priest was nervous as he walked across the playground towards the church of Christ the King. Trevor afterwards wrote:

> I didn't know when I first arrived how I was going to cope with it all because I had this vast parish to look after, with about seven churches and a large number of schools, including the largest primary school in South Africa, St Cyprians. On the day I arrived there, the doors of the church opened and about two thousand children poured out; and I thought, 'How ever am I going to get to know any of them?'

Sophiatown was a sleazy and exciting township built on a rocky hill about five miles west of Johannesburg. It was a collection of shanties, which resembled an Italian village in Umbria. It boasted the only swimming pool for African children in Johannesburg. From a distance, the place was charming: smoke curled into a pink sky, gum trees littered streets tightly packed with red-roofed houses. Walking through

Sophiatown, with its narrow, unpaved streets and dozens of shanties crowded with families, was like stumbling across the wrong part of Naples. Despite its poverty, Sophiatown had a special character for Africans; it was a bohemian and chaotic place, full of gangsters who modelled themselves on American movie stars like John Wayne and Humphrey Bogart. Being 6,000 feet above sea level, its altitude made people nervy and irritable; its squalor and degradation, which could result in forty people sharing a single tap, could make people feel murderous. There were at least three murders every weekend in the township. A child might grow up good in Sophiatown, but never innocent.

Sophiatown was part of the Western Areas townships, along with Martindale and Newclare. The three townships had a total population of around 80,000 people. Sophiatown was originally intended for whites; it was built on land bought by a Pole called Mr Tobiansky at the turn of the century. The township was named after his wife Sophia, and the streets after his children. But Tobiansky's plan was destroyed when the city council built a sewage depot near the land, which white buyers thought repulsive. The Council then built several thousand houses for African builders on ground next to Sophiatown, and called it the Western Native Township. It was surrounded by a tall iron fence and guarded by watchmen. As industry in Johannesburg grew, so more Africans wanted to leave their tribes and live in Sophiatown. Tobiansky, unable to attract whites to the area, split the land and sold plots to Africans, Coloured People, Chinese and Indians who could not afford to buy freeholds in the city.

But in the fifty years since Mr Tobiansky's property dealings, the changes that had occurred in so many African cities struck Johannesburg. The white town spread, and those living in new suburbs were disturbed by the dirt and noise of Sophiatown, which had been safely hidden away. The prospect of rioting never seemed far off. Working-class whites, who lived in comparatively poor areas like Westdene and Newlands, became envious of the large houses owned by the more successful black hucksters in Sophiatown. And most importantly, that plot of land which Mr Tobiansky had bought and sold off had now increased enormously in value; consequently, the city was considering a motion to seize all the land owned by Africans, Coloured People, Indians and Chinese in the western area of Johannesburg. This would mean the end of Sophiatown, one of the few places in South Africa where Africans could purchase their own land.

At first, though, Trevor had other concerns. He was a white missionary priest with a passing interest in politics; his real task was to be in charge of the community's missions in Sophiatown and Orlando. So, first, he needed to get to know the fellow members of the Community who were staying with him at the Priory in Sophiatown, a small bungalow with two front doors and a red tin roof, which was set back from the street. The other brethren were all older than him; there was Fr David Downton, who was in his sixties; Fr Stephen Carter and Fr Matthew Trelawney-Ross, both in their fifties; and Fr Claude Lunniss, who was in his thirties. One fellow priest that Trevor met early on was Fr Leo Rakale, who was six days older than Trevor and a young novice in the Community. Fr Rakale was the first African priest that Trevor had met; he encouraged the tentative Prior, and advised him to learn Xhosa and Tswana so that he could celebrate Mass. In Alan Paton's novel *Cry the Beloved Country*, Fr Rakale is the young priest Theophilius Msimangu and Trevor is Fr Vincent.

Three Mirfield fathers – Nash, Fuller and Thomson – had established the first Community house in a mud hut in the middle of Johannesburg in March 1903, less than a year after the peace treaty that ended the Anglo-Boer war. Twenty years later, about twenty brethren – nearly half the Community – were working either in South Africa or Southern Rhodesia. Right from the outset, the Community supported the rights of blacks, and by 1920 they had trained thirty-one black clergy in the diocese of Pretoria. They preached to the miners and farmers from the Transvaal.

As the Community's missions expanded, so they bought land in Rossentville, a suburb of Johannesburg, and then built the Priory of St Peter, St Agnes School for Girls and St Peter's Secondary School for boys, which would produce most of the outstanding African politicians, lawyers and agitators of that generation. St Peter's, a theological college for black ordinands, was also set up. When Trevor became Superintendent of St Peter's, Oliver Tambo, the future African Congress leader, was teaching physics there; the two men became great friends.

The Community had also been put in charge of St John's College, a smart public school for four hundred white pupils which had faced financial ruin but was now thriving. It was here that Raymond Raynes had been an inexperienced housemaster of the prep school, and taught Latin and Divinity in the main school. Raynes had also moved the Community's headquarters from Rossentville to Sophiatown, which was some miles away and closer to Johannesburg.

By 1938, when Raymond Raynes had been Provincial for six years, the mission had built seven schools and three nursery schools which catered for over 6,000 children. Five years later, when Trevor arrived to continue Raynes's work, the Community was in charge of much of the education, religion and social conditions of urban Africans around Johannesburg. Indeed, African children were dependent on the Church and other missions for their education. With the exception of a couple of schools in Transvaal, the Government would not build schools for the natives, and less than half of them received any education at all. It was no surprise to the Mirfield Fathers that today's child turned into tomorrow's gangster.

Along with the schools, there were the churches to look after. Sophiatown, the largest parish in the Johannesburg diocese, had two churches. Orlando had three, and later added two more. Pimville, the 'ghastliest slum of the lot', had one church and there was another in Kliptown, which was several miles away. So all the Africans in Johannesburg, except for those living either in shacks at the bottom of white people's houses or the city centre or Alexandra, were Trevor's parishioners.

Trevor also needed to deal with the wider church in Johannesburg. There were wealthy whites in Johannesburg, with liveried black servants and houses with verandas, who needed guidance from Trevor. There were well-meaning white liberals, many of them Jewish, who worked for worthy organizations like the South African Institute for International Relations. There was Geoffrey Clayton, the ugly and squat Archbishop of Cape Town, who induced the young man into his new responsibilities using St Paul's words to Timothy as his text: 'Let no man despise thy youth.'

Trevor was also following a great man. Many people had been bereaved by the recall of Raymond Raynes; big parties had been laid on for him, and on leaving he was given a watch, sixteen jackal skins and a shield decorated with feathers. He, too, was upset, and said in a farewell speech: 'I do not want to go away, but I must do as I am told. I leave Africa with this thought in my mind, that one day the great African Church will bring back the European people of this country to the Christianity that so many of them have forsaken or have never really believed. I wish I could take a black child home with me to

England.' He added: 'Do not be sad, I will send a new father to you. Out of all the fathers, I will find one who will look after you.'

Three months after Trevor arrived, Sophiatown was to suffer a second departure. Dorothy Maud, part of the breed of strong-willed aristocrats who did good works, was also leaving to test her religious vocation back in England. Maud, who in her early thirties had come to South Africa in 1926, befriended Raynes and set up a mission house in Sophiatown, which had five bedrooms, a chapel and a sitting room. The house, which was opposite the Priory, was called 'Ekutuleni' (the Zulu word for the Place of Peacemaking). Apart from a small Roman Catholic mission, the women churchworkers of Ekutuleni, and the brethren of the CR were the only Europeans in a township of 70,000 souls. Maud and Raynes together built three churches, seven schools and three nursery schools, which catered for over 6,000 children. They expanded the hospital and built a swimming pool. They demanded water, lighting, clean water and proper roads. They fought for the poor and defended them in courts and police stations and the City Council. When Raynes left, Maud remarked that she had never seen him lose his patience with anyone – except the City Council.

And, in 1935, they built the church of Christ the King. A rich baker called Mr Smith, who was facing retirement, contacted Raynes and explained that he wanted to thank the Africans for helping him to make his fortune. Raymond told an architect that he wanted a church which would house a thousand worshippers, and was cheap. He wanted it to be the biggest and most beautiful building in the place. The church was built with red brick walls and a red roof; it looked like a holy garage, and was always open. Mass at dawn was attended by thirty or forty communicants – old ladies in black smocks, men in grubby clothes on their way to work, boys in schools uniform. At the eleven o'clock Mass on Sundays, there would be 1,500 people present, absorbed by the incense and smoke and the music. People would queue for big services like Good Friday.

The CR's work demonstrated that it was possible in the townships to develop the genuinely working-class Anglo-Catholicism which priests back home had always wished to create, but rarely did. In poor South Africa, High Anglicanism, removed from the peculiarities of the English scene which left it pickled in adolescent naughtiness, came of age.

In January 1944, Trevor wrote his first impressions of Sophiatown in a letter for *The CR*, the journal of the Community:

First of all: the Church. That must come first, because it simply dominates Sophiatown, whatever way you look at it. If you come in from town from the Mayfair direction, you take a bend in the road, and there, away to your right, is Sophia, with its corrugated iron roofs, looking quite colourful and respectable: with one or two other church towers rising from among them: but, standing right up, is the tower of Christ the King. On an evening, if you look up from New Clare, it is rather reminiscent, to my mind, of some Italian town clustering round the campanile of its church. Anyhow, no one has any excuse for being ignorant as to where they ought to come to worship. It is a most lovely church, I think: light and colourful and quite unmistakably Catholic; and the beauty of it is that it holds so many people and they can all see the altar. It needs to hold a good many, too, thank God, for they do come to Mass in a glorious way: generally a bit late, it is true, but by the end of the service filling up the main body of the church. There's no need to urge the congregation to join in the singing, either! I had been told beforehand that they sang in three or four different languages at once, but I didn't quite realize that they sing in harmony by nature. They really sing 'with the heart': it is most moving. Africans have undoubtedly a natural reverence. I don't think that I am idealizing that side of things, for it strikes people at once and so clearly. It was especially striking at the first Mass I saw in Christ the King, when nearly a thousand of our school children were in church for their weekly School Mass. I am sure that their silence and stillness were unforced, yet they were far more marked than one observes in England. It's such a joy to drop into church some time after school ends and to find, as one so often does, little groups of children 'doing the round' of altars and shrines, kneeling down quite unselfconsciously to recite the 'Baba wedu' (Our Father) aloud, and then, with a bob, moving off to the next altar or statue. It is something I have always longed to see: a church which is really and truly part of their daily life.

He added:

> It's quite hard at first to refrain from saying, at the beginning of
> each new day, 'What a lovely morning!' But the sunshine is the
> breath of life, I think, and it must account a great deal for the
> amazing gaiety and *joie de vivre* of some of our people who live
> in the foulest conditions you can imagine. I've seen a bit of the
> London slums (round the Elephant and Castle), but nothing I've
> seen can really touch some of the yards behind Griffith Road in
> New Clare. The other day Miss Maud found a room 12ft by
> 14ft, where thirteen people were sleeping: unable to lie down,
> but propped against the walls. I took some boys from one of the
> big European schools (King Edward's) down to see one of those
> yards, and on the way back I said: 'You see it's not easy for people
> to be good, living in those conditions,' and one of them
> answered, 'It's a wonder to me that they can even live.'

Trevor led a disciplined and sacramental life, saying the Divine Office
seven times a day. He would rise by 5.15 a.m., and be in church fifteen
minutes later. Prayer, including Mass, went on for two hours, and breakfast would be held in silence. Terce followed, and he would be in his
office at the Priory by 8.30 a.m. A long queue of people would sit on a
bench outside, and come to him with their troubles. Fathers would owe
money to their landlords and be threatened with eviction, while their
wayward children would join gangs and extort money. Trevor, along
with the other brethren, would try to appease the landlords. Children
would run up the hill and shout 'Arrested' and one of the Mirfield
fathers would rush down to the courtroom and help those arrested,
many for not carrying the right travel documents. The brethren would
be called to break up knife fights between drunken gangs. The telephone at the Priory would ring constantly, informing the Fathers that a
house was on fire or that a baby was due to be delivered.

Sophiatown was full of tales of drunkenness and adultery and
violence; the brethren would be called upon to defend the Church's
position, while not sounding sanctimonious. As Prior, Trevor would
regularly visit one of the community schools, and take a Scripture
lesson or cheer up a demoralized teacher. He started a little guild of
servers at the altar, and up to one hundred of them would meet once
a week. There was also the daily round of parish life: baptisms,

weddings and funerals, pastoral visits to the sick and the troubled in their corrugated shacks. People were attracted by his laughter and warmth; Desmond Tutu, later Archbishop of Cape Town and then a 9-year-old urchin, remembered Trevor meeting his mother, an ill-educated cook at a hostel for blind black women: 'I was standing with her on the hostel veranda when this tall white man, in a flowing black cassock, swept past. He doffed his hat to my mother in greeting. I was quite taken aback; a white man raising his hat to a black woman! Such things did not happen in real life. I learned much later that the man was Father Trevor Huddleston.'

After dealing with mundane problems, Trevor would have lunch at 12.30 p.m. He would them spend the afternoon in meetings with officials about schools and money and food. He would try to arrive back at the Priory by 6.30 p.m., for evensong and supper followed by a servers' meeting or a choir practice or a church guild. At 9.30 p.m. there would be Compline, followed by the Great Silence which would be interrupted by the noise of drunken shouting and scavengers' carts and noisy laughter from the yard behind the Mission.

Trevor drove himself hard, and was often exhausted. But when he was tired or in low spirits, he would seek out Sophiatown's children. Trevor adored children; and they in turn loved his childishness and natural manner. Day and night, they would tramp through Sophia-town's dusty streets, greeting strangers in a friendly and trusting manner. Much of his anger against cruelty came from his affinity with children, whom he believed were held back in education and health. In *Naught for Your Comfort*, he describes in an unembarrassed way his love of them:

> The Sophiatown creature is the most friendly creature on earth, and the most trusting. God knows why it should be so, but it is. You will be walking across the playground and suddenly feel a tug at your sleeve or a pressure against your knee: and then there will be a sticky hand in yours. 'Hello, Farther, hallo, Seester, how are you? Hallo, hallo, hallo . . .' You have come back from Johannesburg, as I have done a thousand times, fed up and sick with weariness from that soulless city, and immediately you are caught in a rush and scurry of feet: in faces pressed against your car window: in arms stretching up to reach yours whether you like it or not. You are home.

Trevor began to settle, and slowly this shy and aloof man came to identify with a very different type of people. He was still unworldly, awkward in his movements as he tramped through the township with his large hands and feet. The role of following Raymond Raynes's life was stretching him and making him tired. But he was becoming tougher and able to cope with the constant demands placed upon him. He began to smoke heavily and chatted happily to people, who found him charming and debonair where they found Raynes quiet and forbidding. He enjoyed being in charge of a large group of workers, but knew that he was a Christian priest and not an activist or voluntary worker; his prayers and daily Mass and monastic offices were the centre of his life, from which he gained his strength.

In a television interview many years later, Trevor recalled his time in South Africa: 'I learned everything. When I went to South Africa I was totally immature. I had had the usual upper middle-class education, school, then university, then theological college. I learned everything from Sophiatown. It was one of the most vital places on earth. I think that the main characteristic of the African people is this extraordinary zest for life at all kinds of levels. I loved every minute of my life there.'

In November 1943, ten weeks after his arrival, Trevor made his first contribution to the diocesan synod. It would be the start of a difficult relationship with Geoffrey Clayton, the Bishop of Johannesburg.

9

The Church in Africa

BY NOVEMBER 1943, a brusque and often ungracious man had occupied one of the most sensitive positions in the Anglican Church for nine years – the Bishop of Johannesburg. He was called Geoffrey Clayton.

Clayton, who would be appointed Archbishop of Cape Town in 1948, was himself the son of a bishop and was educated at Rugby School, where William Temple, the future Archbishop of Canterbury, was one of his contemporaries. After becoming a fellow and dean of St Mary's, Cambridge, he renounced the academic life and worked as a parish priest in Chesterfield. In Adrian Hastings' masterly description, he was

> an ecclesiastical statesman, shrewd, masterly, somewhat insensitive, a straight Anglo-Catholic, without doubts and without any striking originality of mind, entirely confident in the pattern of ministry which put the Church and religious things very decidedly first. He had the deepest suspicion of any priest who saw things differently, particularly those whose apparent concern was with the needs of the world rather than the Church.

The unmarried Clayton was a heroic smoker, puritanical on sex and an avoider of women. 'It isn't that I hate women,' he once said, 'I just can't tell one from the other.' He was incapable of relating to blacks or women or the poor, but was guided by an iron sense of duty. He would rise at six o'clock, and before seven he was at his Chapel where he said Matins, celebrated the Eucharist and read his daily Meditation. He would work steadily through the day, doing his letters, keeping his engagements and working on his speeches until, often, two o'clock in the morning. He lived with pain, and hobbled around on one foot.

Like many Englishmen, Clayton was haunted by one question: what shall we do with the natives? This question, which had preoccupied intelligent churchmen and politicians for years, became more momentous after the Boer War. Before the Boer War, the colour question in South Africa had remained more or less dormant; most Church work had been carried out in British colonies like Natal, where the government was paternalist and liberal in outlook. For the latter part of the nineteenth century, South Africa was a beautiful and, compared to other African nations, temperate country, where relations between black and white were unequal but peaceful.

But tension rose after the Boer War. A fresh and newly elected Liberal government had swept to power and was keen to do business with the Boers, the Afrikaner people who had fought bravely against the British, and lost. The Boers wanted to be separated from both the blacks and the British, who had arrived with the opening of the gold mines. Four centuries previously, the Afrikaners had arrived in South Africa after suffering religious persecution; now they wanted to re-establish biblical values in the white civilization they called their Promised Land.

A new constitution was drawn up. With the Treaty of Vereeniging in 1902, the government sought to bring together the four separate states of South Africa – the Cape Colony, which was administered by a Governor-General like every other British colony; Natal, another British colony; and both the Boer states, the Orange Free State and the Transvaal Republic– into a union.

Feelings towards this new constitution can be shown in correspondence between John Xavier Merriman, the anti-imperialist Englishman and Prime Minister of the Cape Colony, and General Smuts, the Attorney General of the Transvaal. Writing to Smuts about the planned constitution on 4 March 1906, Merriman said:

> I do not like the natives at all and I wish we had no black man in South Africa. But there they are, our lot is cast with them by an overruling Providence and the only question is how to shape our course so as to maintain the supremacy of our race and at the same time do our duty.

Smuts's reply, one week later, betrayed his anxiety:

> I am entirely with you on the Native question. I sympathize pro-
> foundly with the Native races of South Africa, whose land it was
> before we came to force a policy of dispossession on them. And
> it ought to be the policy of all parties to do justice to the Natives
> and to take wise and prudent measures for their civilization and
> improvement. But I don't believe in politics for them . . . so far
> as the Natives are concerned, politics will to my mind only have
> an unsettling influence. When I consider the political future of
> the natives of South Africa I must say I look into shadows and
> darkness.

The four states fought among themselves for supremacy. The Cape
Colony, which was led by Merriman, fought for a 'liberal civilization'.
The other three wanted white suffrage, arguing that Africans should
vote for a separate electoral roll, if at all. Merriman protested against
the inclusion of a Christian prayer in a constitution which entrenched
the colour bar. But it was the Boer Transvaal, under the control of
Smuts and Botha, who dominated the cabinet in the first fifteen years
of the country's existence as an independent state. The extremists did
not prosper immediately; both men were moderates, and Smuts in
particular retained a High Tory scepticism about the value of politics,
seeing no connection between political rights and social justice.

Yet, slowly, the Liberal Government began to erode African votes
in the country and Africans began to lose a foothold in their own
country. The government began to see segregation as the answer to
problems caused by disunity. So, the only way to maintain peace and
preserve white civilization was to separate the races completely –
geographically, economically, socially, politically.

At the beginning of the century, Africans had been able to cast a
vote in the Cape Colony. This was more remarkable than it seems; at
the same time women in Great Britain were not allowed to take part
in General Elections. But a constitution was emerging which deprived
Africans of the vote; by 1913, the year that Trevor was born, the first
serious piece of apartheid legislation – the Natives Land Act – was
passed. This stripped Africans of all rights in 87 per cent of the land
area in South Africa, leaving them with the remainder to occupy and
grow. Two years earlier, in 1911, the Liberal Government had intro-

duced the Mines and Works Act, which placed a wide range of skilled jobs on the railways and down the mines beyond black people, thus forcing them into cheap labour. From now on, certificates would be handed out for skilled jobs, and 'Coloured Persons' in the Transvaal and the Orange Free State would not be given these certificates. Those that were issued to people in Cape and Natal were not to be recognized. Suddenly, a whole generation was growing up with Trevor which knew nothing of life before the colour bar.

Then the Native (Urban Areas) Act was passed. This regulated the presence of Africans in urban areas. Local authorities would provide housing for Africans; in return, Africans would live on the outskirts of white urban and industrial areas. Authorities placed themselves in charge of regulating African business and overseeing the Pass Laws, in which Africans who were drunk or idle or no longer any use as servants would be deported to the Reserves. But in Johannesburg, where cheap and eager labour was always needed, the law was only enforced intermittently until the end of the 1940s.

Of course, there was opposition to these Acts. One leading opponent was Sol Plaatje, a simple herd boy educated by Lutheran missionaries. In 1917, Plaatje came to England with a group of delegates from the South African Native National Congress, which was formed in 1912 and later emerged as the African National Congress in 1923. He arranged to meet Lloyd George, which disturbed civil servants who saw their Prime Minister as an unreliable and emotional Welshman moved too easily by causes. They were right to be worried; Lloyd George wrote a letter to General Smuts, reflecting the hurt that Plaatje and his followers had felt, and added: 'I am sure that you will be impressed by them, and I am equally sure that you will be able to remove the impression which seems to rest there at the moment, that they cannot get people in authority to listen to them with sympathy.' Smuts's reply was terse. Having dismissed Plaatje and his followers as 'subversives', he added: 'We do not need to be told what we are supposed to do.'

It would be easy to overstate the impact of these Acts on African people. Of course, the Acts caused suspicion between the races in South Africa, but there was little mutual loathing . Of course, Africans were banned from taking certain jobs or forming trade unions or travelling in certain areas. Yes, blacks did outnumber whites by five to one, while whites owned four-fifths of the land. Yet pre-war missionaries like Raymond Raynes were not too disheartened; they believed that black people, with the education that they provided, would improve their status and be accepted by the ruling white minority.

Raynes was a typical white churchman of his time. While he felt that the Church should respond to certain acts of injustice carried out by the state, he did not perceive a general link between his religious concerns and wider political ones. His task was local; he would say Mass and teach in schools and tend the sick. Certainly, he would have scorned radicals like white communists, for communism was synonymous with atheism. Raynes's work in South Africa was low key; it was his nature to be cautious and build bridges with the English-speaking people, although not with the Afrikaners – on whom he had no effect at all.

The Church's attitude towards the growing issue of race was anguished and gentlemanly, but largely ineffectual. This was not always the case; there had been spates of open hostility towards the natives. In 1909 a lawyer from Cape Town, William Schreiner, issued an 'Appeal to Parliament and Government of Great Britain and Ireland' which highlighted the 'racist' provisions of the draft South African Act. Randall Davidson, the Archbishop of Canterbury, argued in the House of Lords that limits should be imposed on black people in South Africa that 'correspond with those we impose on our children', as the vast majority of South Africa's population would be unfit to share equal citizenship with whites. Great Britain was the imperial power, and the South Africa Bill was passed by the House of Commons in August 1909.

But many of the clergymen in South Africa were more knowledgeable than their leaders. In 1924 General Hertzog took control of the government as head of a Nationalist and Labour administration. He was not an extremist, and bided his time until he could command a two-thirds majority vote in Parliament before removing the Africans from the Common Roll. The General's appointment coincided with the resurgence of a distinctly Socialist streak in the Church of England; William Temple headed up the 'Life and Liberty' movement in England and there was much championing of the underprivileged. South Africa was suddenly full of clergymen of real stature – Talbot of Pretoria, Karney of Johannesburg, Carey of Bloemfontein – men who had served as army chaplains in the war and were angry that peace had not improved social conditions. Even these men, though, were not so concerned with political rights as fair play.

Here is an excerpt from Bishop Walter Carey's memoirs:

> It never crossed minds that Christianity embraced the abolition of slums or a fair wage for a fair day's work. We looked after people's souls; we taught them to pray, to be moral; to worship; to use the sacraments – and so, if they kept themselves from a naughty world they would go to heaven. I felt that I didn't want to keep free from the naughty world, I wanted to convert it and make England a paradise – a living, loving part of Christ's kingdom; and that embraced housing, slums, wages, hours, conditions of life, holidays – everything. All had to be transformed.

This was not mainstream Anglican opinion. Of course, it would be easy to caricature the Church of England's view of the 'coloured' question as hot air from silly fat men in gaiters. In fact, church leaders in Africa had been influenced by George Bell and J. H. Oldham as well as Archbishop Temple, by the Oxford Conference of 1937 on 'Church, Community and State' at which the formation of the World Council of Churches was agreed, at the Malvern Conference of 1941. A few years later, the churches were even more outspoken and angry; by September 1948, the Catholic Bishop of Cape Town, Mgr Hennemann, could describe apartheid in a letter read to all Catholic churches as 'noxious, unChristian and destructive' and then condemn 'attacks on the personal liberties and dignity of the non-white citizen'.

But even the most radical of priests was constrained by virtue of his position. Despite all its protests, the Church was operating from a position of strength and needed to be wary. All the mainstream churches were suffering from a post-colonial hangover, with many of their schools and hospitals being subsidized. The way they worshipped, they way they were funded, the way they ritually denounced communism – everything betrayed their reliance on the State. Some churches were happy to comply with the colour bar; St George's, Salisbury, was an excellent whites-only missionary school. The black parishes were poor and the white parishes were rich. African priests were cold-shouldered by their white colleagues; in the Congo black clergy approached a white presbytery by the back door and were barred from the room where white Europeans were partying. One

Anglican clergyman took his black servant to Holy Communion in a white parish; half the parish resigned at this provocative act, and the cleric was forced to skulk back to England. There were special parishes for blacks who had been shunned from white congregation; there were special parishes for minority groups of Coloureds and Indians. South Africans were born separately; they lived separately; they died separately.

The most sympathetic of whites were reduced to 'ambulance' work. They would give clothes and blankets and food to the poor blacks. They would set up schools and hospitals and training schemes. They taught black women how to feed their children properly, and protect them from disease. They wanted the shanty towns to be bull-dozed, for black workers to be paid properly, for the Pass Laws to be relaxed. They used cunning and charm to improve conditions for black people.

But most did not want real change, and were treated with a bemused contempt by white people who saw them as a threat, and by angry blacks who saw them as an impediment to full democracy. These well-meaning, self-loathing whites acted with a mixture of caution and concern – two traits which characterized Archbishop Clayton's report *The Church and the Nation*.

10

The Church and the Nation

IN 1941 GEOFFREY CLAYTON SET UP a Bishop's Commission with the task of 'defining what it believes to be the mind of Christ for this land'. He appointed nine committees to look at difficult topics, including education, religious disunity and Coloured Peoples. The bishop took himself off to Swaziland, where he worked away at the report for many hours a day. The report, called *The Church and the Nation*, was presented to the Synod on 15 November 1943. It was a typical church report; it created an enormous fuss, but achieved little long-term effect.

Trevor, who had only been in the country for ten weeks, did not disagree with the gist of Clayton's findings. At the Synod, he was in the company of some of South Africa's finest priests, including Arthur Blaxall, who with his wife Florence worked with the deaf and blind, and Maurice Clack, who was priest-in-charge of St Alban's Coloured Mission. Few present could find fault with the report; it was produced by a large and capable commission and was certainly the Church's boldest attempt to tackle the creeping system of apartheid. Its main recommendation – to widen votes to all African, Coloured and Indian men and women – was seen at the time as revolutionary. In its different outbursts – at one stage, it called for the African Mineworkers Union to be recognized – the report went much further than could be expected from an Anglican archbishop. The headmaster and writer Alan Paton, both friend and sparring partner of Trevor and a future chairman of the Liberal Party, said: 'I must record that being a member of the Bishop's Commission was one of the seminal events of my life, after which I was never the same again . . . having lived for thirty-eight years in the dark, the Commission opened a door for me and I went through into the light.'

But the report was flawed in one major way. Although there were minor problems too – the report was written by whites for whites; Clayton had made no attempt to find out what black people thought – these were understandable lapses and could be forgiven. What really irked critics was that Clayton had adopted a gradualist approach to the 'colour bar' problem, at a time when even moderate black African leaders were demanding something more urgent.

Trevor was furious at Clayton's lacklustre approach. The report had called for a 'gradual removal of the colour bar'. But this approach was too languid for an absolutist like Trevor: if the colour bar was wrong, then it should be removed immediately. And still the problems went deeper: one clause in the report stated: 'We are aware that to implement its findings demands first of all a change of heart within the nation.' So, the bishop was asked, did this mean that the imple-mentation must wait? Till when? This year? Next year? Never?

But Trevor, who could be formidable when he needed to, had met his match. Clayton, furious at the upstart's defiance, jumped to his feet and sounded forth: 'The Church is not here primarily to serve society. Its prime duty is to worship God and obey Him. And if it is God's will that we should serve society in this or that way, then it is our duty to do it. Let us therefore be very careful that it is God's will that we are trying to obey, and that we are not merely trying to make the Church do something that we want to be done. And let me make it quite clear that I appointed this Commission because I believed that it might be God's will that we should serve society in this and that way.'

So, in the contrast between the flamboyant Trevor and the wilfully colourless Clayton, there was one common bond. Both men were courageous; both men saw the role of the Church in South Africa in a completely different light.

Clayton has been treated unfairly by history, and caricatured as a dyspeptic conservative eager to uphold white rule. This is grotesque; he was certainly grumpy, but he did believe that it was the duty of the Church to meddle in the affairs of the nation and society. However, he never trusted anyone who shared his views, and in particular Young Turks like Trevor. He hated Trevor criticizing the Church; in a way, he was the Church and believed that when Trevor was criticizing the Church, he was criticizing him. He was right, of course.

And it would be easy to place Trevor in a heroic light, casting the young priest as a reckless rebel fighting the forces of foetid conservatism. But serious questions need to be asked before we accept such an image. Why was Trevor happy to confront Clayton after only ten weeks in South Africa? Why did he act in such a precipitous way? Why did he not listen to the words of his Superior Raymond Raynes, who in his farewell letter had cautioned Trevor to be unendingly patient? Trevor could not have begun to understand the delicate complexities of senior ecclesiastical office in South Africa. He was also aware of the need to be obedient to his bishop, who is entrusted with maintaining the unity of the Church. Fr John Briscoe, one of Trevor's mentors back in Wells, had maintained that 'To be a bishop you must be resilient, ambiguous, accommodating and with a mind so broad that it can accept anything and change at all times to suit modern conditions' – but then Briscoe was an anonymous parish priest from rural Somerset, and Clayton held one of the most important positions in the Anglican Communion.

Clayton needed to move firmly, but slowly. He knew that the stipends of black clergy depended on the giving of white laity. In any dangerous political situation, there will be clergy who believe that the first duty of the Church is to carry on in the face of the conflicts that surround it; and also those who believe that the Church must fight injustices by tooth and claw. Clayton belonged to the first camp; Trevor to the second. But it is easy for those without responsibility to be prophetic.

Clayton was also opposed by Michael Scott, the neurotic thorn in Clayton's assured side. Scott, an Anglican curate tortured by religious doubt and sexual guilt, had arrived in South Africa the same year as Trevor. But while Trevor settled into a geographically limited ministry in Sophiatown, Scott led a freelance and peripatetic ministry. Within a few months of arriving in South Africa, this diffident and nervous man was helping to organize, and become chairman of, a national non-party organization called the Campaign for Right and Justice – only to see it overrun by Communists. A deeply unusual man, Scott was unable to keep appointments or mention to his Superiors where he was. He would exert a deep and sometimes unsettling influence on Trevor. Michael Scott later wrote:

I felt overcome by a sense of betrayal and frustration in what seemed the overwhelming forces of oppression both on the Government side and in the Opposition. Against these our methods seemed so puny and were made even more ineffectual by the intriguing methods and cynicism of the Communists towards everything that was not controlled by them or harnessed to their own cause. Their support, though, was in a sense a kiss of death. I felt instinctively from that time that there was no recourse left open to me but the path of passive resistance. I felt betrayed by my own church. Though, admittedly, my tactics had been at fault, they had not been so much at fault as to give the hierarchy any justifiable pretext for their lack of support, if not open opposition, to what we were trying to do.

But Trevor was, in his own words, 'very naïve and very young' and far behind Scott in his understanding of the issues which presented themselves. Scott had a certain edge, a certain anarchism, which Huddleston admired and respected. But it didn't take Trevor long to get to grips with social and political issues. Nor did it take him long to irritate those people in ecclesiastical authority either. What Clayton would begin to loathe was Trevor's public identification with a political party like the African National Congress.

Michael Scott was based in the Coloured Mission of Johannesburg, which covered much of the same territory as the African parishes of Sophiatown, Orlando and Pimville to which Trevor had just been appointed priest-in-charge. The two firebrand priests would meet at various diocesan meetings and commissions. This tall and rangy loner was a recognizable figure in the squalid and violent Johannesburg back streets. Scott believed that there were two kinds of Christianity – one supported the status quo and the other provided a divine instrument for change. Scott didn't mutter about injustice; he took practical steps. He envisaged a programme which would deal with the problems of migratory labour, the ravaged countryside, the increase in crime and poverty and malnutrition. He believed that the Church needed to go further than *The Church and the Nation* report – Clayton saw Scott's own Campaign for Right and Justice as a direct threat to his own Commission's findings, and a direct challenge to his authority. Clayton was happy to denounce injustice from the pulpit, but blanched from the idea that people might assemble in a trade union and do something about it.

Scott flirted with all types of organizations – trade unions, trade councils, legal aid bureaux, political congresses and even the South

African Communist Party. Clayton had a little sympathy for Scott, but, like the Archbishop of Canterbury Geoffrey Fisher, he believed that it wasn't the role of the Church to take a strong position against the State. Clayton believed that there was a profound difference between the Church and the world, and to forget that was to forget the Gospel.

At Michael Scott's funeral many years later, Trevor reminisced that 'my close association with Michael, when we were both living and working in Sophiatown and Orlando, is now so far distant. Those "blue remembered hills" of our angry days of commitment to the struggle of human rights and human dignity in South Africa – thrilling and exhilarating, at least to me – are forty years ago.'

He then added: 'In spite of the impact he made, not only in Africa but in Asia, in the forum of the United Nations and in this country – he was in fact a very private person. He was surely one of those rare individuals whose "spiritual power and interior consecration to God" (to quote from the letter of Mother Geraldine, Mother Superior of the Sisters of St Margaret) were the primal spring of all that he achieved in action. It was that spiritual power and interior consecration to God that gave to all he did its validity.'

He then quoted again from Geraldine's statement, written nearly thirty years before:

It is his transparent purity of soul and inflexible integrity of purpose coupled with his gentleness and complete self-forget-fulness that makes him so like his Master – and gives one even in the most mundane and hectic surroundings an extraordinary sense of peace and of the Presence of God . . .

Clayton . . . was . . . conservative about the role of the Church against the State . . . He agreed with Archbishop Geoffrey Fisher – or Fisher agreed with him – that it wasn't the business of the Church of England or the universal Church to take on a strong position. This was something that the Church of the Province must deal with where it was . . . the sort of attitude was absolutely universal . . . Scott and I only came to the other position by having to live with the situation . . . the attitude of the white leadership was paternalistic. And you get very good paternalists who really loved the African in that sense, but who were never prepared to take that jump and be involved in the political action [of the time] . . . that seemed to be to them not the sort of thing the Church should be about.

Clayton's reaction to both men was straightforward. He would, eventually, banish them both. Scott was harder to deal with, because he did not belong to any religious order. But Trevor, as a monk, had taken an oath of obedience. Clayton put pressure on his Superior in the Community of the Resurrection, the order to which Trevor belonged, to withdraw him from the country. It was the Church, and not the state, which had banished Trevor from South Africa because of his political activities. The state, though, could not have been very far behind.

Trevor, to Clayton's fury, was certainly effective. Many people who came across him were struck by his aristocratic nature. With this nature came a certain arrogance, which irritated his archbishop and infuriated the state authorities. But it lent him a level of valour and determination which he would not otherwise have had. He was bold and charismatic and good-looking, which always helps. And he adored being in the limelight, which again irritated Archbishop Clayton.

And there would always be one critical advantage that Scott and Trevor held over Clayton. They both lived amongst the slum-ridden shacks of Johannesburg, where they baptized sick babies and scolded miscreants and comforted the unhappy and the bereaved. It was this first-hand knowledge which would always wrong-foot their critics. As Trevor said: 'Scott and I only came to the other position by having to live with the situation.'

For all his well-intentioned sermonizing, Bishop Clayton was unable to understand the urban African. He lived in Bishop's House, Westcliff, a large newly-built house with a large garden and gardeners. His position was characteristically Anglican. In the mid-nineteenth century, the bishops were unable to understand the effects of the Industrial Revolution on the workers because they had never worked down the mines or in a mill. Most clergy reaction to the First World War was easily dismissed, for it came from priests who had never fought in a trench. Geoffrey Clayton was an impressive man, but his distance from the squalor and degradation of urban Africa reduced him to a recognizable figure – the *bien-pensant* cleric. For all his faults, the same could never be said of Trevor.

11

Growing Anger

SHORTLY AFTER ARRIVING IN SOPHIATOWN, Trevor had written an excitable letter back to Mirfield:

> We've had two rather exciting incidents out here lately. One is 'Shanty Town', the other is the 'Teachers' Demonstration' . . . Shanty Town began on Lady Day. We'd just finished the Guild Enrolment at St Mary's, Orlando, when we saw the first string of people carrying beds, and other bits of household goods, on their heads or in their arms, in a procession, with banners flying, walking towards the Municipal Hall. They were the sub-tenants in Orlando, who had grown really desperate at the long delay in providing any houses, and had decided to take the law into their own hands and squat on municipal ground until the authorities acted . . . The Teachers' Demonstration was mainly a long procession, with banners etc., but it attracted literally thousands of teachers, parents, etc., protesting for more pay, more schools and more food for the children.

Sophiatown's residents were desperate and angry. They were one generation away from that generation of rural Africans who, in the words of the historian W. M. MacMillan, 'were dragging along at the very lowest level of bare subsistence, blighted by ill-health and starvation, endemic typhus and almost chronic scurvy'. Six years later, conditions had worsened, and rural Africans were faced with a clear choice: walk or starve. Walk they did, to the mines and factories of the Reef, the industrial belt of the Witwatersrand, where gold was discovered. But these workers were poorly educated and badly paid and they had nowhere to live. Those who worked as servants lived in wealthy white areas, in sheds at the bottom of manicured gardens. Within ten years of the 1930s, the population of Johannesburg had doubled; those who did not live in the heart of the city congregated to townships like Orlando and Sophiatown, where there was rampant prostitution, disease, drunkenness and an infant mortality rate ten times the national average. Workers in Sophiatown would often commute two or three hours each way into work, returning to shacks with no water or light or sanitation.

So Trevor realized that he was living in a tale of two cities. On the one hand, there was the city of the Europeans, which was built on the perilous foundation of gold. On the other hand, there was the city of the Africans, which was growing fast and outstripping its white brother. In Trevor's eyes, the greatest problem facing the Africans was frustration – intellectual, physical and spiritual.

Johannesburg had spawned terrible slum conditions in a remarkably short space of time. In the sixty years since it had emerged as a mining camp for the Gold Rush, it had been tainted by the sinking backyards of the townships of Sophiatown and Alexandra, the breeze-blocks shelters of Orlando and the shanties of Jabavu. People argued that this was the result of world shortages in building materials. But Trevor saw it differently; he believed that present conditions had been caused by a criminal lack of vision in past years, with Lazarus lying at the gate unheeded and full of sores while Dives fared sumptuously and built himself skyscrapers and pleasure gardens. Trevor saw the physical frustration of the African race, a people which used their bodily strength and skill every day in the shops, the factories and gardens of the city, while not being allowed to build their own homes.

While Trevor was working in Sophiatown, there were plans to build generous recreational facilities for the Africans. But he was suspicious of such plans, believing that if they remained unfulfilled they would cause more deep-rooted feelings of bitterness than if they had never been conceived. After all, it was not the City Council that could provide the football fields, the clubs and the swimming baths which Johannesburg's residents needed. And it was not the City Council that could halt the crime wave by providing a healthy outlet for African youth – it was the citizens of Johannesburg themselves.

Africans were also intellectually frustrated. The average African desired education, but in Johannesburg only one out of every four children could find a place in school. Although Africans had been granted secondary education, one of the secondary schools in the City had seven hundred children in six classrooms. That same school had produced a generation of children with results as high as their European counterparts, but there were no professional jobs for them to achieve. One of their leaders wrote: 'Amongst the urbanized and educated Africans there is a growing spirit of bitterness against the European which is sowing far and wide the seeds of mistrust and suspicion.' The God-given gift of intellect had been allowed to blossom, only to be laid waste and trampled underfoot.

But even worse than physical and intellectual frustration was the frustration of the spirit. What the African longed for more than anything was freedom. Some people believed that the African's anger was whipped up from outside forces. But Trevor saw that it was a result of government policy, which denied to the African the only thing which he cared about – his spiritual liberty.

Trevor, though, was not blind to whites in the way that Raynes was. He believed that whites and blacks should help each other. He believed that the African should have the right to elect his own representative to the City Council; to have a full share in the government of his own city. That the African advisory boards should have real power, rather than proffer advice which was politely ignored. He also believed that the African should be encouraged to use all his powers – as builder, as craftsman, as civil servant, as tradesman – for the benefit of his own people. Only then could one appreciate his worth to society. It was useless having a vocational school for Africans if there was no vocation for them to fulfil when their training was complete. He also called for an increase in social service provision and a 'drastic revision' of the Pass Laws. This would be revolutionary; it would remove the cruel discrimination between white and black; the haunting fear of search and arrest which hung over every African from the day he left school; the disrepute into which the courts of law had fallen because all distinction between the gravity of the crime had been blurred by indiscriminate arrest.

In a sermon preached at the end of 1946 in the Cathedral Church of St Mary the Virgin, to celebrate the Diamond Jubilee of the city, Trevor Huddleston said: 'It is only if we have faith in the kind of city that God means Johannesburg to be, only if we realize that every earthly city is but an image of the true City to which we belong, only if we have the courage to "go out not knowing whither we go", yet determined to obey the call – that we, with our fellow citizens of every race, shall know the things which belong unto our peace.'

The Second World War had also provoked much growing anger and resistance. In 1939, the newly appointed Prime Minister General Smuts had said: 'The Union of South Africa . . . takes its stand for the defence of freedom, and the destruction of Hitlerism and all that it implies.' Most black Africans were patriotic and supported this move, knowing that Hitler's keenest acolytes were also the strongest supporters of segregation. The ANC supported Smuts's position, while arguing that it was time to consider the 'expediency' of allowing African and other non-European races into full citizenships. But, when the war ended in 1945, whites received £5 in cash and a clothing allowance of £25; their fellow African soldiers received £2, and a khaki suit worth £2.

Crass gestures like this infuriated a new generation of black activists, who were reaching maturity by the time Trevor arrived in South Africa. Their anger was stoked by the movements for national liberation in a dozen African countries, who were now seeing that the days of European domination were drawing to a close. South Africa had avoided the unstable fate of many other African countries, who reacted to the European exodus from their land by establishing violent and corrupt regimes. Somehow, the white liberal vision that Raynes had held – that of a benign equality between black and white achieved through mission schools and sympathetic businesses – had not been realized.

And it was the Church that had helped them on their way by sowing the seeds of rebellion. By educating men and women in their mission schools and encouraging them to realize their potential, they were responsible for creating their own tensions and difficulties. Suddenly, there were whole tranches of highly educated and articulate people who were unable to achieve positions of responsibility and power.

Black activists had once been assuaged by the words of Winston Churchill's Atlantic Charter, which supported the rights of all people to choose their own government and to 'live out their lives in freedom from fear and want'. Lord Lugard, Churchill's High Commissioner in West Africa, reflected British feeling at the time: 'For two or three generations we can show the Negro what we are: then we shall be asked to go away. Then we shall leave the land to those it belongs to.' Equally, the activists knew that Britain especially, which had extricated itself with difficulty from Middle East and Arab possessions, was in no mood to fight black nationalist demands. Indeed, the British Government in particular was working with the churches and the liberal intelligentsia to ensure a peaceful withdrawal from Africa. It would be Church thinking that contributed to the largely peaceful withdrawal from the British, French and Belgian empires in Africa over the next few years.

Confronting from the pulpit was one thing. Trevor, the shy priest who kept his counsel, realized that he needed to inform the white people of South Africa – and, indeed, the world – about the reality of life in Sophiatown.

In order to achieve this, publicity was vital. Many people assumed that they knew the facts, when what they grasped was a version of them. Many white people in Johannesburg were sympathetic to Trevor's causes, but still preferred not to know, or face, or even deny them. In his position as a priest, he knew about the suffering of his flock, and knew that others must know as well. Yet he knew nobody in the media.

One day, he walked into the grimy offices in Johannesburg of *The Star*, an evening paper read widely by the English-speaking people of the Transvaal. He asked to speak to a reporter. It was a naïve but bold step; he was asking for help on a subject upon which he was ignorant. It also led to one of the most important friendships of his life. The reporter he met was Olga Horowitz.

In her early years, Olga, who was born in Dublin but raised in Kimberley, South Africa, had thought that it was natural that a black person should walk in the gutter. She was the first woman reporter on the Kimberley newspaper, where she interviewed General Smuts; she then went to Johannesburg in 1942 and joined *The Star*. When Trevor entered the offices, he saw Olga sitting at a large open-plan reporters' room in *The Star*. She was at her typewriter, cigarette in her mouth and fingers ready for action. Olga always wrote directly onto her typewriter. All Trevor had to do was to tell her his story.

After that first visit and first story, Trevor would come back to Olga again and again. 'To know him was to love him', she said. 'He would come into my office articulate, sincere, angry. One day he came in on the edge of a diabetic coma, exhausted. "Olga," he said, as he collapsed into a chair, "get me some food immediately." Some people think that Trevor is publicity mad. Well, I have never known him mad on publicity for himself. He was mad on publicity for the things that were his daily concern.' When returning to his car from Pretoria, he would reach the outskirts of Johannesburg and find *Star* posters with banner headlines, which he knew referred to his interview with Olga that morning. The interviews led to letters and telephone calls of support and abuse. But it did promote the cause; Trevor was never a good preacher, but he was able to spread the message.

Trevor also needed to learn about the complexities of the situation, and not think and write glibly. He would need to learn from journalists like Olga Horowitz, who taught him to write clearly. He would tell her about conflicts he was engaged in with landlords. There were 40,000 homeless people in Johannesburg, many of whom worked in the city. They were the people on whom the city depended. To house these people, shacks were built in back areas of existing houses, in places like Sophiatown and Alexandra. There was a huge health risk, with so many people in the shacks; the local authority warned the landlords, who put whole families onto the streets.

Trevor would also tell Olga about the Africa Children's Feeding Scheme, which he had helped. The scheme had begun at the end of 1945, when a young European woman went to Mass at Sophiatown on Sunday, and then wrote a letter to *The Star* about the 'Belsen Brats' whom she had seen in the streets of Sophiatown. Trevor also realized that white schoolchildren were entitled to a free midday meal whereas black children had no right to anything. Reading about this in *The Star*, the conscience of white Johannesburg was stirred, and Trevor called a public meeting to co-ordinate an attack on child hunger. In due course, 5,000 children a day were fed. The publicity led to the relief of hunger, and centres for feeding were established in every Johannesburg location. He would speak of particular incidents involving certain people – like Jonas, who was arrested and charged with being a vagrant; when Trevor visited him that day in his police station and asked him: 'Where is your school pass?' he replied: 'They tore it up.' The wastepaper basket was still there and Trevor found the pass in four pieces; when he refused to surrender it he was arrested. A few days later he had a full apology from the Commandant.

Trevor knew that he was unknown and despised. But he also knew that his only weapon was publicity, which he used to the full. A young African priest, a member of the Community, had just returned after his ordination and was arrested and handcuffed at nine o'clock in the morning – he had no pass. He was brought to Trevor at the Priory, and the policeman said: 'I'll arrest every bloody kaffir in the place if they break the law.' Trevor went that afternoon to report the incident to the Commandant, who was furious that the story had already appeared in *The Star*. The Commandant then rebuked him, and said gently and wearily: 'As a matter of fact, Father, you are quite right. If I could leave the Force tomorrow, I would. But it's my livelihood and my profession. So what am I to do?'

For the rest of his life, South Africans would ask: 'Was his publicity loyal?' Trevor was keen to show that it was publicity for the sake of a child abandoned at dawn, rather than his own sake. Friends claimed that it was prayer, not publicity, which fuelled Trevor; at the start of a particularly difficult day, he would go to the church of Christ the King half an hour early for prayer. Others, including members of the CR, disagreed, claiming that he was becoming vainglorious and a show-off. They would say that he became the story, rather than the feeding scheme or dilapidated school that he was promoting. Publicity for anyone is dangerous, for it feeds on distortion; for a monk, for whom the greatest part of his life is hidden, it can damage the soul.

In Christmas 1946, in a sermon delivered on the text of Luke 19:42 in the church of St Mary the Virgin, Johannesburg, Trevor voiced his anger: 'These slums, as Fr Basil Jellicoe used to say of the slums of London, are but the outward and visible sign of an inward and spiritual disgrace – the disgrace not of the City Councils of Johannesburg, but of its citizens, who either did not know or did not care to tell the truth. But they are more – they are the sacrament of the physical frustration of the African people, for even now, whilst we use the bodily strength and skill of the African every day in the shops, the factories, the gardens of our city, we will not let him use them to build his own home.'

He then took one step further.

12

Changing Times

ONE EVENING, TOWARDS THE END OF 1948, Trevor was lying in bed with flu when he heard the results of the General Election on the radio. General Smuts had lost the election as leader of his party and his own seat. As every result came flooding in, Trevor realized that the country was undergoing a huge reversal. Suddenly, with the election of a tough Nationalist Government, all the major laws which structured apartheid would be introduced. On hearing that the Nationalist Government had been elected, Trevor wrote to an old friend, the High Commissioner Evelyn Baring: 'Life is very interesting politically at the moment, and it looks as if we may have a first-class crisis on our hands early next year. Yet somehow or other the very fact that they may be so difficult makes one glad to be out here with the Bantu.'

His concerns were not shared by other brethren. With the election of a new government, Raymond Raynes had written: 'I think it is necessary to be careful not to pass judgement too soon and to remember that often what Governments promise or threaten, they find themselves unable to fulfil.' Others were less cautious; someone had written to Raynes, saying: 'There are sinister signs of people anxious to stir up troubled waters . . . but most of the blame goes to the government for their quite indefensible manner of announcing new proposals in addition to the nature of the proposals.'

But the majority of people, too, were initially unaffected by the result. In the six years before the Second World War, the country had been ruled by a coalition under Smuts and Hertzog. This uneasy coalition had been produced by economic rather than political factors. The Churches issued statements and voiced concerns, but politics continued as they always had.

But the Nationalists won the 1948 election on a specific promise to implement a policy of apartheid – to push through laws enforcing complete political, social and economic segregation. Indeed, they were not merely enforcing an ordinary apartheid – the policy of shared status for whites and blacks in separate areas – but one of white power throughout the dominion. Over the next six years, and through a series of Acts – the Group Areas Act, the Population Registration Act, the Suppression of Communism Act, the Criminal Law Amendment Act – they enforced this policy.

And there is no doubt that this new, unapologetic style of politics bemused the Church. The gentle and rather hesitant John Darbyshire, who was Geoffrey Clayton's predecessor as Archbishop of Cape Town, could happily write: 'The main problem is social. Many Europeans have no desire to promote education among the coloured people. It seems to them to enhance the danger of miscegenation.' To many liberal Christians, apartheid was a social rather than political evil; Darbyshire saw the problem as stemming from prejudice among whites and backwardness amongst Africans. He saw education as the answer.

But the Church had misread the extreme intent of the Nationalist Government. In Malan, the government had a great Cape Nationalist; there was something civilized and generous in his outlook. But his cabinet was full of extremists from the Transvaal, and they became increasingly powerful. Although an advocate of apartheid, he would disagree with his northern ministers about the speed and ruthlessness needed to implement such laws. Nevertheless, after the election of his government in 1948, parliament passed measure after measure to implement Nationalist policy. For such segregation to be curtailed, individuals needed to be controlled and liberties needed to be enforced. Therefore the Church objected to every apartheid measure, as it insulted human dignity and reduced the value of a man in the eyes of God. It was setting itself up for a more confrontational position.

And yet the Church remained hesitant. The majority of white missionaries in the 1950s were benign liberals rather than radicals; some of their fellow Christians were more extreme in their support for apartheid. The Dutch Reform Church, for example, betrayed no self-doubt over apartheid. Its missionary approach was similar; it felt that there ought to be no mixing of the races, but that equality and justice ought to be secured for members of each race accordingly. There was a large number of white laymen in other denominations who felt that the Church ought not to trespass into politics, that a traditional social segregation ought to be preserved and that attempts to disrupt this state of affairs could be disastrous. Meanwhile, Christians from different denominations began to view each other with increasing fear, suspicion and hatred.

Trevor, meanwhile, would push himself onwards with his daily work. There was much sniping over his love of publicity. Yet Trevor continued to believe that he should confront the people of South Africa – and, indeed, the widest public that he knew – with the facts of life that he was facing in Sophiatown. But he was being forced into making political speeches, and on an international level rather than the national level he had been used to up to now. In all this, he was doing exactly what Raymond Raynes had done, but he was a better writer and public speaker and was able to chat people up; the press is a dangerous weapon, but with Trevor's guile and charm he was able to win them over. He would ring them up about any controversial opinion. He would appear in interviews and speeches and on billboards and irritate the African and Liberal forces opposed to him. He was becoming a public figure.

13

A Marked Man

TREVOR WAS TRANSFERRED TO ROSSENTVILLE, in Johannesburg, in January 1949. He was appointed Provincial of the Community in South Africa. This was a terrible wrench for Trevor, but his move was also occurring at a difficult time for the Community in Africa. First, they had to deal with Orlando, which now had a population of 100,000 people and was the fifth largest in the Union. The Community had looked after it since Sophiatown, but they knew by 1947 that they would have to hand it back to the diocese or build a house with at least three brethren to run it. There was pressure from home, but Fr Huddleston wrote from South Africa: 'It seems to me that, if there is to be any withdrawal, it is now the turn of the Home Province to retrench.'

Back in England, Raynes was aware of rising political tension. Since the election of the Nationalist Government in 1949, the discontent of the Africans had turned into hopelessness, the talk of struggle was now about political rights rather than schools. Raynes, as vocal in his support for Africans as Trevor was, said when called to action: 'Under the circumstances restraint at the moment is called for . . . It is also essential to remember that we are not in a position to stand aside and denounce the policy of the government in any spirit of self-righteousness. Too many opportunities for improving the situation have been lost in the past – either through fear or apathy, and sometimes deliberately refused on grounds of penitence.'

Trevor was aware of the enormous tension between the Community and the rest of the diocese caused by the fact that so much money was being poured into Sophiatown and Orlando while the rest of the diocese was going short. There were also general complaints about the ritualism and strange liturgical practices which seemed out of keeping with the benignly English Catholicism of the CR.

And there were deeper concerns. Many people believed that the Community was actively siding with the Africans in the forthcoming struggle. Having relinquished control of St John's, the Community had had little to do with Europeans; they had in fact turned down offers of white parishes in Rossentville and Germiston. Indeed, this lack of interest would cause huge problems in the wake of Fr Huddleston's recall.

The move to Rossentville was deeply distressing to Trevor. Although he was ostensibly very loyal to Raynes ('It has been wonderfully encouraging to know that one has the whole support of the Community out here at every step, and especially to have your advice and encouragement', he wrote to his Superior in 1949), there is no doubt that he was dismayed at leaving Sophiatown. He always said that the six years in Sophiatown were the happiest of his life, where he was known by 'Die Jerry', with his close cropped hair – a tall cassocked figure strolling through the townships surrounded by the sticky paws of children. The journalist Anthony Sampson, who was publishing *Drum* magazine, remembers his ease, his ability to get on with black and white, his quiet strength.

Meeting Huddleston at a Johannesburg cocktail party, with his warm social ease, his feeling for people and his gentle tolerance, it was difficult to imagine him against the austere and rigid background of a Yorkshire monastery preoccupied with the business of prayer. Huddleston's public life seemed so practical and comprehensible, so much what others would wish to have done if they had the courage and the strength.

Sampson recalls an occasion when he went to visit Trevor in his cell at Rossetenville, and found him surrounded by photographs of St Peter's boys, theological volumes, the *Church Times* and *Drum* magazine. He used his cell for everything – sitting room, classroom, office and study:

Huddleston came in, a tall, dignified figure, wearing his long black cassock, with a worn leather belt round his waist, and a cross dangling from one side. He had a long face with a deep chin, greying, close-cropped hair, and direct eyes. He spoke with a simple directness.

In an interview with the *Observer* in 1955, Trevor wrote:

> The impression [Sophiatown] made on me was one of immense vitality and gaiety, in spite of everything. I felt completely *au fait* with the people, shrewd and quick-witted like the people of Camberwell [South London, where he had been on a mission]. It is a community, not an abstraction like Orlando, in spite of its backyard shacks. There was something tremendously alive and real about the whole show there . . . I was there to run a parish, with three others, but it did seem to me that one couldn't do the job at all without getting involved in these social problems. Fr Raynes had set the pace . . . We are the only Europeans who ever lived in Sophiatown, the only white people.

Anthony Sampson remembers the sight of Trevor, wandering through bread queues in the early morning, listening to meetings, separating knife fights between tsotsis, starting a cocoa club for young children. He raised funds for a swimming pool at Orlando, attended African functions and Congress gatherings, European cocktail parties and fundraising meetings, and burial services. He was the only white person who could walk through locations alone at night, except for the police. He was promiscuous in his friendship; he would dine with Sir Ernest Oppenheimer, and stayed with Sir Evelyn Baring. He was a close friend of Oliver Tambo, Secretary of the African Congress, and Yusuf Cachalia, Secretary of the Indian Congress. Most important visitors to South Africa would make their way to Huddleston's cell.

Unlike some of his brethren, he did not think that it was odd that he should involve himself in politics. Accused of being a troublemaker and agitator, he would reply: 'The Christian is always, if he is true to his calling, an agitator.' He preached one sermon at Christ the King in Sophiatown on the theme: 'He that loseth his life for my sake shall find it.' He told the assembled congregation: 'It reminds us that at the heart of our religion there lies a principle in absolute contradiction to the principles by which the world speaks and thinks and acts.'

And so, gradually but inexorably, Trevor became caught up in African politics. Many of his African friends were in Congress and they came to him for advice and companionship; as he began, through speeches and talks and newspaper columns, to oppose government legislation, so the Anglican monk shared the same platform as Congress. As people became more defiant, so Trevor became more confused. Could he, as a Christian priest, deliberately support the flouting of laws? Could he sit on the same platform as people very different from himself, including Marxists and Nationalists? Should he support passive resistance as a means of protest?

Such questions confused and irritated Trevor, but he knew that they would need to be resolved. A meeting was held in February 1953 to protest against the new Acts to suppress the defiance campaign. He was the only white figure, addressing the sea of black faces of the nine hundred Congress delegates at the Trades Hall, Johannesburg. He spoke in simple, short phrases, pausing at the end of each one for the Zulu interpreter: 'It has been the teaching of the Church through the centuries . . . that when government degenerates into tyranny . . . laws cease to be binding upon its subjects.' He ended: 'The future of South Africa is in your hands, that is certain . . . I pray God he may give you your strength . . . *I identify myself entirely with your struggle.*'

As he hurried out of the hall at the end of the service, he muttered to a journalist friend: 'I've been trying to pluck up courage to say that for months . . . I'm glad I've taken the plunge.'

But such straightforward identification made him a marked man. He began to be seen as the cause of any African opposition. He was shown the copy of an English newsletter, which said, under the heading of 'Dangerous Men': 'Huddleston is either the dupe of Communists, or worse, he may know what he is doing.' Trevor was refreshingly frank on the subject: 'I'm convinced that Communism is not a serious danger in South Africa,' he said, 'otherwise I wouldn't be doing what I am . . . It'll be a terrible thing if I am wrong.'

So Huddleston became followed by the police, who would meet him at airports and wait outside the houses of people who he visited and search the rooms of his hosts. Congress meetings would be raided and the names of everyone present would be taken as they filed out. Police cameramen took photographs of the audience row by row.

Huddleston was under pressure. 'They seem to be closing in . . . I find it difficult to get a platform now. People are scared by the police, and I can't blame them: they politely cancel their invitations to speak. It's hard enough getting somewhere to exhibit photographs.' But he denied any real interest in politics; sitting in a classroom at St Peter's writing out passes for his schoolboys to go into town so that the police would not stop them, he would say: 'People say I'm a politician . . . but all I'm interested in, really, is people: particularly these people.'

Whereas some CR members were not natural schoolmasters, Trevor certainly was. He would soon stalk around the school, his cassock flowing as he berated a boy or took a Scripture lesson or spoke at Assembly. 'Anthony, when are you going to take some pictures of our jazz band?' he would ask. 'Jake Tuli's giving a boxing demonstration next week', 'I've arranged a debate between a white school and St Peter's', 'You might like to do a feature about our printing press: Lady Oppenheimer has just given us some Perpetua . . .'!

But soon none of this would matter.

14

Turning Point

ON 28 JUNE 1953, Sunday in Sophiatown was a typical day. The weather was bright and clear, as it is when a city is 6,000 feet above sea level. Fr Huddleston had been living in South Africa for a decade. He had lived along the people of Sophiatown and was now their recognized leader. Now they would turn to him when they needed someone to chair their Western Areas Protest Committee and its inaugural meeting that Sunday morning – in the Odin Cinema.

The meeting was caused by the threatened Western Areas Removal Scheme, which would finally be put into practice in February 1955. Under the scheme, all the residents of Sophiatown would be moved six miles away to Meadowlands. All the houses and huts owned by the Africans would be pulled down, and the cleared area would be re-developed as a white district. The whole process was defended as a slum clearance scheme, although no Africans were consulted about the scheme. While it is true that Sophiatown was a slum and some clearance was welcomed by some Africans, the real reasons behind the government's actions were not hard to fathom. Sophiatown was very close to the affluent white suburb of Westdene, and many Africans owned the freeholds of their houses in Sophiatown, which would not be the case in Meadowlands. If the scheme were to be put into practice, all the churches, schools, shops and youth clubs – indeed, everything which had made the place a community – would be razed to the ground.

Trevor decided to make a stand. He felt that if he did not resist now, the battle would be much harder later. So he became chairman of the Western Areas Protest Committee, became friends with leading figures in the African National Congress (ANC), and informed the press of the action he was taking and the speeches that he would be making. He had no legal action to bring against the government; he needed to appeal to the moral sense of the people. Through his actions – his speeches, his letters and articles, the meetings he chaired – he was infuriating and antagonizing the authorities more. Sometimes he forced the authorities to climb down; sometimes he was forced to climb down himself. The authorities began to single out Fr Huddleston for special criticism, and often speeded up the measures which he resisted.

Most of all, the authorities were furious about his relationship with the ANC. The party was the oldest political party in South Africa and worked – ostensibly – to integrate all races into democracy, rather than advance the interests of a political group. It was a modest and insignificant group that had been spurred by the militant youth league, which was formed with the help of Walter Sisulu, Oliver Tambo and Nelson Mandela. They were more militant, calling for strikes and civil disobedience and, by 1952, the direct withdrawal of apartheid legislation. The government clamped down; within seven months, 8,500 protestors had been arrested and imprisoned and new laws were passed which made any acts of protest, or the reporting of them, illegal. Undercover police conducted raids to hunt out subversives; the result was that a total of fifty-two ANC members and many members of the Communist Party of South Africa (SACP) were banned from attending any political gathering.

So Trevor hurried to the Odin Cinema, as soon as Mass was over. As he arrived, there were already over a thousand people filling the cinema, and many more outside. When he reached the vestibule he was met by a group of Europeans who said they were the CID. They were arguing with Indians and Africans, and asserted that they – the CID – had every right to be there. Trevor slipped into a neighbouring shop and telephoned a friend of his from the law, who said that the CID had no such right. Fr Huddleston returned to the cinema and asked them to leave. They slouched off.

As soon as Trevor finished speaking, the doors burst open and a body of police marched up the centre aisle of the cinema and onto the stage, where they arrested Yusuf Cachalia, a prominent leader of the Indian Congress. The people rose to their feet and exploded with anger. Fr Huddleston was aware of the acute danger and the possibility of violence. Also, he knew that he had to deal with the police. Many police were in the doorway, and he was confronted by a policeman with a tommy gun. Other police were in the foyer, and outside there were a hundred or more armed African police. Trevor feared a massacre, as people inside rushed the door. He protested to the officer-in-charge and tried to make him see reason, but was himself threatened with arrest. 'If you will call off the police, I will see that the meeting ends peacefully,' he promised.

The arrest of Yusuf Cachalia was of great significance to Fr Huddleston. From then on, he could no longer be patient. He now needed to use every means available to make known abroad as well as at home the lengths to which South Africa had gone in the matter of suppressing civil and personal liberties. The meeting in the Odin Cinema was crucial, too; Trevor now decided to join the African National Congress.

Trevor's behaviour at the Odin Cinema had endeared him to a new generation of ANC's future activists, including Nelson Mandela and Walter Sisulu. The hatred from others gave him strength; and there was growing loathing between the 'effortlessly' superior leader of the non-voting majority in the townships and the white electorate who applauded the policies of the good life. By this stage, Huddleston was loathed by most whites.

It was a bold step. As his arguments with Archbishop Clayton had shown, Fr Huddleston had believed that the Church was distant from the problems of the people of Sophiatown. Some members of the Community resented his fame; others resented his assumption that the Community had been lethargic in the past, concentrating on 'ambulance work' rather than the cause. But Trevor remained determined; as he wrote:

For the Christian, it is this mystery of identification which finds its expression in the Stable of Bethlehem – God Almighty and Eternal, identifying Himself with man at his most helpless, with man in his utter littleness and poverty. Surely, if the Incarnation means anything at all, it must mean the breaking down of barriers not by words but by deeds, by acts, by identification.

The crisis was brought to a head by two major schemes – the Western Areas Removal Scheme and the Bantu Education Act. The Bantu Education Act, which enjoyed the support of many white liberals, was based on a sympathetic idea. Instead of a broad European education, a new type of 'Bantu' education would be laid on, which would suit the average African in the new South Africa. Many welcomed the Act; the belief that Africans would 'develop along their own lines' in the reserves, with their own education and culture, seemed reasonable to many decent Europeans. Many believed that a case should be made for a more realistic education, which was less dependent on learning by rote.

But the basis of the Bantu Education Act was apartheid, for it forced African children to be educated to a lower state of life. The African National Congress was not impressed: 'Bantu education means slave education. It was designed to create cheap and docile labour for the mines, farms and other similar industries.' The Congress had first planned to boycott the new education, but then decided to postpone action until an alternative schooling could be found.

So missions were forced either to hand over their schools to the government or close them down. Most of the Church schools handed themselves over, as they preferred to have their children poorly educated than not at all. Trevor, as Superintendent of St Peter's, Rossentville – which Raymond Raynes had rebuilt and which was now accepting over 1,500 pupils – knew that young Africans with promise were condemned to a minimal curriculum. The Church had shouldered the burden of educating the African for over seventy years; until 1940 every school in South Africa owed its origin, building and supervision to the Christian missionary. Even fifteen years later, nine in ten schools were Church schools, though dependent on church grants. The Community of the Resurrection ran the largest primary school in South Africa – with over 2,000 pupils – yet only one in three children could find a school place.

The Mission schools were poor and the government schools were wealthy. But by taking over the Church schools, the government would rob them of their independence and vigour. Trevor believed that the whole purpose of the Act was to force children to accept the world of apartheid, so that they would not find it bewildering or depressing when they grew up.

Like other missionaries, Trevor was faced with an impossible question. Should St Peter's continue under the present regime, and teach a syllabus which was considered unChristian – or should he close it down? Certainly, the Anglican establishment – the bishops in

South Africa, except for the bishop of Johannesburg – agreed to lease their mission school buildings to the government. The alternative, they believed, would be to throw many teachers out of employment, and leave many children without any opportunity of any kind of instruction.

But Trevor then made a startling and brave decision; he refused to compromise with the Bantu Education Act. He decided to close the Church schools rather than hand them over to the government. It was this breathtakingly unEnglish refusal to compromise that remains his most definite and lasting contribution to the fight against apartheid. He chose to close down St Peter's rather than hand it over to the Nationalist Government, a courageous decision about a school which he loved. His action was not shared by many of the other churches, among whom opinion on what was best for African children was very divided; all the Catholic and many of the Anglican schools remained open. Within a few months the whole school system built by the Church and the Community in the Transvaal had closed.

In an article he wrote to justify his position, Huddleston said:

It is still happily possible to prefer death to dishonour. St Peter's will die. There is only one path open to the African: it is the path back to tribal culture and tradition: to ethnic groups; to the reserves; to anywhere other than the privileged places habited by the master race. It is because we can't accept such principles that we are closing St Peter's . . . it has been a decision made in anguish and only after the most careful thought and prayer. For it means the end of forty years of labour and devotion, and it means the break-up of a tradition of which we are unashamedly proud.

One old boy, writing about his school, said: 'In weeping for St Peter's, I weep for a new generation of slum kids for whom there will be no escape, as there was for me, through St Peter's.'

Meanwhile, Trevor was facing a special crisis in the nearby township of Newclare, which was in particular trouble, due to fighting between gangs. He writes in *Naught for Your Comfort*: 'Something was stirring beneath that strange mixture of slum and open place, in those crowded backyards. Indian shops were set on fire and looted, perhaps to stir up racial strife between African and Indian.' A black gang which called itself the Communists had entrenched itself at Newclare, and locals replied by forming a civil guard. Men, armed with heavy sticks and moving in groups of a dozen, would patrol the streets after midnight. Meanwhile, bloody clashes continued in Newclare between gangs and residents. But the gangs were not disarmed and two months later the civil guard was declared illegal and conditions became impossible: 'People began to move out of their homes and erect shacks and shelters in the open . . . within a week two hundred families – 1,500 people – were living there, with a public lavatory.'

After much debate, the authorities then tried, with the City Council and the police together, to evict the squatters. People who had been terrorized by gangs were being asked to walk back into terror. Trevor decided to build to save the squatters' children from the worst of the cold, collecting a miserable £300 for their blankets and basic comfort. Meanwhile a tornado hit nearby, and thousands of pounds worth of clothing and food were distributed immediately. This action provoked Trevor to say sardonically: 'I have always felt that this was an interesting comment on the conscience of White Johannesburg. Stirred to immediate and most generous action by a tornado, it could remain utterly impervious to what was happening day after day to hundreds of its own African citizens in its midst.'

Bereft of his own home, his love for Sophiatown remained real and emotional. In Chapter 7 of *Naught for Your Comfort*, he writes in a simple memoir and a rare *apologia pro via sua*:

> The overcrowded rooms . . . wherein whole families must sleep and must perform all their human functions as best they may . . . Again and again, hearing confession, I have asked myself how I can advise these children, how warn them, how comfort them when they have fallen . . . I can shut my eyes and see old, blind Margaret, tapping her way along the street into the darkness which has been hers for many long years. Or there will be old Tryphena Mtembu. She has spent all her years . . . mending sacks and inhaling cement dust into her old lungs so that she is never free from a fierce cough. She lives in a single dark room and 'does' for herself. . . . or Piet, crippled with arthritis, infirm and with no pension after thirty years' work in a furniture shop . . . It would be easy to list a score of others, who have lived in Sophiatown for the better part of their lives . . . folk who live

ordinary lives in extraordinary conditions . . . The only thing
that is meeting the need for a sense of 'community', of 'belonging' in the broken and shattered tribalism of the town-dwelling
African is the Church.

The violence of his protests and the publicity surrounding them made
him enemies on his own side; there were people who agreed with him
in principle, but not with his methods – especially white Church
people who thought that he was being provocative and deliberately
antagonizing the government, when he should have been conciliatory.
But, most seriously, he was in trouble with his own Church.

15

The Beginning of the End

IT WAS A TYPICAL EARLY MORNING in Sophiatown. A few men strolled down the hill to the bus stop. Horses clip-clopped as they drew out of a yard for another day of hawking coal. A baby cried; a cock crowed. In the distance, voices greeted each other in the half-light. It drizzled. But in one sense this was an unusual day. It was 10 February 1955, the day on which the Western Areas Removal Scheme was put into practice.

In the early morning, twenty communicants sat in the chapel of St Mary Magdalene, in the church of Christ the King. Trevor stood at the low altar. 'I will go unto the altar of God, even the God of my joy and gladness.' In *Naught for Your Comfort*, he recalled that February morning, saying: 'It is the beginning of the end of Sophiatown: because from now nothing will ever be the same again in this little corner of South Africa: because today the great removal is beginning, and all the people I know, and the houses they live in will soon be scattered, and Sophiatown itself will crumble into dust.'

Trevor had informed journalists that the police would eject people from their homes. He chatted up journalists and walked past the bus queues in the rain, where people gave the forbidden raised Congress sign and shook his hand. He takes up the story in *Naught for Your Comfort*: 'Suddenly . . . there comes a sound I have never heard in Sophiatown before. It is the sound of men marching . . . A detachment of African police under European command marches raggedly but purposefully past us, down the hill.'

A whole fleet of army lorries drew up. Thousands of police lined the streets, white men and black men with rifles and revolvers. The Commissioner of Police emerged in a VIP car, remaining in hourly

89

contact with the central authorities in Cape Town. Outside the bus station, military lorries were drawn up, piled with the most pathetic possessions that had come from the rows of shacks behind them. Trevor, staring pointedly at the row of cameras in front of him, said to the police: 'Move away there . . . you've no right here . . . get out I'm telling you.'

The police, who said that they were acting on orders from the Ministry of Justice, continued to move Trevor on. Trevor, in turn, held press conferences, gave newspaper interviews, cajoled his prominent friends on the telephone. So when the removal took place that February morning, many foreign journalists from all over the world reported on it, and many of them took photographs of, and took quotes from, Trevor.

The government destroyed Sophiatown for one main reason: white people could not stand living close to so many black people. Many Christians, too, would have been pleased by the damage that was being inflicted on the CR's work in Sophiatown. The intense hatred that the government felt for Trevor – a hatred which he fed on – exacerbated the mutual distrust between South African Calvinists and Anglicans, who continued to insist that they were part of the true Church. Remarkably, nearly twelve years after first arriving in Sophiatown, the young white missionary had been identified as the leader of black protest in the country. No wonder so much of South Africa hated him.

Four months later, on 25 June 1955, the ANC and other anti-government authorities arranged a meeting at Kliptown, a village near Johannesburg. In an attempt to combat oppression, they adopted a Freedom Charter, which clearly set out the Nationalist Movement's demands on wealth and schools and rights. Some 3,000 delegates – blacks, Indians, coloureds, white liberals, communists and churchmen – travelled from all over South Africa to the meeting. There were many police present, who took pictures and wrote down what was said, unless speeches were drowned out by passing trains or disguised in vernacular languages. Opening the meeting, the Chairman Dr Congo announced 'a new feature in the liberation struggle of the people of South Africa. It is Isitwalandwe. There will be here presentations made to individuals who have distinguished themselves in the struggle of the people of South Africa.' The Isitwalandwe was an honour given for outstanding national or war service; indeed, every man who was awarded the honour had achieved the greatest distinction in African society. The three individuals who were awarded the honour were Chief Albert Luthuli, a Congress leader; Dr Y. M. Dadoo, who was head of the South African Indian Congress, and Trevor. Trevor was awarded the Isitwalandwe, because 'he has given us without fear, his courage and services. He has refused to compromise whether in the field of education or freedom of speech.' He was loved for having refused to leave Sophiatown on the day of the Removals, for having stayed with the people and helped to resist the efforts of the police.

Receiving the award, Trevor replied: 'I cannot help feeling sad that of the three people to whom this honour is given, I am the only one who is present to receive it, and I don't know whether it is to be blamed on the part of our friends, the police, or not, but the fact is that I am here.' After a few sideswipes at the Minister of Justice and his friends, Trevor continued:

> Here in Kliptown this afternoon we have only one answer to the government in this country. The government in this country wants to deprive people of their rights, the government in this country uses unconstitutional methods, methods which are used to deprive the majorities of their rights. Here this afternoon . . . we meet openly. We want to discuss freedom. We meet to plan a charter which will be the basis of action for the coming years. Those are the principles we hold so dear, of justice and of peace in our time, and so I thank you from my heart and I wish this Congress of the People every blessing in the years to come. Thank you very much.

The Congress of the People proved to be Trevor's watershed. He was now showing, in public, his support for the ANC. The rest of the Church was simply not prepared to take that jump and to become immersed in the political action of the ANC. It was not what priests were about. Like Michael Scott, Trevor had become one of the few whites who had been accepted as an honorary black by the black people of South Africa. But as black people accepted him, so white people rejected him; they saw him as that worst kind of caricature – the 'interfering cleric'. Anyone who was not in the centre of the Anglican Church in South Africa demonized him – and even sympathetic people in Johannesburg, who were served their supper by black people in white gloves, perceived him as a threat. White people were disturbed and anxious.

As Sophiatown was destroyed and its residents removed to Meadowlands, so there was an upsurge in crime and violence. Most white people, who did not understand the predicament of the Africans, were frightened that their houses would be burnt and their money stolen. Those white people who tried to understand the African – a minority who lived in Johannesburg, many of whom were Jewish and members of the Communist Party – were derided for betraying their own people.

By the spring of 1955, Trevor was under intolerable strain. The Priory at St Peter's was raided and most of his papers were taken away, although the drafts for *Naught for Your Comfort* were hidden, and were eventually safely delivered to London. Trevor was facing the continual threat of imprisonment and arrest and deportation. His friendship with Olga Horowitz, the sympathetic reporter on *The Star*, was viewed with suspicion. He would visit her office, and she would quickly transform an emotional speech or long-winded letter into a terse feature piece, quickly syndicated to newspaper agencies overseas.

There was also Trevor's diabetes. By 1955, he had been diagnosed as diabetic and needed to be treated with a daily dose of insulin. He treated his diabetes with typical courage – 'he rolled with the punches', as one CR member put it – but this illness definitely contributed to the depressions which were to afflict him in later life. Much of Trevor's generation treated pain with a noble indifference, and he was no exception; but his diabetes caused his friends huge concern, and many believed that imprisonment in a South African jail would have led to his death.

In September 1955 Trevor spent his annual summer holidays with the Patons, and spent much of his free time at a small card table, where he wrote *Naught for Your Comfort*, a manuscript about his recent political campaign. He wrote through the day, with few revisions and even fewer breaks. The book would eventually be published and became an international bestseller. The title contained an ironic reference to Alan Paton's *Cry, the Beloved Country: A Story of Comfort in Desolation*. It is a tribute to Trevor that he was able to complete the book in the midst of the huge turmoil that he was facing. The book is the work of a preacher; it is angry and eloquent and passionate.

Huddleston was able to sum up an argument, draw a picture, irritate his opponents and inspire the young by writing clearly, in his neat and feminine hand, what was in his mind. His work rarely needed editing. The journalist Anthony Sampson, who had edited *Drum* magazine, had told him that he should write up his own personal experiences in his own way, and avoid the curse of objective prose. In the end, his editor Robin Denniston only needed to lift what was Chapter 1 from its position near the end of the book. The book is passionate, occasionally incoherent, very direct and honest. In a brief preface, he apologizes to the CR for publishing the book at all.

It was also while he was on holiday with the Patons that he was informed of a decision about his future. The decision all but destroyed him.

16

The Recall

IN NOVEMBER 1955, Trevor was recalled from South Africa to the Community in Mirfield.

He had seemed on the verge of a nervous breakdown for some time; his behaviour was obsessive, and verged on egomania. Trevor was fighting hard and people felt that he might break, or become gravely ill. Some believed that he would be arrested and then disappear into the South African legal system. He faced the constant threat of imprisonment and deportation. His life had been reduced to one of protest, in which he was happy to attack fellow clergy who were working in impossible conditions as well as government officials.

When he, in his own words, 'took the jump' into the ANC, he became despised by the ecclesiastical authorities no less than by the political ones. His papers were seized, his house was ransacked, he was followed everywhere. His upbringing had lent him an assurance, which in turn gave him a stubbornness that infuriated the Archbishop and the authorities. In the words of his sometime ally Alan Paton, Trevor 'had a conviction of the rightness of his views . . . which led him to pursue what he saw as the right, but to condemn and accuse those he saw as being in the wrong'. Paton was uncomfortable with his egotism.

His life was under threat. The politicians had been making apartheid laws since 1948; now, for the first time, they were taking action (forced removals) to enforce those laws. They were not confident that they could actively force it through, and the Minister was in direct contact with the police CO on the ground in Sophiatown. Their chief enemy was Trevor, whom they hated with a passionate loathing. If they could get their hands on him, they would, and they were happy to take the consequences of world opinion. In 1955 the world did not know what was going on in South Africa, and did not take steps to rebuke it.

Trevor was also a South African citizen, and deportation was not an issue. Stories had been circulating of an imam who had mysteriously died while in prison. His captors said that he had slipped in the showers. The death of diabetic Trevor could have been arranged and the world, which had scarcely heard of Sophiatown, would hear no more about him. That was his Superior's fear, and Trevor's death in prison was one that Raynes could not countenance.

But, even in his darkest hours, Trevor could never have imagined being recalled from the place he loved. Of course, he had grown up from the 'very young and very naïve' man who had first arrived in Sophiatown in 1943. He could be astonishingly acute and perceptive and, as he illustrated later in his life, politically sensitive in his dealings with others. However, there was one enemy he could not afford to make in South Africa – Geoffrey Clayton, the Archbishop of Cape Town. Only Clayton, along with the Superior of the CR Raymond Raynes, had the power to recall Trevor. Clayton was the Visitor to the CR, and there was a great deal of co-operation between the Visitor and the Superior.

In June 1954 Raymond Raynes had made a special visit to Johannesburg to see Trevor, believing that Trevor would not be allowed to return to South Africa if he came back to Mirfield for his regular meetings with the Community as the Provincial. In December of that year, Geoffrey Clayton resigned briefly as Visitor to the Community, saying that Trevor had illustrated his contempt for him through countless articles and sermons.

The most famous and damaging of these articles had appeared in the *Observer* newspaper that year. In the article, cheekily entitled 'The Church Sleeps On', Trevor wrote:

> The Church sleeps on. It sleeps on while 60,000 people are moved from their homes in the interests of a fantastic racial policy. It sleeps on while plans are made (and implemented) to transform the education of Africans into a thing called 'Native Education'. It sleeps on while a dictatorship is swiftly being created . . . so that speech and movement and association are no longer free. The Church sleeps on – although it occasionally talks in its sleep and expects (or does it?) the government to listen.

These words were not written to reconcile; they are stripped of deference or politeness. They were intended to condemn and indict and infuriate. Trevor had cut through the Church's official line: that it should not officially take sides; that it should remain broadly neutral, despite the agony and death inflicted on its own people; that its inertia could be justified by theological argument. Trevor, despite the most overwhelming pressure, had refused to budge one inch. Clayton was livid.

Of course, the two men had argued before, and not simply over *The Church and the Nation* report or South African politics. Trevor had already courted trouble when, with a hundred other South African clerics, he wrote a letter to the *Church Times* attacking the Archbishops of Canterbury and York for offering full recognition to the newly reconstituted Church of South India. Trevor, who preached tolerance while remaining theologically illiberal, had once pinned up a notice on the wall of Christ the King when he was Prior: 'This Church is not in communion with the Church of South India.' The Church of South India, which had only been inaugurated in 1947, was seen as dangerously modern; it was not doctrinally Catholic, and the rebels believed that its acceptance would dilute the Anglican faith. The signatories were so furious that they threatened to withdraw the South African Church from Communion with the Provinces.

This time, Trevor was stunned by Clayton's resignation. Knowing that the Archbishop was about to fly off on a journey, Trevor raced to Johannesburg airport and persuaded him to change his mind. Lacerating himself, Trevor wrote to his Superior: 'it was my fault for writing too strongly: I have been pretty wore out [*sic*] by this endless crisis and said too much.' But the damage had been done; Trevor's views on apartheid and theology were viewed suspiciously by the establishment. That same year, Geoffrey Fisher, the Archbishop of Canterbury, had come to inaugurate the Anglican Province of Central Africa at Salisbury Cathedral. He was told that there were two experiences that he must not miss: the Copper Belt and Huddleston. When they met in Penhalonga in May, Fisher told him that his methods were 'entirely wrong'. At supper, the two men had an argument over whether Christians should ever use force. Trevor cited the example of Christ driving the money changers out of the Temple; in turn, Fisher argued that Christ's actions were only 'symbolic'. The two men argued on, but later on in his trip Fisher proclaimed cheerfully to a posse of photographers that 'the score is about deuce' and insisted on being snapped arm in arm with his adversary. Temporarily, they may have been friends, but a few years later Fisher, despite protestations to the contrary, delayed Trevor's appointment to Masasi.

In February 1955 Raynes sent Fr Jonathan Graham to Africa to report on all CR activities there, and particularly the path that Trevor had taken. Raynes already seems to have decided in principle to recall Huddleston. Graham spoke with two fellow priests – Sidebotham and Rakale – with Oliver Tambo (who wept at the idea), and finally with Clayton, who said ambiguously: 'He has too much to give; and what is best for him must be best for the Church.'

Fr Graham, the astringent son of a housemaster at Uppingham who would go on to succeed Raynes as Superior, was uncharacteristically fulsome in his praise of Trevor:

> Though one may first be struck by his affection for Africans and go on to marvel at his unsparing work of service to them, it is not long before one meets evidence of a profound and detailed, if lightly worn, knowledge which lies behind them both . . . He is heart-whole and single-minded and uncomplicated to a degree which is the envy of lesser men. There are no reservations, no pettiness, no querulousness; everything about him is fresh and wholesome and in perspective and integrated; the whole man is there for everyone's disposal, whether the claimant for his attention is a dirty schoolboy or an Archbishop, an eccentric or a bore . . . Gifts of leadership are there in plenty but they are never displayed, just naturally incorporated into the whole character.

Trevor, sadly, could not repay Fr Graham's compliments; he was so distracted by other events that, in later years, he was unable to remember Graham's visit.

Raynes, then, had made up his mind. But he worried about everything; about Trevor, about South Africa, about talks of splits in the Community. In speaking about South Africa, he had urged restraint when Trevor had urged resistance: 'The most important thing we can do is to make available in England as far as possible the actual facts of the situation which, once they become known, speak for themselves; and to underline the fact that it is by no means the whole truth to say that this is a domestic matter for South Africa.' But he had always, both publicly and privately, supported Trevor, and believed that he was supporting him by taking him back home. Raynes also had to contend with tension in the Community; brethren felt that the CR had become wholly identified with Trevor's work, and that the quiet diligence shown by other members of the Community had been over-looked. Trevor would often say that CR is 'the only family I have', but this was disingenuous; throughout the rest of his life, he longed to be exiled home to South Africa, and often felt trapped and frustrated at Mirfield.

In July 1955, at the General Chapter, Raynes wrote to a friend: 'Say a special prayer for me as I have to make two decisions next week of a very serious nature concerning the Community. It is nothing "awful" – just serious and important.' One of those decisions was the recall of Trevor to Mirfield, where he was to replace the present Novice Guardian, who was an 'old dear', but useless.

Raynes then wrote to Trevor, who was staying at the Patons. Trevor, bound by obedience, replied immediately. He believed that he had been recalled because his Superior had felt that his life was in danger, and that his relationship with Clayton had made it very difficult for him to operate as a Provincial. But, whatever the reasons, Trevor had been wrenched from what he felt he should have been allowed to do. His bereavement was beyond words. He could have done more for South Africa by being recalled than staying there. Some say that he would have been martyred, which would have done more for South Africa than anything else. Yet Trevor never relished the role of leaving. He had been at a place where he was loved and needed, surrounded by people that he loved and needed, which had brought out parts of his being – warmth, love, feeling – that he had lacked before. He was now returning to a dark monastery in West Yorkshire. Despite his intense discipline and, for an emotional man, intense privacy, he never accepted the decision.

Many years later, Trevor explained his decision to obey Raynes:

> I couldn't see the point of taking a vow of obedience and then [disobeying] . . . when it became inconvenient . . . Looking back on it, I'm absolutely certain Raynes was right. If I'd disobeyed, I would have drifted on and got involved in the Treason Trials, and heaven knows what would have happened then . . . But as it happened . . . I got back to Africa after all . . . in a country at the

point of transition from colonialism to independence . . . and I was able to do a lot.

On 24 October 1955 Trevor's recall was publicly announced. People were dumbfounded. Many put great pressure on Raynes (who had also been recalled against his will) to change his mind. Writing from Africa, Trelawney-Ross CR told Raynes that the brethren felt devastated, saying that it was as if Montgomery had been withdrawn just after El Alamein. Africans were signing petitions, forming deputations, begging that Fr Huddleston be allowed to stay. Cassandra of the *Daily Mirror* named Huddleston as his Man of the Year:

> For twelve long years he has fought an untiring, desperate, lonely battle against hatred and intolerance in the worst slums in the world. For twelve long years he has endured the malevolent ill-will of the South African government . . . To watch him, as I have done, working in the squalor of the shanty towns and to see children race up to him is to know he is a great and good man.

Raynes decided to face his critics. In November, he flew out to Johannesburg, where he faced headlines in the African press like 'Do not leave us, Father Huddleston!' In Rossentville, there was a meeting of the Fraternity at which many white supporters refused to speak to Raymond. Raynes patiently explained to delegations of Africans that Fr Huddleston was needed by the Community at home. Many of the Africans, who had known and loved Raynes, could not understand him and were not convinced by his arguments. He would say to them: 'Try not to think of me as a wicked man, only a silly one.' He attended farewell concerts for Fr Trevor, which would have been awkward for him. Many believed that the Superior of the CR had taken away their champion just when he was needed, because it was afraid of the Nationalist Government. To white activists, Trevor's non-violent opposition to apartheid seemed absolutely crucial. A correspondent to *The Star* said: 'Talk to any Bantu and see how his face lights up when the Father's name is mentioned.' Most believed that Dr Malan had been given an unnecessary reprieve.

Raynes was resolute, but anguished. He would only show his suffering to a few close friends. In December, Fr Raynes went to visit Deane and Dorothy Yates in Johannesburg. Deane had been headmaster of St John's College, Johannesburg. The pair were close to both Trevor and Raymond. In an excerpt from an unpublished diary, Dorothy wrote:

> Raymond loves Trevor, and, having himself been in Sophiatown he knows the value of the work Trevor is doing. But he knows about the threats Trevor has received, and some of the numerous people he has talked to believe that Trevor could be imprisoned. He is a diabetic, and a spell in prison without the proper insulin could bring serious illness, or even death. 'I am his Father in God' he says, 'and I feel the responsibility is awesome.'

Dorothy Yates remembers that Fr Raynes did not sleep at all the night he was with them, because of the agony of decision over Trevor.

Deane also remembered meeting with Raymond. He was in bed with a duodenal ulcer, having been headmaster of St John's for fifteen months. It was Raymond's first visit to South Africa since Deane had started at St John's, and he was hoping that they could talk together about St John's. But when Raymond arrived, Deane said:

> [We] saw how tense he was. He did the talking and we just listened. It seemed he was using us as a sounding board. He paced up and down the bedroom, chain smoking, and talking all the time about the tough decision he had to take. This is so vivid in my mind, I could only liken it to Raymond's Garden of Gethsemane. As far as I remember, St John's was not even mentioned.
>
> I am still quite certain that Raymond was gravely concerned about Trevor's diabetes. Of course, there were other reasons which must have influenced him in taking the decision he did, but I still think that when Raymond talked to us it was the problem of the diabetes that was uppermost in his mind.

Any number of theories still remain behind Trevor's recall. Perhaps there was an overwhelmingly strong desire within the Community for him to be the new Novice Guardian, although this seems unlikely. Perhaps Pretoria had put pressure on Raynes, although Raymond, who had faced down thugs before, was not the sort to be cowed. Raynes supported Huddleston, and believed that the more brethren and bishops protested, the better. The two men were different in temperament but shared similar characteristics – an anger which needed to find an enemy, an iron discipline and determination and, above all, a love of Africa. No one who knew Raynes could believe that he was acting at the behest of the Archbishop of Canterbury or the South African/Pretoria government.

Many thought that Clayton had advised Raynes to recall him. This, however, was strenuously denied by Raynes in a sermon which was preached in St Mary's Cathedral, Johannesburg, on 4 December 1955, in which he said:

> Twelve years ago it was my duty, as Superior of the Community, to send one of its members to take charge of the mission at Sophiatown, and I sent Fr Huddleston. I have no need to say much of what Father Huddleston has done since – save this – that I personally and the whole Community thank God for giving us such a brother, and we thank God that he has so continuously and so courageously, yet with persistence, patience and charity, witnessed, by his life, his words and actions, to those fundamental principles which are held and shared by all his Brethren. In a remarkable manner, he has expounded by word and action the Christian approach to the racial, social and political problems of the world, and that in a country where they are most acute.
>
> It has been said that his recall to England is due to the fact that I disagree with him or am embarrassed by his attitude. Nothing could be further from the truth. I remember nothing with which I disagree and I thank God for giving me such a son and brother . . .
>
> It has been continually and persistently suggested that pressure has been brought to bear that he should be removed; the source of the pressure being either Church authorities, big business or the governments of South Africa or the United Kingdom. There has been no pressure from any of these sources. People must either believe me or not . . . On that I can say no more, save that, had there been such pressure, I should not have been much influenced by it . . .
>
> There has, however, been very strong pressure on me to reconsider Fr Huddleston's recall. I have been deeply moved by the representation made to me by people and groups of all races

and of all creeds. I have considered them all most carefully, but I am still convinced that he should return to the home of the Community for the work to which he has been appointed.

It is the duty of the Superior to safeguard the life of the Community in all its aspects and, further, to seek its increase, growth and development, and this, not for its own comfort and security, but that it may serve God and the Church more strongly . . . The position of Novice Master in any Religious Order is one of the utmost importance; a thing which it is perhaps not easy to understand for those outside. For long I have thought that Fr Huddleston was the right person – an opinion supported by responsible people whom I have consulted. There are some who urge that, though this is true, this is not the time. They may be right: but equally the Community may be right.

In all this, strategy and long-term policy must not be over-looked, and to move a leader from one part of the field to another, which may appear to be less important, is often required. The decision to do so is no easy one, and no-one is infallible. I must accept the fact that I may be mistaken. I can only say that I am seeking to do what I believe to be right, and to God I must answer for it. He is a merciful judge, who knows the secrets of our hearts. I know, and it is heavy on my heart, what personal loss to very many Fr Huddleston's departure must mean. Yet on earth and in the Church Militant such partings and separations are inevitable and necessary in this our pilgrimage. On this personal matter I have said enough.

There may be other reasons, too. Raynes may have been jealous of Trevor's fame. He was certainly concerned for his health. But, most of all, he was worried for his soul. Trevor wanted to be a martyr; he wished to die in prison. Such a desire would be deeply damaging to his soul. One should always ask questions about people who want to be martyrs rather than rejoice in the role that they have been given. As Martial wrote, 'No hero to me, is the man who, by easy shedding of his blood, purchases fame. My hero is he who, without death, can win praise.'

There was also a strong belief that Trevor was doing the work of the Africans. The sheer strength of his personality, the fact that he was willing to go to prison and die for them, gave the people confidence and made them stronger. But, at the same time, it made Africans tend to lean on him, when they should have been fighting for themselves.

Was it silly of Raynes to claim that Trevor was recalled because he was to be made Novice Guardian? The role was very important. In 1955 the Community needed a new Novice Guardian. No one at Mirfield was believed to be suitable. By appointing Trevor, he was saying that the future of the Community rested in the hands of Trevor. The situation was unusual, made stranger by the fact that there was a large number of novices and their training depended on the Community. They needed to look for someone abroad. Trevor was that man.

But, as the writer Nicholas Mosley puts it from a distance of fifty years:

> Raynes always maintained that the Community needed a new Novice Guardian at Mirfield, but it was unwise and absurd of Raynes to say that. I feel that there are two strands to his recall; Raynes felt that he was responsible for both his physical and spiritual welfare; he felt he was going hell-bent to be a martyr.
>
> In Africa, Trevor found an enormous confidence and strength and this gave him the power to take everyone on and not to count the cost. Raynes thought that he was being a one-man band; that in effect his mission was affecting other parts of the Anglican Church and community. Raynes also liked Clayton, who was worried about what Trevor was actually doing. Raynes was worried that if Trevor did his public show then Clayton might find it awkward to be a Visitor to the Community.

The CR historian Alan Wilkinson agrees:

> Raynes realised that Trevor was at the end of his tether and would land in trouble and was facing emotional and physical exhaustion. One of Raynes' main motives was to preserve him from death in prison and physical and mental collapse. There were great worries about his safety in prison and that he was becoming embroiled in political activities.
>
> As Superior, Raynes needed to look after all the brethren. Raynes was worried that his vocation was at risk. Raynes didn't want Trevor stereotyped as a political activist. There were signs that he was becoming totally focused on the issue in a very

individualistic way – a very Protestant way. Whereas the Communal or Catholic way was more appropriate.

Aereld Stubbs, a member of the CR and a friend of Trevor's, says: 'In the Community, there was a feeling that the whole Sophiatown epic had been hi-jacked by Trevor, who was not well known until the book came out. He was living at such a pitch, and something had to give. For Raynes, obedience came first and personalities came later; Trevor, however, always had the art of the personal. Trevor never got over his recall, but he lived so much in the present moment that he would never have allowed you to believe that he hadn't got over it.'

The former Conservative MP Harry Greenway, who knew Trevor well, understood how painful Trevor's recall was: 'Africa generates passion and if you have a passion and it's taken away from you, the strain of maintaining that effort can give you some relief, but at the same time the passion does not go. The passion never left him, and he would only have to hear an African choir singing or performing; he didn't wear his heart on his sleeve, but people knew that he would be affected by it.'

He adds: 'All the time, he was dealing with people stuck in poverty who haven't got anything. The poor have a simplicity and a vision which the clutter of riches may impede; they are struggling for clothes and food and they have an openness and a passion which other people may lack. There is no bullshit about them; they are good, straight-forward people. I can see why Trevor found it so hard to leave.'

One question lingers. How could someone as intelligent and intuitive as Raynes seriously think that he was serving the Community's best interests? Anthony Sampson spoke to Raynes for over three hours on the evening of 23 January 1956: 'Trevor had shot his bolt, and was in danger of putting others in trouble. Now Raynes felt that Huddleston, despite his great sorrow at leaving, was inwardly relieved at his recall, after the great strain and frustration.' Raynes was convinced that Trevor's soul was in danger as he was becoming a national protest leader, despite his monastic vows and unwillingness to accept such a destiny. He told a close friend: 'They would have taken him away and made him king.'

And what happened to Clayton? The two men did not immediately communicate after his departure. Huddleston, with considerable charity, paid a special visit to St John's to say goodbye to his Archbishop, and received 'little more than a grunt'. He found this very painful; after all, Trevor had written to the same man in 1948: 'These past six years have been far and away the happiest of my life. Laus Deo! And certainly part of their happiness had been due to the very cordial relationship with you, and to the knowledge that – even in disagreement – I could always count on your wisdom, patience and affection.'

The Archbishop replied that they were different types of people, and could not respond in the same way. The two had never seen eye to eye, and Trevor distrusted Clayton's pietism and could not understand many of the attitudes of the other bishops of the Church of the Province of South.

The two men did communicate once Trevor was safely back in England. In September 1955, shortly before Trevor was recalled, the government had responded to the Congress of the People by swooping on the offices of fifty organizations and the houses of five hundred people. By December 1956, one hundred and fifty-six members of the Congress Movement had been arrested and charged with treason – the run-up to the Treason Trials had properly begun.

On 6 December 1956, a number of prominent Anglicans – including Oliver Tambo and Helen Joseph – were arrested and charged with treason. The Treason Trial, which was to run from 1956 until 1961, was the longest and largest in South African history, revealed the remarkable political qualities of Nelson Mandela and ended in fiasco. From the safety of Mirfield, Trevor read that Clayton, Reeves and other leading Anglicans had lent their support to a defence fund in South Africa. Trevor, in turn, had been contacted by Christian Action, who had asked him to write to the *Observer* to ask support for the fund in this country.

Desolate and isolated, Trevor would write wildly excitable letters to Alan Paton, asking his help in returning to South Africa (against the will of his Superior, if necessary) so that he, too, could stand trial. Paton informed the sympathetic Bishop Ambrose Reeves of Johannesburg, who tried to calm Trevor down, reminding him of his vows and adding 'on no account should you contemplate disobedience'. Even Trevor's most loyal supporters were frustrated at his manic behaviour, and believed with some justification that Huddleston and Canon John Collins were more sympathetic to the aims of the South African Communists than the views of Liberal Moderation. Paton was furious that Christians, encouraged by Trevor, gave large sums of money to political extremists in South Africa, while the Liberal Party, which studiously avoided violence, was starved of funds. Paton was to endure this situation stoically for years.

Trevor also wrote to Clayton, saying that he was disturbed at the turn of events and felt guilty that he was not present at the Treason Trial. Clayton wrote back, pithily: 'In my opinion it would be unwise to assume that the Government had no valid evidence at all against any of those who have been arrested. It is indeed very difficult to suppose that some who have been arrested are guilty of high treason. But there are many about whom I know nothing at all.'

There was then a second set of letters, which were even more revealing about Clayton's attitude towards Trevor. Clayton started by saying that he doubted that Trevor had any evidence which would aid those facing trial. He then warned, brutally but accurately, against 'the desire to put oneself in the limelight and a sense of frustration which comes to a man when he ceases to be in the limelight'. Furthermore, he warned against the 'temptation to believe that one is indispensable. The devil persuades other people to tell one that one is that when it is not true.'

Clayton was concerned that Trevor was planning to leave the CR and return to South Africa. Trevor, perhaps disingenuously, denied that this was the case. Clayton ended his letter:

> I can see that you are sorely tempted. I am sure that it is the temptations of the devil, though lots of people whose opinion you value would not recognize it as such, but they would regard you as acting heroically [*sic*] . . . I believe that they are wrong.

The exiled Trevor accepted with grace Clayton's withering remarks about his love of the limelight and belief that he was indispensable. He finished, though, by launching his own defence:

> I still believe (and cannot say otherwise) that the Church is not facing [the issue of race relations] . . . as courageously as she should. Where I have resented your criticisms and attitudes towards me (and I beg you to believe that I've often resented them wrongly too) it has been because it has seemed to me that you wished me silent and submissive when I could not be. At

least I have always tried to be frank with you too. But I could often and much more easily have been a yes-man.

Yet, towards the end of his life, Clayton defied the law, and urged others to do likewise. He urged all to oppose the Native Laws Amendment Act, which would enforce the separation of black and white protest. On Shrove Tuesday, 5 March 1957, the bishops arrived. On Ash Wednesday, they considered a draft letter to the Prime Minister. After the bishops decided on a final draft, Clayton took the arm of Ambrose Reeves, the Bishop of Johannesburg, and said to him: 'Reeves, I don't want to go to prison. I'm an old man. I don't want to end my days in prison. But I'll go if I have to.'

Early on Thursday morning, the bishops left the Archbishop. After a Mass and breakfast, he busied himself with mundane tasks. At twenty past three, Clayton collapsed on the floor of his study and died.

17

Back in England

TREVOR SAID FAREWELL TO SOUTH AFRICA in early March 1956, four months after his recall had been announced to the world. Hundreds of children lined the airport to say goodbye as he left the country. Many television crews, including the mighty American television company CBS, filmed his departure. Soldiers lurched around with rifles, but Trevor remained unflappable. He turned to the children as he was about to board the steps to his aeroplane. 'Have courage. The Lord is always with us,' he said.

It would have been cruel to send Trevor straight back to West Yorkshire. Instead, he went straight to New York, where inquisitive customs officials asked him whether he had ever been a Communist; McCarthyism was rife, and both he and his writer friend Alan Paton had been described to the US authorities as Communists by the South African government. He visited New York and Connecticut, where he told dinner guests about Christian schools in South Africa. His publishers held a press conference to publicize the book; *Life* magazine commissioned him to write about the Huddleston jazz band. The religious magazine *Presbyterian Life* paid for him to have a trip to the Deep South, where he met Martin Luther King Jr in Montgomery, Alabama. He visited Mississippi, where one activist after another told him of the atrocities that blacks were facing. He then hitched a ride in a taxi to meet Louis 'Satchmo' Armstrong and told him about the young trumpet-playing protégé Huge Masekela. Armstrong then handed over his instrument, which Trevor had sent back to South Africa.

He returned to New York, where he had lunch with Eleanor Roosevelt and was photographed in various stages of piety by the famous Karsh of Ottawa. Meanwhile, reviews of *Naught for Your Comfort* were being published in the British newspapers; Trevor described them as 'very flattering and long'. The *Manchester Guardian*, which breathed religious scepticism, described *Naught for Your Comfort* as 'a noble book, a superb book, to be read by anyone who cares about race (or any human relations). It vibrates with humanity.' The *Daily Mirror* put it more simply: 'I beg you to read his book; a supremely eloquent and burning indictment. Trevor Huddleston is a man with a zest and joy for life; and, most blessed attribute in a priest, a sense of humour and a taste for laughter.' His old friend Michael Scott, writing in the *Observer*, said:

> Here is a book which comes straight out of the crucible which is modern Johannesburg. He never loses his hold on the things that are excellent, as he moves about among so much that is irredeemably tragic, and sometimes foul and cruel and corrupt. It is his faith that helps us to see these victims of a social order as infinitely precious in the sight of God.

A less gushing response came from a South African government information officer Alexander Steward, who defended the Nationalist Government and attacked Trevor's work in *You Are Wrong, Father Huddleston*. Steward was a persuasive if shrill writer, and his book illustrated the level of hatred which Trevor attracted during his last few years in South Africa. In the book, Steward draws a distinction between two types of missionary in South Africa. The majority, he writes, are 'quiet men who have devoted their lives tirelessly and with single-minded purpose. Their endeavour has been to serve with love to all and ill-will to none.' He then turns to the minority, the 'political missionaries'. These men, he says, 'too have sought the advancement of black people, but in their effort to achieve it they have treated with contempt the interests of others whose home is equally Africa'. Missionaries like Trevor, he says, offer no advice or encouragement to people facing the daily reality of life in South Africa: 'His [Trevor's] argument is destructive and hollow through and through', he concludes.

For the first time, Trevor began to feel that he might enjoy life after South Africa. He was being fêted and revered and listened to, and he loved it. By April, he had returned to England, and he spoke to reporters at the Community's house in the village of Hemingford Grey, near Cambridge. He chatted to Raymond Raynes, and both men compared their press cuttings and the number of prominent meetings they had attended. Two pressure groups – Christian Action and the Africa Bureau – funded a series of meetings held all over the country at which Trevor spoke. Suddenly, *Naught for Your Comfort* – along with Paton's *Cry, the Beloved Country* and Anthony Sampson's *Drum: A Venture into the New Africa* – was bringing the distant problems of Africa and Christianity to a generation full of ideals and curiosity; a monk who was unknown outside the shanty towns of South Africa was talking about causes that very few people knew or understood, but were keen to discover. The book was difficult to obtain in Johannesburg, but many locals over there found out about 'Die Jerry' from impoverished local newspapers which were recycling foreign stories.

In dreary old England, far away from the sunshine and joy of Africa, Trevor spoke to packed houses at the Central Hall, Westminster, the Albert Hall, St Paul's Cathedral and to undergraduates at Oxford and Cambridge, where an overflow meeting had to be set up. He addressed a huge public meeting in Manchester's Trade Hall, and another at Bradford, where he tried to convince a packed audience that it was important that the Church in South Africa did not identify itself with white civilization. He discussed obedience on a BBC religious show with Major A. Farrar-Hockley. He suggested that the MCC should stop sending Test cricketers to South Africa. He spent three days visiting Cardiff, in order to refute a suggestion made by a South African minister that the slums in Tiger Bay were worse than Sophiatown. Suddenly, people were seeing that the timid and compromised Church of England was capable of producing people like Trevor Huddleston, and that there must be more to this strange institution than they had previously thought. He taught a new generation about taking up the Cross and denying yourself. Next to the Pope, he was the most photographed Christian on the planet.

Ken Leech, an Anglican priest who has worked in London's East End for much of his life, heard Trevor speak at Manchester's Trade Hall at the age of 17. He said: 'He was tremendously impressive. I came from a non-Christian family, and Trevor and his book *Naught for Your Comfort* were huge turning points in me coming to Christ. Whenever he spoke, there was a great power emanating from him.

Thousands of people would turn up at the meeting; he made a great impact on Christians and also on monasticism. He made grand and passionate if long-winded speeches; he was able to pack four sermons into one. Certainly, 1956 was the great year in his life.' Trevor was never an academic speaker. He was not an intellectual and was very impatient with them. But when he led a mission to Oxford University, students were impressed by his passionate presentation of Christianity, if not by its intellectual content.

And so to Yorkshire. He had dined with Eleanor Roosevelt, written an international bestseller, made speeches that Cambridge undergraduates had queued for hours to hear and appeared in newspapers all over the world; now he was back where he had been in 1939, needing permission to go for a walk or post a letter. His anguish and depression were evident. But, then, he was prepared for it; back in February 1956, before he left Africa, he had asked his great friend Molly Baring whether he was going to 'ever adapt to the West Riding? I just cannot begin to think . . . As things are at present I see nothing but darkness . . . I do want to be good about it, but I just find it fearfully hard going. And I cannot see the point.'

18

Novice Guardian

'ENGLAND IS NO LONGER MY HOME and never will be. I am an African.' Despite Trevor's melodramatic protests, he had arrived back in Mirfield to take up his position as Novice Guardian. But after the madness and violence of South Africa, this post would offer him few challenges, and he was in no fit state to assume the position. Some argue that he needed to return to Mirfield and re-discover his vocation, some go further, and say that his refusal to accept being Novice Guardian was the single greatest tragedy in his life, damaged as he was by a need for the limelight and a loathing of the routine. But it is hard to see how such an arrangement could have ever worked out. He just longed to be with the people that he loved – nearly all black, mostly children – in the land which he loved.

People still remember Trevor when he first returned from Africa. They talk of a man destroyed by grief, as if he had overcome some major surgery while losing a vital part of himself. When people spoke to him he sounded interested and friendly, but even a man with his iron will was unable to disguise his love of Sophiatown and the terrible homesickness which it brought. Africa was his great love and it nearly killed him to come back, yet he didn't whinge about his grief in public; a man of his generation learnt to hide emotion, and it was only when his face lit up on hearing the word 'Africa' that one could sense just how hurt he had been by his exile.

So he missed Africa terribly. But there were other, more practical reasons why he was unsuitable to be Novice Guardian. Since his return from Africa, and the publication of *Naught for Your Comfort*, he had been inundated with invitations from schools and universities, political parties and churches, both at home and abroad. They wanted him to talk about South Africa and protest and priesthood. He preferred to talk about the Gospel, but clever questioners would divert him onto Sophiatown and his conflicts with the Nationalist Government. His addresses to pupils at most boys' and girls' public schools, and to many comprehensives around the country, are remembered today. With other clergy, he led a mission to Leeds University.

And all these talks and sermons distracted him from Mirfield. Trevor knew that it was here that his obligations lay, however irritating and constricting he found them. When Trevor became Novice Master, Mirfield had its largest novitiate ever – twenty-two in total, half of whom were ordained – and some were unsuitable. Novices need to speak to their Guardian when they are troubled or unsure or lonely, and they look to him for guidance and support, but Trevor was too frenetic and absent to be an effective guide. No man of Trevor's talent would stay as Novice Guardian for long; and yet Raynes had placed him there, with the full intention that he would soon be placed in charge of the whole Community.

Trevor would confess to being a useless Novice Guardian: 'I was given novices from a post-war generation of varied backgrounds – the West Indies, a Yorkshire mill town, Oxford – and I hadn't had time to get the feel of their ideas; I was never sure that I had the right judgement of their vocations . . . I should have weeded out half of them before I started.'

Apart from his enormous workload and love of Africa, there were more personal reasons why Trevor was not suitable for the role. He lacked confidence about the strength of his gifts, and was unwilling to chat to people intimately, and so discern their strengths and weaknesses. He was a shy man, who preferred to address public meetings rather than chat away to people in private. He also had misgivings about the community at Mirfield, and whether it should exist at all in its present state. He felt that some of the novices were running away from the pain of human life and seeking refuge in a gentleman's club. He believed Mirfield lacked austerity, and so the novices were not being prepared for missionary life in South Africa. He was disturbed that some novices, though admiring of him, did not share his obsession with South Africa. For all their friendliness, Africans were not a trusting race, and Trevor was one of the few who had broken through to them. The very man known as Makhalipile – the dauntless one – in

South Africa, felt himself to be the custodian in a club for English Gentlemen. No wonder he felt frustrated.

There were further problems. The Community was facing anxious times. In earlier days, its theology was split between the moderation of Gore and Frere and the zealous enthusiasm of Raynes for more extreme liturgical practices – prostration, frequent confessions, and many altars for individual masses. Raynes had stayed on as Superior for two terms too long, and many brethren shared Trevor's restlessness and disquiet over the Community's direction. Raynes, an ageing and traditional Anglo-Catholic, was quite unaware of how liberal Catholic writers of the 1950s, along with liturgical modernists and avant garde writers, had changed the face of Catholicism on the Continent. The Community, in turn, was unprepared for any effect such intellectual changes would have on their daily life.

Some novices, though, adored him. Fr Jeremy Platt joined the Community at Rossentville, but became a novice when he joined Trevor in England. 'Some of the guys got a bit browned off, because Trevor was away so much; but I thought that objection was stupid. How could we expect a man of his calibre to "stick around like a nanny" all the time? Trevor was simply marvellous and he imbued us with his courage, his integrity, and his devotion to the Lord; and it's been a major thing in my life to have known a man of that calibre.'

Forty years later, and speaking shortly before he died, Jeremy Platt was living in a squatter camp on the outskirts of Johannesburg. He said of Trevor: 'The work that I personally am doing now is repeating, in a way, the pattern of his life in Sophiatown, with his love of the poor. He lived among them, and worked for them and with them, and they perceived the depth of his regard. He's so wise and so loving; so caring. He has given the rest of us a tremendous example.'

In Lent 1957, a tetchy Trevor addressed the CR novitiate. It demonstrates just how deep he felt his failure: 'I am more and more uneasy at the idea of delivering pious addresses when there is nothing immediately to emphasize in our common life: the divorce of piety, devotion or whatever you care to call it, from the common life as a whole: the substitution of ideas of my own for the true working of the Holy Spirit, as he leads you . . . I am horribly aware at present of a terrible barrenness, perhaps the result of a fairly strenuous year, which makes it difficult to give you anything refreshing or new.' Above all, Trevor wanted to return to Africa.

1. Trevor Huddleston, aged 10.
(Used courtesy of The Bodleian Library, University of Oxford)

2. Southwold, 1933. Huddleston (far left) on holiday from Oxford with friends.

(Used courtesy of The Bodleian Library, University of Oxford)

3. Sophiatown, 1948. High Church Anglicanism in Southern Africa.
(Used courtesy of UWC-Robben Island Museum Mayibuye Archives)

4. Kliptown, 1955. Huddleston addresses the Congress of the People.
(Used courtesy of UWC-Robben Island Museum Mayibuye Archives)

5. Raymond Raynes, circa 1960.
(Used courtesy of House of the Resurrection, Mirfeld)

6. Archbishop Desmond Tutu, February 2002.
(Used courtesy of Associated Press)

7. Stepney, 1972.

(Used courtesy of UWC-Robben Island Museum Mayibuye Archives)

8. Huddleston with Nelson Mandela during a Vote for Freedom rally. Glasgow, 1993.
(Used courtesy of PA Photos)

9. Huddleston after receiving his Knighthood
in the 1998 New Year's Honours for his contribution to
ending the apartheid regime in South Africa.
(Used courtesy of PA Photos)

But, first, there would be further change in the Community. Raynes, who many brethren found to be a startling figure with no small talk and a boring obsession with religion, had never treated his own life seriously. It would be far-fetched to say that he acted with a death wish, but the loss of his beloved brother in the First World War had changed his view of his life. He lived a life of the Cross; 'A Christian, if he is a proper one, is a man who is wholly alive, a full-blooded man, living under the sign of the Cross. The whole of our life, every part of it, is our cross and our way of redemption.' Unlike Trevor who was a diabetic and took the necessary precautions, Raynes had a total disregard for his health, and rather than eat full meals would graze on bread and butter and pickles and doughnuts. He would drink gin, and eat crackers.

And he was now close to death. Meanwhile, in late 1957, Trevor went on a quick and successful tour of Ireland, where he entertained people with nine full-length sermons and two public addresses and held meetings with lord mayors and archbishops. He formed an intense and father-like relationship with Mischa Scorer, a Westminster schoolboy, writing on 26 December: 'I do pray for you at every Mass each day, and always after Compline. But more of the time than that, really, for you are much in my thoughts, dear Mischa . . . much love as always.' On 6 February 1958 he admitted that he shared a 'fearful inability to cope with the demands of really secondary interests. I think it is awfully hard to learn priorities and especially so when you've rather let yourself go in the past . . . I really do know your love and trust in me and am immensely grateful.'

But the least satisfactory part of Trevor's life was drawing to a close. Raynes was dying, and the newly elected Superior Jonathan Graham knew that Trevor could not combine his work as a preacher with being Novice Guardian. So he placed Trevor in charge of the Priory House in Notting Hill, West London, where he was to remain for two years.

19

Notting Hill

TREVOR ARRIVED IN NOTTING HILL on the day that the race riots broke out.

It is always assumed that the riots in Notting Hill were the first race riots in Britain, although this is not true; there were serious incidents in Liverpool and Cardiff in 1919, and a smattering of anti-Irish and anti-Jewish disturbances in nineteenth-century London and Nottingham. But the events in Notting Hill in 1958, which took place at the end of August, were the first clear evidence of Britain's race problem.

And yet the race riots were not typical. The area where the rioting took place contained very few black people, yet myths persisted that Notting Hill was a 'black ghetto' – which is why the riots occurred. Most of the rioters were young men from white working-class districts. Strange groups roamed around the area – the Union Movement (the successor of the British Union of Fascists), the National Labour Party and the White Defence League. The Union Movement would boast Sir Oswald Mosley as its candidate at the 1959 General Election.

So from an unhappy situation in West Yorkshire, Trevor was thrust into a more tense environment in West London. But he was a happier man; based down in London, and freed from the entrails of Mirfield, he was able to socialize and preach and address public meetings, mainly on matters of race and the rioting that had stemmed from it. Trevor, who always had a remarkable gift for friendship, befriended a group of nuns, and especially Mother Clare, the Superior of the Deaconesses at St Andrew's House, in the slums near Portobello Road. Africa, of course, remained his true love; even Trevor, who had the monastic capacity for self-discipline and a wonderful ability to look forward, could not help but reminisce about Africa.

He was realistic about himself. In order to survive and not break down, he needed to be kept busy and, by doing so, push Africa to the back of his mind. He tried to make his new life as strenuous as possible, and would maintain his monastic discipline; he would be the first into chapel in the morning, and pray before he went to bed. Yet soon Trevor, who was single-minded and obsessive by nature, became tired of regurgitating old speeches about South Africa and felt un-motivated in Notting Hill, where there was no real outlet for his enormous talents and energies.

But, as ever, there were compensations. In London, he found himself fêted by secular liberals, who adored his radical populism and air of theatricality. One of them, the Royal Court playwright John Osborne, recounts meeting Trevor and being entranced by the monk's 'personal aura of saintliness'. He describes Trevor's appearance as 'cropped, scarred to the bone of suffering, with the same unblinking gaze of fallen sainthood, gouged by anguish, impervious even to grace. It was the mask of transparent nobility.'

In the same passage from his autobiography, Osborne then describes a supper he attended at the Priory with the theatrical producer George Devine and Trevor. Brutally perceptive as ever, Osborne notes: 'Like many priests, most bishops and all politicians, Huddleston, it seemed to me, was possessed by a driving vanity. Such a frailty underlined rather than diminished his inhuman perfection.'

On 12 June 1959 Raynes died. He had been seriously ill for many months, but his life would have been longer were it not for his mania for work and contempt for a balanced diet – a luxury Trevor, who suffered from diabetes, could not afford. Before his death, Raynes had spent many miserable months in Mirfield. Five days after his death, Trevor wrote to his friend Molly Baring: 'I saw him twice in hospital, desperately tired. Never has the veil seemed so thin. I just cannot feel him other than as marvellously near.' The two men had been bound by one great love – Africa – and Raynes had defined Trevor's life, by sending him to Africa and then recalling him. Now, with Raynes dead, Trevor was completely at a loss – with no proper job or role in the Community, he had lost much of his enthusiasm and drive.

His African friends despaired. Hugh Masakela, who visited him in England, wrote: 'Our relationship was not the same as it was in South

Africa where I would sit on your knee almost every day and pour out my heart to you . . . It was impossible to establish the same old wonderful atmosphere.'

Many people were convinced that Trevor, for his own sake, should stop languishing in West London and return to Africa, though not South Africa, from where he was strictly forbidden. Three people in particular supported this initiative: Fr Andrew Blair, a member of the CR who had advised him to go to Swindon; Fr Jonathan Graham, the Superior; and Evelyn Baring, Lord Howick, who had known Trevor since 1944 and had just ceased to be Governor of Kenya.

In October 1959, the new Superior wrote to Huddleston's long-term friend Sir Evelyn Baring, who was the government's chief administrator in African affairs. In his letter, he said that he was 'much exercised in his mind about Huddleston's future'. For the last three years that Trevor had been at home, he had been on a frenetic tour of the country and had been surrounded by hordes of people who were keen to be his disciples. He was being pulled between his private and public life, with Africa on the sidelines. Now, he needed to return to Africa.

Lord Howick wrote back:

Trevor . . . can never in England be as irreplaceable as he could be in Africa. This is particularly so because it takes years for any European to build up a position of trust with Africans, and Trevor has only done it over a long period . . . What about Tanzania? It is about to become independent, with a pathetically small number of educated Africans, a general social and economic backwardness, compared with West Africa or even Kenya, a host of problems to the eastern side of Africa . . . I believe that Trevor's appointment in the fairly near future to, say, Tanzania, might have a profound influence on a large part of the African continent.

One month later, the diocese of Masasi in Tanzania fell vacant.

20

Masasi

TREVOR'S APPOINTMENT AS BISHOP OF MASASI in Tanzania was controversial and tortuous. When the diocese fell vacant in January 1960, his name was put forward as a successor to Bishop Wilfred Mark. He had received the backing of many eminent churchmen, including Richard Wood, MP, who was President of the Universities' Mission to Central Africa. In addition, Canon Gerald Broomfield, who was General Secretary of UMCA, was adamant that there was no native African qualified at the time to take over the role of Archbishop and so put forward Trevor's name.

However, Geoffrey Fisher, the Archbishop of Canterbury, had clashed with Trevor before and was underwhelmed at the prospect of Trevor becoming bishop. He wrote a sceptical letter to a group of African bishops, sounding them out. In the letter, he conceded that although Trevor undoubtedly had 'devotion, prophetic powers and outstanding ability', he was not 'always wise and statesmanlike' in his support of blacks in South Africa.

The Archbishop then wrote a further letter:

I write a confidential letter to you and your fellow diocesan bishops about the appointment of a bishop to the diocese of Masasi. I feel bound to say now (though with a heavy heart) that I should find myself unable to nominate him (Huddleston) to the Bishopric even if all of you wanted me to do so. He is a friend and a devoted person, and he has mobilized a great many people to pray for South Africa in this crisis, but he has identified himself with political objectives, namely to turn the present South African Government out of office.

And then the Archbishop washed his hands of the appointment. 'That does not mean that the bishops must not appoint him. It does mean, I fear, that if you want him for Masasi you must advise me to leave the See vacant till the Province is in being, and you must then yourselves appoint and consecrate him.'

Trevor was distraught at Fisher's tactics. He considered withdrawing, and wrote to his great friend Molly Baring, the wife of Lord Howick: 'Although I do see Geoffrey Fisher's point of view, I find it quite desperately hard not to be sore about his taking this line.' He then added, poignantly, 'For me, it means so very much – perhaps my last chance of ever getting back to Africa to a job that would be so immensely worthwhile and to which I would give my whole life and being.'

But Trevor need not have worried; by this time, the Archbishop had shifted his position. Canon Broomfield wrote to Archbishop Fisher, saying that they were considering appointing him and that Trevor had given them an assurance that his meddling in South African affairs would not be repeated in East Africa. Broomfield added that the bishops in East Africa now hoped that Archbishop Fisher would come round to their point of view. 'I do feel very strongly,' he said, 'having held various posts in Africa, that Trevor Huddleston's appointment would prove of great value to the Church in East Africa.' Fisher was magnanimous in defeat, and wrote a letter offering him his full support if East Africa wanted him as a bishop. 'You must not worry about the past; the slate has been wiped clean,' he added.

Trevor was relieved. He was thrilled both to return to Africa and to escape from both England and his Community. Before he left for Masasi, he wrote an open letter to his fellow brethren in the CR quarterly on 4 August 1960. It betrayed the guilt and anxiety he felt in relinquishing his duty to the Community.

I am indeed deeply sorry for everything in word or deed of mine that has injured CR. I know I have often tried the patience and perhaps hurt the good name of the Community by my imperiousness and by worse things. I shall do my utmost as a prelate brother to make reparation for that. I do hope to be able under God to do good work as a bishop in Africa and so perhaps to restore what damage I have done. But above all I'm just overwhelmingly thankful for the love and forbearance of everyone.

Trevor's relationship with his own Community was like a marriage which thrives on separation.

Trevor, who could equally be naïve and acute about politics, was aware that his appointment would cause difficulties in Masasi. Many Africans outside the Church resented being led by another white bishop; many inside the Church were furious that no African would be sharing in the diocese. Many thought it peculiar that Lambeth was appointing a new bishop for Masasi, when the diocese was on the verge of getting the power to elect its own bishops.

Not that these difficulties caused Trevor much concern; he was just thrilled to be returning to Africa. Just before leaving for Africa, he gave an interview to his favourite newspaper, the *Observer*. In the interview, he made it clear that his time in Africa was in the past – a typically robust stance from someone suspicious of nostalgia. 'I really have no more to say about South Africa. I said it years ago,' he averred. He also denied that he was disappointed about his new posting, as if Masasi was a come-down after South Africa. He replied with typical fervour: 'It couldn't be an anti-climax. A bishop is a truly pastoral figure: his work is truly pastoral. I shall be out and about my diocese all the time, and in touch with people.' He was soon to find out just how true this prediction would be.

21

A Tense Backwater

TREVOR SAILED INTO THE HARBOUR of Mombasa on a Sunday morning, 1 October 1960. He had spent three weeks in a crowded and noisy ship where he was cold-shouldered by many of the South Africans who recognized him on board. He made himself promise that he would never travel by passenger liner again. On arrival, he found that his consecration had been delayed due to an outbreak of polio in the area. He became petulant and threatened to return on the next boat; then he calmed down and apologized. He was consecrated on St Andrew's Day at St Nicholas's Church, Dar Es Salaam, and was enthroned on 7 December.

Trevor had responsibility for a diocese the size of England. It was a scattered area, with only two major towns which were both situated on the coast – the port towns of Mtwara and Lindi. The diocese fell between two rivers, the Rufiji and the Ruvuma. For six months of the year it rained continually, and many of the roads into the villages became impassable to cars and lorries. Everything moved very slowly. In many ways, then, Masasi was a typical diocese in a poor and remote part of East Africa, and all the parishes which Trevor looked after were little country villages scattered over a wide area. Positioned in the south-eastern part of Tanganyika, or Tanzania as it became known after it united with Zanzibar in 1964, it was completely different from the African townships of Johannesburg and the Reef. Trevor, who had been brought up in London and had worked in urban parishes, now needed to understand about the rural life and his parishioners, who were peasant farmers. Masasi was very different from South Africa in another crucial respect; whilst South Africa was orientated towards the West, there was a greater openness and sense of freedom and movement in Tanzania. Here, Africans were aware that they were building their own society; it was revelatory for Trevor to see this miracle occurring under his very nose. The African in South Africa adopted an attitude of servility which was unthinkable in an independent African country.

Tanzania was fuelled by baffling tribal enmities, but Trevor had one great advantage in going there. He knew Julius Nyerere, who was leader of the party which took over as the government at the time of independence. When Trevor arrived in East Africa, Nyerere was already Chief Minister, and both men had met when sharing a platform at the launching of the Anti-Apartheid Movement in London. Nyerere emerged as the socialist ruler of a one-party state in 1961; both men would become great friends.

Trevor, as ever, arrived at a crucial time. It was the last year before independence, and therefore the last year of the colonial regime. He was learning to live in a country which was discovering its own identity as a free, sovereign state. When he arrived in Masasi, it had a typical colonial set-up: District Commissioner, Assistant District Commissioner, District Medical Officer, District Veterinary Officer – all of them white. After independence in 1961, they all withdrew within a few months. Trevor's criticism of the colonial establishment was never total, but he always felt that it did absolutely nothing to prepare the people for independence. When the British colonial civil servants withdrew, the only educated person in the administrative headquarters in Masasi was an Asian filing clerk. So Trevor started as a bishop under the old administration and, unlike other colonies, relationships with the British Colonial Service were very cordial. Trevor's theory on such good relations was simplistic but seductive; Tanzania was such a wonderful country that those sent to administer it fell in love with it, and enjoyed the people.

Of its population of 750,000 people, there were 137,000 Christians, just under half of whom were Anglican. In only one sense was it unusual, although the Anglican Church had been in the area for over eighty years, it did not form part of the colonial establishment. Christians had come to Masasi before colonialism; missionaries had come to Tanzania when it was still an African tribal area. There were no Germans present – they were the first true colonialists in Tanganyika – the Arabs and the Portuguese arrived on the coast, but the interior was tribal. So Christianity in Masasi was not prestigious or patrician;

it came from the poor and was for the poor. Trevor would compare it to English Christianity of a century before; a priest would step out of his door and tend to dying children whose faces were ravaged by poverty. There was little time in Masasi for the polished in-fighting that exists in cathedral closes or General Synods. The Anglicans formed a large minority in a predominately Muslim area. Islam, in this part of East Africa, was not overbearing and was conventional – you could visit any village in the Masasi district, and you would be hard pushed to find a mosque. People called themselves Muslim without realizing its implications: just like most Christians, in fact. But it was open to exploitation by extremists, and zealots could make the life of Christians very difficult.

Masasi's geographical position was unfortunate; it was situated between the wealthy farming regions of Kenya and the British-controlled land of Rhodesia. It lacked roads or electricity or natural resources or ambition. Served by generations of idealistic doctors, teachers and missionaries, Masasi had become the most literate part of Tanzania, while remaining very poor. The Church here, just like South Africa, had inadvertently sown frustration in its flock; through its decrepit but vibrant schools, it produced highly motivated people with no prospects. The Church also contributed enormously to health services; Trevor supported this patronage, as he believed that the closure of schools and hospitals would limit the contact that villagers had with the Church.

Life here was very simple; people rarely left their villages. Yet people needed to remain mobile because of droughts, or because wild animals were destroying their crops and meant they needed to move on. The Church would come to these small, illiterate villages and give them meaning. It brought a sense of moral law and obligation which was clearer than Islam or paganism. Where Anglican Christianity existed, it was rooted firmly in the Anglo-Catholic tradition; a large number of African priests and laity taught and practised a sacramental religion. Although a traditional Anglo-Catholic, Trevor remained concerned that the Church had become too preoccupied with life's inessentials and would alienate huge swathes of people who were undergoing the full attack of secularism.

So Masasi was a sleepy backwater, but it was also tense, as it faced real turmoil on the eve of independence. By the late 1950s in East Africa, anti-colonial movements had brought freedom and independence without a glimmer of peace or prosperity. The growing resentment of the West – embodied, in many eyes, by the Church – aligned with a growing nationalist movement would result in Julius Nyerere becoming leader of a one-party state after independence in 1961. In Western Africa, the Nationalist Movement had prospered, while producing boorish and brutal leaders. In the South, Rhodesia had resisted black nationalism and allowed white supremacy to entrench itself. The Portuguese, French and Belgians were keen to get rid of their former territories, which had become an appalling burden.

There were religious difficulties, too. Most of the power in Masasi lay in Muslim hands; it was Muslims who held most official posts and resented the presence of Christian missionaries, whether they be Catholic, Anglican or Protestant Evangelicals. Converts had been killed by a small but poisonous group of Muslim extremists. There was also a strong Roman Catholic presence, embodied by a group of German Benedictines who lived in comparative luxury (they had their own electrical generator!) and who enticed Anglican converts by offering them a better quality of life. One of Trevor's major concerns while at Masasi was the poaching of Anglicans – many of whom practised a more ornate and rarefied religion than their Roman counterparts – by the more affluent Roman missions. In Masasi, however, it was never forgotten that Islam was the major, indigenous religion which belonged to the people; Christianity was there to offer succour to those who felt that they were destined for hell, to provide health and care through the regions, and to cast a dubious eye over some of the stranger rites practised by Islam, such as male circumcision.

A few months after arriving, Trevor wrote a letter to Fr Hubert Northcott, an old friend and fellow member of CR. He was settled in his house and working as a bishop, but still there were problems. This was illustrated by some of the distress he was feeling:

Communications are so much less developed than anywhere else in South Africa. I went to a little place this week called Liwale – about 120 miles from Masasi – where there is a tiny Christian community in the midst of a strong Muslim area and often cut off completely by rivers and floods. Ours is the first Church ever to be built in these parts – a little round and thatch affair – spotlessly clean. And when it was dedicated a year or two ago the Muslim population threatened, with clubs, to destroy it. However, it held its own, and it was a moving experience to say Mass there and to give Communion to about twenty men, women and children. I'm often reminded of that sort of life (without Landrovers, of course) that Aidan and Columba must have known – wild country, wild animals, very simple people, no great churches, much insecurity and a great sea of paganism around. It's rather thrilling – but awfully daunting too and I feel so utterly ill-equipped. You will understand what a terrific strain it can be when you want, so much, to communicate freely and fully the Gospel and you are held back because of language difficulties and lack of knowledge. I honestly can't imagine a bigger contrast than his life as compared to life in London! I am, of course, quite extraordinarily alone, even when I'm at home: and I have, too, some corking great problems to solve somehow (including a debt of £10,000 and a clergy paid at the rate of £5–£7 an hour). So I confess that there are days when I get a bit into the doldrums. But I can truthfully say I don't want to be anywhere else but where I am – even in the dark bits. And I know I must expect confusion and bewilderment for my first year – at least sometimes. I have so much to make up for it, including some really first-class fellow priests and workers. But do pray!

Trevor settled to life as a missionary bishop in an isolated and occasionally volatile corner of East Africa. Apart from officiating at deeply ceremonial services, he would spend much of his time alone, driving in his battered Renault along battered tracks in order to reach the remotest villages. On arrival, he would celebrate Eucharist, hold confirmations, sort out a school's administrative or financial problems, deal with shortages of supplies – before returning to Masasi for more meetings and interviews. He would relax by reading theology and biographies, and novelists like Margaret Drabble and Graham Greene.

So, outwardly at least, he appeared to be cheerful and effective. As soon as he arrived, Trevor realized that he needed to set himself three clear objectives: to rid the diocese of its debts and make sure that its buildings were in good repair; to make sure that the diocese was part of the Church of the Province of East Africa, so that his successor's appointment would be made by the bishops of the Province, and not Canterbury; and to make sure that there was real African leadership in the diocese. He needed to work himself out of a job.

22

The Missionary Bishop

TREVOR KNEW THAT HE WOULD FACE three personal challenges when he was appointed Bishop of Masasi. First, he had lived in a Community all his life, and now he was going to be alone. Of course, one of the costs of leadership is loneliness, but Trevor faced additional sorrows: in Swindon, South Africa and Notting Hill he had been surrounded by clergy and fellow brethren – now he was truly alone. Although his monastic training had prepared him for solitude, he knew that he would find it very tough – and he did. Second, he needed to learn the new language of Swahili. Without it, he would not even be able to talk to his own clergy. Trevor was now 49 and was not a natural linguist; he was not a child, who has the simple advantage of moving around and listening. He would sit down and learn tenses and verbs and find the whole process a terrible ordeal, which he overcame through industry and prayer. He would practise his Swahili with the children who came to his house. Finally, Trevor's previous experience had been limited to urban areas; he was now thrust into a rural diocese of which he had no experience at all, to a people that he had no understanding of, and in a direction that he was unsure of. He would look after churches, hospitals and schools.

But prayer, as ever, sustained him. Trevor could be obstreperous and belligerent – especially when he was tired and cast down by his diabetes – but he always remained an old-fashioned Man of God. As he himself said on one occasion: 'The only thing that has given me any sense of purpose and direction in my life has been the Gospel.' He would say that being a bishop with the Gospel is bad enough, but that he could not conceive of anything worse than a life without the Gospel. As he wryly noted: 'What would it be – some status symbol?'

Trevor, who would read his prayers alongside the daily readings of the Gospel, knew that his prayer life had changed enormously over the years. He would look back to his time as a young novice, when the safeguarding of the hours was the main preoccupation for him. His life had moved on, and his prayer life was no longer so rule-bound. However, he believed that his early years as a Mirfield novice during the Second World War had instilled in him a discipline which had never left him – even when he was thrust out in the African bush.

If Trevor's view of his prayers was no longer so rule-bound, so his sense of the mission of the Church had also changed. It was in Masasi that Trevor's religious views began to change. Here, he was learning that the Church was not making converts. He felt that it had become settled in its ways and too scared of upsetting the balance of things. Masasi was changing; its people were responding to Western influences and programmes of development were being launched. Meanwhile, as Masasi was making huge strides in terms of development, and as its people listened to radio and television, Trevor felt that it was vital that the Church followed likewise. Of course, it was easier to go on preaching what your father taught you, and yet fail to see its relevance to the lives of its adherents.

In Tanzania, Trevor was thrilled to see the Church throw off its Western forms of worship and embrace the introduction of African forms of worship. He would tear his hair out at inappropriate Catholic traditions being foisted on unwitting villagers. Every Easter, there would be the Veneration of the Cross, when people would kiss the figure of Jesus on Good Friday. But he realized that in Eastern Africa the kiss was virtually unknown, and that it was not part of African custom in the very least. So when people say that on Good Friday people must 'kiss the cross' – well, what did they mean? It was not meaningful to them, so how could it be used? Trevor cited with pleasure a Roman Catholic Community of African nuns with a very enlightened Superior. Instead of silent adoration of the Blessed Sacrament, they would dance in front of the sacrament and salute in their traditional ways. This was a good development, but it could not be achieved by a Western missionary.

Trevor, though, adored sacramental religion, and believed that it was crucial for Africa. A generation of African priests had been raised with sacramental religion, and then taught it to their parishioners. It meant, therefore, in every village or every main centre there was a priest. In the diocese of Masasi, the Eucharist was a daily occurrence, which was not true in many large areas of the mission field because of the shortage of clergy. So, the sacramental element of faith was important. But Trevor felt that it was not connected with the reality of life for a poor villager; it was becoming a small ritual, a kind of superstition, a kind of law. It was concentrating on the non-essentials, the externals.

He also knew that the principal task for the white religious was one of 'disengagement'. Even to missionaries like himself, it was not immediately obvious how closely entangled with the concept of 'white superiority' was the faith that he had come to preach and share. Africans believed that Christianity was symptomatic of the dishonesty of the West; it preached Love and it practised power. It was important, he felt, for the Western Church to be disengaged, not to be too closely identified with the social order of Western civilization.

And here, Trevor's solitude certainly helped. He was alone and not part of a Western religious community like the Franciscans or the Mirfield Fathers. He believed that the time had passed for that form of religious life to grip the African as he felt that it ought to. So, it was time to change. He believed that African archbishops ought to come and worship in English or American dioceses, and would not rule out the role of the expatriate. Often, in his time in Masasi, he said that he hated the idea of all Europeans pulling out; he just felt that the English Church needed more sense of the immediacy of God, as the African Church needed expatriates of one kind or the other for a long time to come. But these expatriates, he added, were not traditional missionaries like himself, but people who worked out there as a technical assistance officer to the government, or a doctor, nurse and teacher – he hoped there would be room for them always.

Trevor knew that he was a white outsider taking charge of an area that was hurtling towards independence and resented the influence of outsiders. So he was determined that his successor should be African, and that once a succession was announced he would depart. In order to prepare for a one-party state, Trevor also knew that he would have to hand over control of the school system, which was still in the power of the Church.

By 1961, the Europeans were beginning to withdraw from Tanzania. President Nyerere faced an enormous task; he had to provide an administration for a country twice the size of France. Now, he had to lean on all the schoolteachers, doctors and nurses that the country relied on and hope that they would forge a brave, new independent state.

And here the Arusha Declaration, named after a large town in the north of Tanzania, becomes significant. No one can understand Trevor's time in Masasi unless one understands the Declaration. It may read like a tired and dated Socialist tract now, but at the time it was revolutionary. The Declaration was based on the idea of self-sufficiency; that Tanzania was poor and would remain poor for a long time to come; that it was no good relying on 'foreign aid' to get rich quick, for all donations were tied.

Self-reliance ran through the tract. It emphasized the proper use of land and leadership and labour, and called upon voluntary agencies like the Church to follow its example. The Declaration accepted that its people lived in a poor country with few natural resources: no oil, and little mineral wealth; but the people had the land, and all that could be produced from that. They did not want to be dependent on foreign aid; they wanted to be independent. The government, under the leadership of Julius Nyerere, made one enormous demand on its people: in a modern world and surrounded by richer countries eager to loan money, it was to stand alone.

This idealism had practical consequences. In most countries, national service is just a matter of military service; in Tanzania, every young man had to give two years of service to his country. He would do six months of training – service camps, drilling and marching – and then he would enter his profession. Any salary that he might have earned during those two years would then go back into helping the country.

There were further consequences, in order to get rid of corruption and fudge the line between the rich and the rest. A law was passed which would make it impossible for a member of parliament, a member of a ruling party or a civil servant, to earn more than one salary. No public servant could own a property and then draw rent from it; he could either own a property, or cease to be a public servant. It sounds incredibly dated, but such measures were drawn up in a light of socialist zeal. But socialism here did not mean faded notions of

Communism, or the 1960s Labour Party's idea of redistribution; it was based on African socialism, or Ujamaa – the notion of 'family-hood' which had its roots in the African way of life, with its emphasis on the extended family.

In Masasi, as the nation prepared for independence, Trevor knew that he needed to concentrate on education. Early on in his episco-pate, he had been determined to hand over church schools to the education authorities, but a swift transition was never possible. Schools which were Africanized too early would damage the educa-tion of their pupils; an articulate group of male African teachers resented any attempt by the Church to stall or prevaricate over the handover. Trevor would argue: 'the Church is here to serve in any way it can, but no longer to manage or govern . . . This, as I see it, is the logical extension of the Arusha Declaration.' Yet money remained a problem; if the Government wanted to occupy church schools, then it needed to compel the unions to hand over the money. Trevor refused to pass control of the schools over to grasping politicians.

Education was a major source of contention throughout Trevor's time in Masasi. All education had been run by the missionaries; as bishop and therefore head missionary, he was in charge of their man-agement and finance. He was in a hugely powerful position, and he needed to persuade local district councils, who were happy to criticize the Church for being rich and colonial, to pay the dues which they owed to local church schools. Much of his depression resulted from his inability to persuade authorities to hand over their money, and the criticism he attracted for his perceived prevarication.

Political battles over education wearied Trevor. Often, he felt low and cross and disheartened. Masasi itself was little more than a fair-sized clearing in the scrub, with a police station, a garage, a few houses, a long cathedral and the hospital and Mission of Mkomaindo. It was here, in a steep thatched house, which was surrounded by high grass and was close to the cathedral, that Trevor lived. He lived in four rooms, one of which was a private chapel. The roof was thatch and the rain often fell in. The house lacked basic home comforts; Trevor, though an ascetic by nature, felt depressed at the simplicity of his living and the lack of friendship. He was lonely, and drained by the continual tension he felt with the German Benedictines. His diabetes, too, continued to cause concern; he had suffered two blackouts while overdosing on insulin. Before leaving for a trip abroad, he wrote:

I can find no sort of joy in going . . . it has been a very full two
years . . . I have learnt a great deal. I have made many mistakes.
I have failed over and over again in charity so that I could almost
despair. Yet I do believe God has called me, and in spite of two
years of failure I want to go on.

In July 1963 it had been twenty years since he had set out for South
Africa, but he was overwhelmed by a sense of failure. He was famous
around the world, and would take care to personally answer the
hundreds of letters which he would receive over the month, yet his
depression remained. In his log book, he wrote: 'I cannot shake off
this constant worry and depression, and each day seems to add some
new cause or anxiety, and I don't know how much of this is my fault
or not. Moreover, I am lonelier than I have ever been . . . Life is
strangely, utterly empty of joy and peace.' His loneliness and sense of
isolation were compounded by the chaos in South Africa, with the
acquittal of all the defendants in the Treason Trial – including names
like Walter Sisulu and Nelson Mandela – only for them to be re-
arrested one year later.

But he still continued to impress. The *Daily Mirror* journalist Cassandra, who was always a great admirer from the days they had met in
Sophiatown, travelled to visit him from Jerusalem, where he had been
covering the trial of Adolf Eichmannn. He began his article with the
immortal lines: 'From the darkness of the trial of Adolf Eichmann in
Jerusalem come with me into the sun – from the abyss of evil to sanity
and saintliness.'

In a first-class piece of tabloid journalism, Cassandra followed
Trevor around his hospital, run by the gifted and devoted Dr Taylor
who performed all of the operating herself. It was, he wrote, a heroic
but pathetic sight. 'Here were few trivial ailments. Tuberculosis is an
active, ravaging scourge – the curse of this remote part of Central
Africa. Malaria is commonplace. Leprosy is well-known.'

Noting that Trevor combined tenderness with toughness, he again
contrasted the world he had left to the world he was now visiting: 'For
compassion, read infinite cruelty. For care and healing, read deportation, starvation, torture and the gas chamber.'

Trevor's other great contribution during his time at Masasi was in
the field of personal health care. As Cassandra observed, Masasi's
patients were not obsessed with Western concerns like stress or

dietary problems; no, they were worried about tuberculosis and leprosy and malaria. He would spend much time administering the medical centres in the area. At the Mkomaindo Hospital, which was close to where he lived, he used all his charm to sign up four eye specialists, who agreed to undertake hospital work under the umbrella of the United Society for the Propagation of the Gospel (USPG). The doctors there were also helped by four Dutch doctors.

Lack of funds was always a chief concern for Trevor, and when he was Bishop of Masasi he would make regular fundraising trips to the United Kingdom and the United States. There is no doubt that these trips raised a lot of money and yielded many voluntary workers, but Trevor always felt uneasy about them, and resented the pressure they placed him under. More deeply, he was seen by many as a regular source of income, which undermined his great faith in the Arusha Declaration and the sense of self-reliance.

The political situation in Masasi continued to be as precarious as ever, and during an attempted coup d'état in January 1964, Nyerere had been forced to call in the help of departing British forces to return and discipline his own troops. In order to preserve his own power, Nyerere was compelled to link the countries of Zanzibar and Tanganyika, a problem given that Zanzibar was ruled by a military dictator with fascist leanings.

Trevor, meanwhile, kept his head down and proceeded with his work, making speeches and leading missions and arguing with education officers and visiting all the parishes in his enormous diocese. As ever, his energy was enormous and he was never still; always jumping up to perform some task or to fetch someone or to remain tireless. A man of immediate action, his energy was formidable. He needed to deal with obstreperous teachers, who were resigning over pay and conditions. And still Trevor rose at 5:30 a.m., and tried to say part of the Rosary daily and carry on with studying his Swahili.

He continued to negotiate the handover of schools from Church control to local authority, but remained unsure about his future: 'I wish I had more real love for this place, but there is so little love in it, in my opinion.' Following a visit three months before from the BBC TV crew headed by Erskine Childers, he wrote an article for the *Observer* which was published on 19 December. He wrote: 'To me it is an immense privilege to be part of this moment of African history, even if it is only for a while until my African successor is chosen and takes over.' Although homesick for Sophiatown, he recognized that he felt at home in Tanzania, whereas in South Africa, although life was more exciting and exhilarating, he felt that he could never belong.

Meanwhile, ecclesiastical gossip had reached full pitch back home. He was certainly not destined for one job; Jonathan Graham, his Superior, had died young, but was replaced by Hugh Bishop, who was himself to depart from the Community in some scandal a few years later. He was tipped about a possible appointment at Liverpool, and possibly his knowledge of worldwide Anglicanism could have secured a nomination to Canterbury. Meanwhile, the BBC TV show was broadcast, and Trevor received more fan mail.

The journalist, Joe Rogaly, who had been commissioned by Collins the publishers to write a biography of Trevor, said: 'The real lesson (which Huddleston knows), is that this mission plus the Benedictines (which is ten times as big an employer) makes up the only decent target for young trades' union men – and, I might add, government officials – to work on; the rest is bush.'

Perhaps Trevor was happiest at Mass. It was certainly here where, with incense swirling and wearing a jewelled cope, with its two golden peaks, wrote Rogaly, he is 'giving an essentially bored people – with little to do or see all day in the dust – some great colour and excitement and emotional experience'. It was in services like this that Trevor, who often confessed to being depressed, felt that everything was all right. Trevor offered to resign; his eventual successor said that they were sorry that he had ever uttered such words, and asked him never to speak of such things again. Trevor was comforted.

Life resumed its ordinary patterns – heat, cold, rain, mud, trips with children, meetings, visitors, safaris to parishes, letters, periodic tiredness. He remained depressed: 'will this gloomy tunnel never end?' and on 23 May 'simply overwhelmed with depression . . . I get more and more alone. I wouldn't mind if I felt I was doing the diocese any good. But I don't and I'm not . . . I am wholly and unreservedly depressed.'

Throughout 1968, he veered from deep satisfaction to deep depression. By 20 February, 'a most distressing meeting' had left Huddleston feeling barren. 'It seems to me almost hopeless to try and convey my own feelings of despair over the lack of real love in the diocese.' He then told Archbishop Beecher of his decision to resign by 30 November 1970 at the latest. On 28 May 1970 he was invited to become Bishop of Stepney.

23

Stepney

HIS DECISION HAD BEEN ABRUPT, but he was sad to leave. In a resignation address to assembled Anglican clergy in Masasi on 13 June 1968, he conceded that his audience might think that he no longer loved them and that he had betrayed them. This, he assured them, was not the case: 'I come to say good-bye and I do so with a heavy heart. I came to Africa twenty-five years ago. Therefore nearly all my work has been with Africans and for the African church. Africa is where my heart is and where it will always be.'

But, he added: 'I believe God does call men to show their love for people, for places and for the work even of his church, by leaving all these in His hands: by not holding it fast oneself.'

Trevor believed that he had been an unsuccessful Bishop of Masasi. He knew that he would be the last English bishop in Masasi; he also knew that from now on Masasi would need to look after itself or it would die. It was in pressing Masasi to be independent that Trevor believed he had failed, and failed deeply. As a bishop, he knew that he should bear responsibility, and not seek to blame other people. He knew that, even to the white missionary, it was not obvious how closely connected his faith was with the idea of 'white superiority' that he had come to preach and share. Yet throughout his time in Masasi, he had understood more than most just how many younger Africans had viewed the Church with scorn rather than gratitude. They saw in the white priest a symbol of all that was dishonest; a faith that proclaimed to be based on love was judged by the behaviour of its believers, many of whom practised power rather than love. He had needed to show that the missionary Church, the white Church, was no longer linked to the social order of a white European civilization.

Of course, the irony was that the strength of the Church overseas had always lain in its institutions – its fine schools, its splendid hospitals, its glorious churches. And he was aware of how the Church, through these institutions, could protect its flock against the power of the State. But he also realized that these bodies by themselves could not convert a single person to the Catholic Faith – this power lay in supernatural love, which came from a humility born of penitence. He realized that black Africa could not hope to accept Christianity unless its adherents were prepared to pay the price of which they spoke so glibly – the price of a religion whose heart and centre was the scandal of the Cross. And Trevor still tried to examine where he had erred. Had he learnt Swahili at too late an age? Did Christians in Masasi, seeing the money which Trevor has generated from other people outside their country, feel no need to give themselves? Was Trevor himself the problem? As he conceded: 'I came to see that it was my own leadership that was wrong; that, somehow, even though in England, America, Zambia, Nairobi, I could move people to give me their trust, I could not do so here in Masasi.'

And he ended: 'He [God] will overrule all my mistakes and all my failures and sins since I came here. I ask your forgiveness, each single one, for any thing I have said or done to hurt you. And I assure you of my prayers every day in the years that lie ahead.'

Much of Trevor's frustration in Masasi had stemmed from his high doctrine of Christian leadership. He did not believe that he could offer answers to all problems, but he felt he was there to offer guidance to the problems which paralyse people in life. He also knew that he could not lead if he didn't speak the language of its flock; one of the troubles of the Church was that not enough of its leaders were able to talk the language of people who were troubled. As a young priest in South Africa, his criticism of Clayton had originated from this; the Archbishop had the right ideas, but he spoke the wrong language because the source of his experience was wrong. If a man needed to lead, then he needed to show involvement, and in the front line. Leadership was involvement, not power.

It was all very well for Trevor to return from Africa, but nothing of real excitement awaited him in England. Of course, he wanted to remain a bishop, despite his suspicion of the self-seeking and compromised. After all, it had been his childhood ambition, from the days when he dressed up to hear confession and conduct Communion and irritate his sister. But there were very few opportunities available. It was unlikely that Canterbury, York, London, Durham or Winchester would accept him; most senior clergy saw him as a rebellious nuisance who was poor at paperwork. And yet, while he was at Stepney, he was considered by the more imaginative onlookers to be a leading contender for Canterbury; while leading bishops were considered grey and worthy, Trevor was both highly regarded and charismatic.

Indeed, throughout Trevor's life the Church of England never found a suitable position for a man of his stature. Of course, Trevor may well have been a victim of Establishment whispers; he wasn't clubbable, he loathed the fact that the national church was established by an Act of Parliament, and he was completely unsympathetic towards the modern Church, with its endless committees and heaps of paperwork that were part of the territory with synod government. He distrusted red tape.

Trevor's irritation went beyond the mere irritation of not being offered a proper job, or the love and hate relationship that most Anglican clergy feel towards the Church they have spent their life serving. He would make persistent attacks on the 'Establishment'. He would inveigh against the lethargy and complacency of the national Church. Working as a religious, and one who had spent much of his working life overseas, he never understood just how the Church of England worked. His patrician manner and formidable charm were very English, as was his love of Africa and despair of his native country; yet, in his inability to understand his own Church, he was on his own.

But where, in all honesty, could Trevor to go? He could not bear the prospect of returning to Mirfield, where his brethren would have found him extremely tiresome. He would have loved to return to Sophiatown, but this was out of the question. Another foreign posting might have been available, but Trevor had spent eight lonely and gruelling years in Masasi, and a spell in England might just have been right for him. And at this crucial point in his life, just when he began to feel as stranded as he was when he was made Novice Master at Mirfield, Trevor was lucky – just as the offer to go to Masasi had appeared, so he was fortunate when Dr Robert Stopford, an educationalist and the Bishop of London, invited him to become Bishop of Stepney.

Trevor was the most famous living Anglican priest in the world, and yet the Church had recognized his talents by offering him a minor see in the East End of London. Stepney was on a par with Kensington and Willesden; Trevor was a suffragan bishop rather than a diocesan bishop. But, in ecclesiastical terms, Stepney had always been seen as a stepping stone: Cosmo Lang, once Archbishop of Canterbury, had served as a bishop there. And in many ways, Stepney was the ideal constituency for someone of Trevor's outlook, and most local priests greeted his appointment with delight; he was known to loathe racism and support group ministry. He was now responsible for three of London's most testing boroughs – Tower Hamlets, Hackney and Islington – and ninety-four churches, many of them spikily Anglo-Catholic and run by generations of tough East End priests with an instinctive disgust of authority and love of rebellion.

London priests could be difficult. But, more seriously, there was deep tension in Stepney between the races. Feuds would erupt between West Indian and Bengali families, many of whose children attended the same schools. The National Front, ever alert to stoking dispute, was influential in the Brick Lane area, and clergy would arrange for Asian youths to learn how to box in the Repton club, where they could stand up to white youths. Meanwhile, Bethnal Green was a white enclave and a place of recruitment for generations of National Front members. The pubs around Bethnal Green would be dotted with members of the fascist group Column 88, huddling over tables as they plotted their latest attack. Many of the churches were white and conservative and as direct in their manner as Trevor; churchgoing white parents resented their children going to schools which were full of black children. Trevor was equally authoritative in return and would often say that he wanted to be the Pope and close down all the churches in Bethnal Green.

Trevor's first move was sound. He became the first Bishop of Stepney to actually live in the area; his immediate predecessor had lived in Gray's Inn, and generations before had lived in Amen Court, and were canons of nearby St Paul's Cathedral. Using his customary mixture of will and charm, Trevor persuaded the Church Commissioners to buy an attractive four-storey terrace house at 400 Commercial Road, next to a maternity hospital in the heart of the East End. From the outside, the house was covered with fumes and filthy grime, but inside it was tidy and well maintained. There were a few items of plain furniture, some pictures on the wall which had been given by artists, and in his study a low range of bookshelves upon which were placed photographs of Africans whom he had known and loved.

It was very typical of Trevor that he should choose to live and work in the centre of things. Day and night heavy lorries pounded along Commercial Road where he lived, buses stopped outside his door and the local bookmaker and newsagent were his local neighbours. He made himself available to endless callers who came for advice and counsel, from the writer Margaret Drabble and the politician Frank Longford to the lowliest child who was worried about his family or homework or just keen to chat and watch television. He was often absent, but the devout couple Win and Eddie, who cooked for Trevor and cleaned the house, would cope with the rascals.

In Stepney, as in Africa, he took his parish work very seriously, and saw himself as a parish priest. 'I am not a monk', he would grumble during his infrequent stays at Mirfield; he relished contact with the outside world, and most particularly children. Within an hour or so of hearing that one of his clergy or a member of their family was ill or in hospital, he would rush off to their bedside to minister to them. His vocation had made much of his life lonely and low-spirited, but it also brought him tremendous freedom; he could afford to be single-minded about his work, without the worry of a wife to appease and children to feed and scold.

Nor did he need to worry about making a living; he was unclut-tered with possessions; every penny from his writings and broadcasts went into a charitable trust which made him able, when he would retire from Stepney after ten years, to respond to a call from the diocese of Mauritius to help them out with a little local difficulty. Trevor was industrious, but never accommodated himself to the work of an English bishop, which meant spending much time in stifling rooms bossing people on committees and pastoral groups.

As a cleric, he would take care of things that other bishops might have ignored, and he listened to his clergy. He was devoid of the affected manner which struck many other English bishops. Early on he was told that his sermons were too meaty and lacked the personal touch. Trevor listened, and said that he would change his style 'I am afraid of just uttering clichés on such occasions,' he said. After the next sermon, he turned and asked: 'Was that better?'

He had always found preparing sermons hard work and could never have followed the custom of many of his colleagues of having a 'sermon for the month'. On one occasion, after preaching a very forthright sermon at the induction of a priest at Bethnal Green, a member of the congregation wrote thanking him for the sermon. He replied: 'Thank you for your note; it was so encouraging. People tell me when they think I am wrong, but rarely when they think I have got it right. Even bishops need encouragement.' He did need encouragement and appreciated it when it was given.

His sermons were passionate and informed. Speaking in St Mary's, Cambridge, towards the end of 1971, on the text: 'Why does this generation ask for a sign?' he found an answer in St Mark's account of the feeding of the 5,000, where 'a vast crowd of people, who had come out of the villages to hear Him, had found themselves on the hillside without food and yet they all ate to their hearts' content, and seven baskets were left over'. Huddleston compared himself to the young Nazarene who, according to Saint Mark, 'sighed deeply to himself'.

He stated: 'It was a sign of anger with a generation too obstinate, too self-concerned, too parochial to recognise the sources and implications of the wonders done in it. And here you see he touches at the very heart and core of the mystery of faith.'

And then he added: 'To one coming back from Africa there appears here to be a generation bored with the trivialities of affluence, a generation disgusted by the deviance of party-political attitudes . . . we wear mankind as our skin and yet we are prepared to tear one another apart on behalf of this nationalism or that, of this idea of race or that.'

A passionate man, he would speak of his despair at the lacklustre approach of people to the Gospel. At Mirfield's Commemoration Day earlier in the year, he spoke again about signs: 'Why does this generation ask for a sign? They are seeking security rather than faith. Why does the Church ask for a sign? Success, increased church attendance . . . ' 'The Sign', Huddleston declared, 'is the Lord Jesus Himself, the Living Lord who called Mary Magdalene, "Mary"; who called Thomas, "Touch me"; who called Simon Peter: "Do you love me?"'

He would talk about the need for Christians to act. Speaking at St Mark's, Victoria Park, he told the congregation: 'From time to time from within the institutional Church and from outside it, men are raised by God whose sole purpose appears to be to demonstrate the meaning of power as a spiritual reality.' He then pointed out that

Martin Luther King had been assassinated on the same day three years earlier. 'To accept a situation and to do nothing about it – as if God's will were only to be found in what is static: this is profoundly unChristian.'

He led an organized and structured day. After praying every morning from six to seven, he would hold a Communion Service, followed by breakfast. He would then walk up to his first floor study, where from eight until nine he would open the post and read *The Times* with classical music blaring out on the radio. At nine o'clock his secretary, Mrs Sutton, would arrive, followed by his part-time chaplain Revd Julian Scharf.

Once a month, he would meet up with his fellow clergy, and most particularly the Venerable George Timms, the Archdeacon of Hackney, and three rural deans (who looked after one of his diocese's three boroughs). Trevor would try to keep his morning as free as possible so that he could keep up with his heavy correspondence. Most afternoons, he would have appointments every half-hour from two o'clock until leaving in the early evening for a meeting and then dinner, often with a London notable like a Labour MP or the head-master of Westminster School.

He kept the first floor room as a study for himself. While peering over his books – Trevor enjoyed modern fiction and new biographies – he would write articles for the newspapers and deal with his correspondence. Along with personal letters and bills, his post would be submerged with requests from lobby groups to support their causes and schools to present their prizes. He was happy to speak to schools and would lend his name to many humanitarian causes.

As a monk, Trevor had always accepted that his life would be regulated by prayer; it gave him strength and purpose. But there were also medical reasons why he needed to lead an ordered life; as a diabetic since 1946, he had to watch how much sleep he got and would try and achieve his allotted seven hours by getting to bed by eleven o'clock. Trevor was luckier than most diabetics, for he could tolerate a large dose of insulin and did not have to worry too much about his diet. But he needed to be careful; he would relax by taking every Friday off work, and go and visit friends or enjoy long walks. Like his father, he was also a keen fisherman.

Trevor spent much of his initial years dealing with the racial problems of Stepney. It contained many generations of white East

End families; there was also an influx of immigrants from the Caribbean and East Bengal, which would later be East Pakistan. Many of these immigrants were hard-working but poor. They were easily identified by their religion and their language, and they struggled to lead ordered lives in English society. Their presence was resented by many of the white working class, who were worried they would lose their jobs and their way of life.

Trevor was a supporter of immigration, and would later argue in pamphlets that the East End had been re-invigorated by the Jews and Hugenots who had escaped persecution in mainland Europe. But subtle pamphleteering meant little when immigrants carrying bags of shopping down the Brick Lane were abused in the streets, and kicked and robbed. Diplomats in East Pakistan House complained that there was 'growing hysteria' against Pakistanis in the area. Asians would be sworn at and spat upon by white youths, many of whom lived in Bethnal Green and Shoreditch, two London districts where Oswald Mosley had recruited his Black Shirts in the 1930s. It was in Trevor's constituency that Mosley had planned his great march which ended in the Battle of Cable Street, when the police lost control and fascist sympathizers were seized upon by Jewish and Irish groups.

So Trevor spent much of his first couple of years in protest meetings and leading delegations to the House of Commons; indeed, his life was following the same course that it had before the Nationalist Government came to power in South Africa in 1948 and started bringing in repressive laws. By 1970, after a series of nasty incidents, one reporter from the *Observer* wrote: 'Any Asian careless enough to be walking the streets alone at night is a fool.' But the Asian community, with the help of Trevor, began to fight back. Obeying Trevor's advice, they organized themselves in local and national groups, as the state was unable to protect them. To this day, racism, though often exaggerated by both special interest groups and the communities themselves, still persists; however, the Bangladeshi community is now well established.

Much working-class resentment had been stirred up, or at least articulated, by Enoch Powell, the Conservative Member for Wolverhampton, who in April 1968 made his infamous 'rivers of blood' speech in which he called for voluntary repatriation for Caribbean immigrants. In an acerbic aside – and surely a reference to characters like Huddleston – he attacked 'those who indulge the luxuries of pharisaic and self-righteousness, so long as it is at the expense of others'. Canon John Collins, an old Africa friend of Trevor's, arranged for the two bulldogs, who admired each other's passion and certainties, to meet. They debated Christian duty and race on television; honours were drawn. Trevor continued to write articles on race, religion and politics, and received much hate mail, which hurt him. While he was at Stepney, he did much work on radio and television, and was a magnificent broadcaster – he spoke simply, clearly and forcefully. If the BBC phoned to ask him to talk on race relations, he would make more time to do it – immediately, if necessary. His face on the screen validated his words. He looked, said one viewer, as though he was being crucified on behalf of the oppressed. He may have appeared the sacrificial victim, but it was not a role he chose with relish; he felt criticism, badly. The *Church Times* reported his words:

> During the past two years I have received more consistent abuse because of my well-known attitudes to race, colour and the arms issue than ever I received in my twelve years in South Africa . . . I have often thought of returning to those parts of the world – the hungry world – than to remain here if one has to accept this kind of profitless abuse.

His views on Africa alarmed moderate Tories. In November 1970 he spoke in support of Dennis Healey against arms trafficking with South Africa at the Cambridge Union, starting from the premise that 'what is morally wrong cannot be politically right'. He went into battle with the new Conservative administration over its African policies. He quoted a letter he had written to *The Times* earlier in the year, attacking the Tory Government's indifference to black African opinion, which meant that 'it can have no claim to moral authority in this country'. These words infuriated Lord Hailsham and other thinking Conservatives. He then challenged his audience and government ministers with the words of Leo Tolstoy: 'I sat on a man's back choking him and making him carry me, yet assure myself and others that I am sorry for him and wish to lighten his load by all possible means – except by getting off his back.'

Yet for all his forcefulness, Trevor could appear as isolated as a tragic hero in a Paul Scott novel. It wasn't just the rancid hatreds of London streets which disturbed Trevor. After Tanganyika, he was uncomfortable with the frenetic pace of London life. In crowds, he would turn to his friends and ask them where all the people were rushing off to. Certainly, they were in no hurry for church; Trevor found it hard to settle into a London parish where most educated and uneducated people were indifferent to the Gospel of Christ. He had come from a country where his status was revered to a place where bishops were ignored. He was homesick for the sunshine, the friendship, the excitement of life in South Africa. Trevor came from a brave and unsentimental generation, but few who knew him doubted that his heart rested in Africa, and in particular the 'great emptiness of its skies above the silence of the veldt'. It was to this that he remained closest.

Looking back at this spell in his life, it must have been ghastly for him to return to grey London. He had found it easier to pray under the wide open skies of Masasi, but now he was making do with the noise and fumes of Commercial Road. As ever, he found solace in the company of children, who clung onto his cassock with their dirty paws and roamed around his house. He threw himself into setting up adventure playgrounds and community projects for children.

But it wasn't only the racism, or the pace of life, which Trevor found difficult. His years in Africa had hardened him; he was unsympathetic towards families who pleaded poverty. He had come to a country where shops were bursting with goods, where East End children would tell him that they were going to get Christmas presents costing £70 – a good year's wage in Masasi. And yet the parents of the same children would tell him that they were poor. In Masasi, children would exist on one meal a day; the greatest treat in their lives was to hitch a lift in Trevor's Landrover and, on their way down to the sea, stop on the way and have a plate of rice and some fish, swimming in the gravy in which it was cooked. He would be in charge of schools where people would come to school, not on a full stomach, but having to wait until school was over to walk the two or three miles back home. It was then that they received their full meal.

It would take Trevor a while to adjust to the 'affluence of the deprived'. He had forgotten that it is easier to be poor in a hot country, that to have no money in a rich country with little belief in community or sharing is the purest form of misery. In a Third World country, there would be values of sharing and community which did not apply in the First World.

He would talk about the poverty on London streets. 'The Good Samaritan came where man was – in the ditch – and took care of him. I recognize vast areas of deprivation within our affluent society; and I recognize them more clearly the longer I work in Stepney. There is plenty of room for the exercise of compassion here. But – I ask myself – does it really compare with the needs, the hunger, the absolute poverty of the Third World?'

But he would also talk about his uneasiness at remaining in Britain. 'Perhaps the real motive behind my desire to return is a sense of guilt, the knowledge that, like Dives, I am well clothed and "fare sumptuously every day" whilst my brother "lies at the gate full of sores". I have, in a sense, run away from him.' His fixation with Africa began to irritate others. Was his heart elsewhere?, they asked. For some time, he had been treated with suspicion by the white community and fellow High Anglicans, many of whom felt that he favoured blacks over them. Perhaps he was going in the same direction as his old Superior Raymond Raynes, of whom it was said that he had three topics of conversation: bishops, blacks and British Railways. Trevor had Catholic taste but even sympathetic colleagues tired of him obsessing about black South Africa. Many people in the East End believed that Huddleston's heart was really in South Africa; this distraction caused much resentment amongst his parishioners.

Trevor realized that he could be repetitious. In an early speech he gave at St Dunstan's, Stepney, he said:

Today I come among you as a newcomer . . . I have everything to learn . . . My experience as a bishop has been the glorious one of caring for parts of the great African Christian community. The diocese I have just left (and I know you will understand me if I say that my heart is still there) is different in almost every respect from the diocese to which I have now come – vast in area (the size of England), sparse in population (about the same as Stepney). Entirely rural with no sizeable towns: its people for the most part earning no salary at all but living on what they could grow . . . a typical part of the undeveloped world . . . I need emphasize the contrast no further. I only make it clear because it would . . . be foolish to look at the work which you and I are going to do together until I have had time to understand our common problems and opportunities.

So Trevor was happiest being a pastor and dealing with victims; he hated wasting time by passing resolutions and being tied up in administration. He couldn't believe that he was expected to spend so much time, for instance, dealing with the closure of redundant churches. In addition, he was being worn down by opponents within his own Church. Trevor had changed over the years, and the austere Anglo-Catholic who stared out from the cover of *Naught for Your Comfort* had given way to a calmer ecumenist. This new attitude infuriated the febrile diocese of London, an untamed beast at the best of times. He angered the powerful Anglo-Catholic caucus on the Diocesan Synod, Bishops' Council and Finance Committee, the leaders of which were laymen. Many of them were adamant that he had lost all credibility as a Catholic. Trevor, in return, felt that many Anglo-Catholics were stuck in a time warp; he became more political at Stepney, felt theologically and ecclesiologically threatened by Mirfield and wanted to withdraw from the Community.

He could not contain his impatience with the diocesan procedure, the 'establishment', and as a result he would give them opportunities to harass him as they did. When he attended diocesan committees, he was urged to be cautious and bide his time. But this was against his nature; he felt that a bishop could achieve a lot more if he was not content to be a democrat. Trevor was an authoritative socialist who felt trapped by the Church's red tape.

His naïveté could be startling. In Trevor's eyes, the big man was always wrong and the small man was always right. He would throw himself into situations when he needed to be careful. One school in his diocese sacked a teacher for, according to the press, publishing poems by the children he taught without the permission of the governors. In fact the teacher was a member of a far-left political organization and had engineered a confrontation. The day after his dismissal, Trevor was interviewed and said, without having consulted the Chairman of the Governors who was the rector of Stepney, 'The Governors are incredibly stupid' and much more in that vein. The case dragged on for weeks; there was no way that Trevor could act as a reconciler, for he had publicly taken sides in a case about which he knew very little. He disputed with his governors, but did not take sides.

So as a bishop, many found him infuriating. But he remained loved by a large number of people who saw him for what he was – a man of prayer. Trevor would encourage all wings of the Church and there could be real affection for him among the clergy and their families and the lay group. He was in favour of the ordination of women and especially keen on Evangelicals, whom he felt were more down to earth than their Catholic counterparts. David Sheppard, the former Bishop of Liverpool and steeped in the Evangelical tradition, remembers the early years well:

Twice a year, after I was appointed Bishop of Woolwich in 1968, we would take a quiet day together and go walking. He had not been long at Stepney and I think we both found it a help to be able to share thoughts about priorities as bishops in our inner city areas. Trevor was both rooted in a deep Catholic spirituality and concern for God's justice in the whole world – especially on behalf of the poor . . .

We felt a considerable kinship, although we came from different traditions. I was from the Evangelical tradition and he was from the Catholic tradition. Both of us had a sense of social justice which came from the soul of the Church. We did meet up about three times a year and walk and pray together. I was closer to him than any other bishop. We set up a joint working party and came to it from different points of view. We felt that local leadership needed to be encouraged there. Trevor had a dream of local people being ordained and six of them were ordained in Bethnal Green. Trevor, though, was happy; he was not one to worry about status. Stepney would also help him; he was very well informed and well connected so that he would constantly surprise people by recounting in a casual way the people he had met in politics, in the arts, in places of power and influence, and he could call up support from an army of such people when required – whether it be to aid a young journalist's career or raise fundraising for a project.

He was a good bishop; he liked to be personal and upfront to people in church. He was lively and colloquial and warm and friendly to most people. One day every week Trevor opened his house to his clergy and they would come to him with their problems. He was very hands-on like that.

Trevor was happiest dealing with one issue and then moving on. While his diabetes could make him tired and irritable, most of his parishioners found him a very warm person from whom emanated great power; he could be both awesome and ascetic and he had a real presence to him. But, for a man who was gifted with extraordinary charisma, Trevor was also deeply shy; some of his priests complained that he was not good at relating to working-class people and did not find him easy to talk to. As one priest puts it: 'He was not good at socializing; he would have one cup of tea at events and then disappear; some found him aloof and patrician and he was not an easy mixer. I don't know if there was anyone really close to him; I never felt him engage when I spoke to him. Michael Ramsey would be happy to barge into pubs; Trevor was kind, but frightening to some and aloof and often overbooked; he had so many commitments.' So, he was happy to carry out his Episcopal functions, working himself as hard as ever in a sometimes frustrating and sometimes fulfilling role. He would visit schools and encourage his clergy and say his prayers. He continued to work with the Anti-Apartheid Movement, to which he had been appointed vice-chairman in 1969. He would preach at festivals, in cathedrals and university chapels, catch up with old friends, visit parishioners in prison, attend bishops' meetings. And then, one day in early 1974, everything came to an abrupt halt.

24

Collapse

ON THE MORNING OF 3 APRIL 1974, the new Bishop of London, Gerald Ellison, received an urgent telephone message from Trevor. When the Bishop rang back in the afternoon, a hysterical Trevor said that a mother had made allegations about his behaviour with her two schoolboy sons, who used to play regularly at 400 Commercial Road. The allegation concerned sexual harassment, and was made at a time when little was known or thought about the subject. With his solicitor present, the police interviewed Trevor for half an hour in his office; on departing, the police indicated that the matter would be left on the files and that a report had been sent to the Director of Public Prosecutions (DPP). Trevor then read to the Bishop a statement which had been prepared in conversation with his solicitors and then given to the police.

He told the Bishop that he was physically, mentally and spiritually exhausted – his voice had given out and he had cancelled all Holy Week engagements. He said that he was going to recuperate with old friends in Richmond. The Bishop then forwarded a plan to the DPP, saying that he hoped that a decision could be reached quickly because of the tremendous strain both on Trevor and on a diocese which needed leadership.

Trevor knew that he could rely on the support of Ellison. Ellison was utterly different from Trevor: he was a Trollopean monarchist who would treasure a sweet wrapper which he had picked up when playing parlour games with the Royal Family; yet, crucially, he was able to sympathize with clerics so very different from him. In this crisis, he was a great friend to Trevor.

And Trevor needed enormous amounts of sympathy, for he had been caught at his weakest moment. On hearing of the allegations,

Trevor suffered a major nervous breakdown; he lay in his bed and needed to be looked after. Of course, he had suffered periods of depression before – it would be psychologically unusual for such an energetic and driven man as Trevor not to suffer from 'blue devils', and, rather like Winston Churchill, his life of ceaseless toil and activity was, at least partly, a flight from melancholia.

Famously, Trevor was a restless figure, and would be consumed by any task he was performing. The author Nicholas Mosley once invited him down to the country for the weekend. On the Sunday morning, Mosley popped his head around the door and asked Trevor if he would like to accompany him to their little village church, where he was to read a lesson:

> Trevor replied: 'I will come, but I won't sit with you, but near the door.' Within a quarter of an hour he had gone. When I returned home after church, he was walking furiously up and down the lawn. I said to him: 'Trevor, are you alright?' He replied: 'I can't bear pious people, normal church-going people.'

This was a typical response from Trevor, but his nervous collapse was in a different league altogether. There were rumours that he was about to be committed to a psychiatric clinic. To worried parishioners, Trevor's secretary told a half-truth; the Bishop was recuperating after 'a bad attack of laryngitis'. It is certainly true that Trevor did suffer from a bad attack of laryngitis, which had been caused in turn by his diabetes. But it was not laryngitis which caused him to be so unwell; the laryngitis had been sparked off by the allegations made by the East End mother.

His breakdown was caused by the allegations, but his response betrayed little self-knowledge; he was the last to analyse his feelings and was never good at understanding the pressures which dictate people's behaviour. As a modern shrink would put it, Trevor was not self-aware. He had always been suspicious of psychologists, and this antipathy was only partly generational – after all, Fr Talbot would regularly send unhappy novices to see a psychotherapist. No, his response was more temperamental than generational.

Introspection often paralyses and Trevor's distaste for exploring the self made him one of the most effective priests of his generation. But many of his friends believed that such a laudable distaste for exploring the self masked a deeper concern he had with identity and the story of his life. When he lay in bed following his breakdown, he cried out: 'Who am I? I don't want to be this famous person any more.' He realized that his character was being determined by media images of himself and the contrast between the two – the perceived and the real – frightened him.

Certainly, Trevor's chances of promotion had disappeared for ever. No longer would the sympathetic *Guardian* newspaper be able to tip Trevor, 'one of the most uncompromising, most militant and most magnetic of men', to be Harold Wilson's choice as the next Archbishop of Canterbury. Now, the *Sun* newspaper could write that Trevor,

> one of the most popular figures in the Church of England, is no longer being considered as a successor to the Archbishop of Canterbury because of his health. He was suffering from stress and strain with a virus infection . . . His doctors have told him to take a complete rest and he is staying with friends in the country . . . Dr Huddleston is best known for his stand against apartheid. As a priest in Johannesburg he challenged the South African government's policy. As a result he was treated by black Africans as an equal, but by the government as a trouble maker.

The Church of England was then involved in a damage limitation exercise with Fleet Street, who suspected that the Bishop had been struck by rather more than a little illness. The *Sunday Express*, whose editor John Junor loathed Trevor, was particularly restless. On Saturday 13 April a reporter from the newspaper rang John Miles, the chief press officer for the Church of England, and asked him if Trevor was off duty because of illness and whether he would be likely to return. Miles replied that, yes, he was off duty because he was ill and that he would be returning one day. The reporter then contacted the mother of the children who had made the allegation, realized that the matter was with the DPP and rang Miles again, asking whether this changed his previous statement. Miles said that it did not, for before the trouble blew up Trevor was a sick man who had been ordered to rest.

The Bishop, who was terrified that the story would hit Fleet Street, then rang Prebendary Dewi Morgan, the Rector of St Bride's, to ask for his advice. Morgan, who knew John Junor, said that he would agree to see the editor. Both men agreed that he should see John Junor to ask him not to withdraw, but to let people know if he intended to publish so that all the necessary arrangements could be made. The Bishop told Dewi Morgan that Trevor's sanity and life were at stake. He agreed to see John Junor.

Junor told Morgan that he had seen the papers and was sure that Trevor was guilty. Later on that day, a version of the story was read out to Dewi Morgan by the *Sunday Express* legal adviser, the gist of which was intended to scupper Trevor's chances of ever being promoted to Canterbury. In the event, the story was spiked – much to the relief of Trevor and his friends.

Meanwhile, Trevor had gone to stay at a friend's holiday house in Scotland. He went to see a psychiatrist, who said that if Trevor went into a psychiatric institution – which was par for the course – he would never be the same again. However, if he was allowed to rest and withdraw, he might discover himself again. Trevor, who was hardly able to feed or dress himself, went for long country walks with his hostess and spoke on the telephone every night to the tremendously supportive Gerald Ellison. In his 1974 appointments diary, there were blanks and crossings out for March, April and May – as well as August, which would be normal.

In May 1974, a month after his collapse, Trevor wrote to his bishop:

My dear Gerald,

I shall not attempt in this letter to express all I feel of gratitude, affection and trust towards you. That must wait until I can do so more worthily. I am having a wonderful rest and change – weather perfect almost every day. And certainly I am very much better in all ways. But I am still rather like someone feeling his way across the ice: unsure whether it will bear me. I am so thankful to Tony and Joan Rampton and to my many friends: but I know the best way of showing this will be to get well.

And to other friends he was equally effusive and sensitive. To Canon Ted Roberts he wrote: 'I am certainly enormously better. We've had some perfect weather for walking and have taken advantage of it every day . . . Apparently my diabetes really did swing right out of control, but, thank God, it seems to be back in balance now and has been for the past ten days.'

By September of that year Trevor was deemed fit again. Now, Ellison could write to old friends of Trevor:

> Thank God, we are out of the nightmare, and our fears have proved unfounded. But it was a close run thing! It is good to see Trevor much like his old self. It seems as if he still has some way to go until he is fully recovered. I only hope he won't drive himself too hard or make too great demands upon himself.
>
> I saw him a day or two ago and I thought he was well enough for me to warn him of the dangers which still are present. I did not emphasize the point too strongly, and indeed it would have been impertinent for me to teach him his business. But I thought I was right to let him know that he (for very good reasons, in my view) has powerful critics who would not hesitate to make use of any opportunity given to them if it served their purposes to do so. I think he took the point. One must hope and pray that all will now be well.

But all was not well. Trevor did recover, and by mid-September he was back at work and as busy and engaged as ever. But the innuendo and gossip continued, through the occasional article which appeared in newspapers and magazines right through to the end of his life. The satirical magazine *Private Eye*, for instance, published this article on Friday 20 August 1976:

> Sir Robert Mark has been to see the Bishop of London, Gerald Ellison, over a most delicate matter. It seems that Sir Robert has become concerned over reports from his men about the activities of a certain London churchman. The pillar of the church, who has many coloured immigrants in his diocese, has been engaging in activities of a highly-specialized, not to say illegal, nature. I will keep you posted about developments.

This was a naughty ruse from the magazine, designed to attract people to ring into the newspaper with snippets of gossip.

When the article appeared, the Bishop of Edmonton wrote a letter to Gerald Ellison. It was mid-August, and Bishop Ellison was on holiday. But in a letter to his boss, the Bishop of Edmonton said:

> They are now using these innuendoes in the traditional manner of hoping to smoke something out. I think that there is no more strength to it than that, unless something is terribly wrong and this I do not believe. I am urging a total silence using your absence as excuse. If they can get nothing (unless they are being fed) it will die, but I hope most strongly that you will in no way be disturbed or worried about this on your holidays. It is an old and nasty trick to rake over dead embers in the hope of re-kindling dead fire.

And still the affair rumbled on. Much more serious and potentially damaging was an intervention in September 1979 on Radio 4's *Talking Law* programme, in which the former Attorney General Sam Silkin admitted that special consideration had been given to the plight of the famous. On the radio programme, Silkin referred to one case in particular:

> I won't name the man for obvious reasons. The Director of Public Prosecutions came to me about some allegation in relation to small boys. Although it was entirely within his province, it was something which he could ask the Attorney whether to prosecute or not, he said.
>
> I found that I was in difficulty as the man was very well known. If he had been prosecuted at all it would have ruined his career and his influence. Within the DPP's department everyone thought he would be acquitted though there was clearly evidence.

The press were thrilled when the programme came out. The *Daily Mirror* splashed with its front-page story: 'Famous Mr X and the Law.' Silkin was then pursued by reporters from rival papers, asking whether Mr X was not a named politician, whose contacts with the police were chronicled. Silkin denied that the man was Smith and added that he was not an MP at all. But Mr Silkin did add that Mr X 'was a well-known figure in community work'. Of course, John Junor picked it up immediately, and wrote in his mischievous column the next month:

> Former Attorney General Mr Sam Silkin must have known that he would be unleashing a storm of speculation when he revealed that during his term of office a man prominent in public life had escaped prosecution for sex offences against children because Mr Silkin and the then Director of Public Prosecutions had agreed that he was likely to be acquitted – but would have been ruined by court proceedings.
>
> For that could be another way of saying that the prominent man was not necessarily innocent, but that in any court proceedings it would have been his word against the word of the little children and that a jury would almost certainly have accepted his word.
>
> So who was the man? To begin with, the rumours centred quite unfairly on a well-known MP. Now it is suggested that he was someone high up in the hierarchy of the Church of England. Mr Silkin may still be unwilling to give names. But, if it were a churchman, should he not be prepared to tell us that in return for non-prosecution he was given an assurance that if the man concerned remained in the priesthood, he would never again be in a position in which he had to deal with children either in England or overseas?

Many years later, in the early 1990s, Canon Eric James, in research for his biography of Trevor, went further to investigate claims of wrongdoing involving Trevor. On visits to Tanzania and South Africa in 1991 and 1992, he enquired whether similar allegations had been made before in places where Trevor had worked. After all, it is very rare for people who commit such offences to be guilty only once. There were no allegations or evidence of criminality. Trevor's confessor in Tanzania, who became the Bishop of Masasi, told Canon James: 'I cannot, of course, discuss what Bishop Trevor confessed. I can tell you what he never had need to discuss and that is any criminal offence.'

When the situation in South Africa changed enormously, Canon James took steps to examine the BOSS files to see if there was any material on Bishop Trevor. BOSS would certainly have tried to make an attempt at 'disinformation' where Bishop Trevor was concerned. But the BOSS files had been shredded. Of course, if BOSS had proper evidence, it is unthinkable that they would not have made full use of it and pressed their case to its natural conclusion.

While conducting research into his aborted biography, Canon James encountered Bishop George Ellison, who had warned Canon James not simply to write a hagiography about Trevor – it needed to be a 'warts and all' book. Close to his death, and from his retirement home in Cerne Abbas, Dorset, Ellison travelled up to London to see Canon James. Near the end of his life, he was now free from any episcopal pressure and was very happy to talk about the affair.

When the two men spoke, Bishop Ellison made it clear that the incident involving the two boys was not the reason for Bishop Trevor leaving the diocese of London. Nevertheless he was glad that Trevor was able to leave Stepney and do another Episcopal job – which, he said, he 'did with my full confidence'. He added: 'Ten years as Bishop of Stepney are enough for any man, and the strains and the stresses of those years were evident in Bishop Trevor's last years in Stepney.'

He then revealed to Canon James more about the actual incident. He said that the parents of a child had levelled claims against Bishop Trevor, that the police were involved, and that political enemies of Trevor were involved.

The Bishop then said: 'I want to make it absolutely clear that I have seen no evidence to convince me that Bishop Trevor was ever guilty of a criminal act.' He added: 'Bishop Trevor undoubtedly had many enemies in South Africa and England who were waiting to denigrate him, indeed, to destroy him.'

The Bishop was also clear that neither he, nor his legal advisers, believed that anyone had the right to impede justice if there was any real evidence of guilt. He certainly did not believe in a hierarchical 'cover-up'. The bishop strongly hinted to Canon James that he had taken steps at the highest level to see that Bishop Trevor, as a result of the incident, should not become the subject of a private trial in the courts or by newspaper, and that he did not believe – with the South African situation being what it was – that Bishop Trevor could have justice done to him.

Ellison reiterated his belief that he had seen no evidence of Trevor's guilt. He was also aware, though, that there could be cultural misunderstandings. It was quite common for children in Africa to sit on

Trevor's knee. There is little doubt that such acts were, even in the 1970s and before the onslaught of child legislation, frowned upon in this country.

Archbishop Desmond Tutu, who as a little boy had encountered Trevor, was particularly affronted by the belief that Trevor was a paedophile. On 1 February 1995 he wrote a lengthy letter, saying that any suggestion of Trevor's criminality was outrageous and adding that he could easily gather together a dozen black friends of Trevor's acquaintance – like Walter Makhulu, the Archbishop of Central Africa – who would all testify to the man's innocence. On Valentine's Day 1995 he wrote:

> I have seldom felt more devastated and even soiled by the implication of what your letter suggested. It is utterly unthinkable and indeed totally unacceptable. My own view is that if BOSS had any credible material in their files, they would certainly not have been bashful and coy about using it to discredit Bishop Trevor. He was an enormous thorn in the side of the apartheid regime and was effectively the real spokesman for the anti-apartheid movement for a considerable period. No one did more to keep apartheid on the world's agenda than he and therefore it would have been a devastating victory for the forces of evil and darkness had he been discredited. I don't think they would have been backward in coming forward.
>
> I, like many another of his so-called creatures, sat on his lap. He was wearing a cassock all the time. This was in an office that was a virtual thoroughfare and his desk was at a window and people were constantly passing by to get to the back of the house or coming from there. There was just no opportunity for any untoward conduct, but even more importantly, I can swear categorically that he never fondled me below the belt. I would have remembered it. How ghastly to want to besmirch such a remarkable man, so holy and so good. How utterly despicable and awful.

And still the rumours remain. The biographer Michael-de-la-Noy, writing Trevor's obituary in the *Independent*, alleged that Trevor was moved from Stepney to the Indian Ocean of Mauritius to 'hush up a scandal which will raise few eyebrows today'.

Of course, it would be tempting to dismiss outright the claims against so transparently good a man; except we should consider that the allegations were made at a time when abuse was just not considered the issue that it is today. Trevor's psychological collapse suggests that the allegations touched a raw nerve. Sam Silkin's intervention, too, certainly clouded the issue. There will always be plenty of gossip and hearsay about Trevor's behaviour, especially in Africa, where he would call colleagues 'dearie' and was renowned for his love of small and rather beautiful boys. But was there any substance in the allegations laid against him in April 1974? We shall probably never know the full truth.

25

Back to Work

TREVOR, TRUE TO FORM, recovered, and by the beginning of September 1974 he had resumed his normal duties as a suffragan bishop. Ever since the allegations had been made, Trevor had felt an enormous sense of persecution and loss, but these were feelings to which he was accustomed and he retained the strength to conquer his depressions throughout his life. Besides, Trevor needed to remain warm and humorous and authoritative; as a London bishop with an enormous burden of responsibility, he could not afford to surrender to pity or despair. Instead, he did what he had always done and threw himself into even more work.

There was certainly plenty of work to do. In Stepney, he needed to confront the secular city as he had confronted race in South Africa and poverty in South Tanzania. This was the age of the *dirigiste* planner, and Trevor was seeing at first hand how old communities were being threatened by endless redevelopment and how the lives of the poor in a rich culture – or 'deprivation in affluence' as he termed it – were threatened by that loss of community. In his sermons, he would point alarming facts out to his congregation: in his diocese, one child in four was placed in front of the courts before the age of 17, one child in twenty-nine was placed in care because of the breakdown of their family; and Stepney had the highest truancy, unemployment and illegitimacy rate of any diocese in the country.

Of course, Trevor had worked with the poor for most of his life and understood the terrible conditions which they endured. What alarmed him about Stepney was the loss of comradeship. The destruction of terraced housing and their replacement by hideous high-rise tower blocks; the complete uprooting of traditional communities; the building of vast roads which literally divided old communities in two; the destruction of playing space for children; the flight of the young and ambitious from their streets, leaving behind only the old with their loneliness. The destruction of community – that sense of the early Church that they had all things in common – meant everything to Trevor, and its loss was deeply painful to him.

He addressed parishes, promoted home-grown ministries from the East End, offered comfort to wayward priests, visited old friends, heard confessions, attended various meetings of old friends, and spoke at Synods and other clergy gatherings. He began to speak more on morals and public life, and in a direct and unpompous manner about the benefits of restraint and the horrors of promiscuity.

It might seem strange that Trevor, most at ease in a world of private monasticism and public politics, would be concerned about a nation's morals. He was one of those clerics who would drink and socialize with actors and writers and lawyers and politicians and teachers. Many of his friends, while sharing his political views, did not begin to grasp the religious impulse behind them. They were mystified by the monasticism which lay at the heart of his being. And it was this monasticism which separated him from others and gave him the strength to utter views which were repugnant to many.

Now, Trevor was too worldly and self-critical a character to moralize to other people about their own sexual weaknesses. But he did feel that it was his duty, as a Christian priest, to issue forth when he believed that someone was mistaken in their views. He would criticize the Church for its loose attitude to sexual morality, saying that Christian chastity was not a prohibition but an affirmation – an affirmation that the soul and body were closely related, that the body was so influenced by the soul that it should be treated as having an innate dignity. Christians, he said, believed in the resurrection of the body, and not just the immortality of the soul alone. He then added:

> Therefore we know, and we rejoice in knowing, that the con-
> flicts and tensions, the joys and sorrows, which are part of the
> human condition here, are not meaningless, disconnected expe-
> riences, but are the very stuff of Love. And amongst them the
> needs for self-discipline and restraint are recognizably of
> supreme importance. Without them, love can degenerate into
> lust; affection into selfishness; surrender into defeat.

Man is made for the vision of God – that is all that he is made for. And chastity is the discipline of love by which he attains it, not in Heaven but here and how. It is certainly harder than contraception, but rather more worthwhile.

Trevor would advocate without fear the virtue of discipline which had guided his tempestuous and unrestrained character. He would use one of his favourite examples. An artist has a vision which can be obscured by a failure in discipline; the musician has a vision which is muffled by a failure in discipline. Likewise the human being has a vision, to make his soul with God; and this purpose, too, is weakened by an absence of self-control.

Trevor's belief in chastity was at odds with the mood of the time. He just could not understand how friends of his, who would openly support the rights of the Bantu in South Africa, could demand a relaxation of the sexual laws in this country. People would say that it was unrealistic and too hard to expect people to be chaste; Trevor replied that chastity should be expected because it was so hard. He added that an attack on apartheid was a religious attack, and Western liberals' arguments were weakened by their failure to understand this. England was too trapped in what he termed a 'secular-humanist ethic', and so her voice would be ignored when she spoke out on major moral conflicts in the world.

Trevor was never the trendy vicar of conservative imagination. An authoritative socialist, a misguided obsessive, a naïve militant perhaps – but he was not soft or compromising. With passion and clarity, he used his position in Stepney to attack secular humanism in the same manner that he condemned Verwoerd's policies, lambasted the weakness of the British Government or highlighted the lethargy of the national Church. He would make ferocious attacks on what he termed the liberal-humanist ethic, saying that it always chose the soft option and avoided the hard way. It could do no other, for such an ethic was based on a wholly pragmatic view of human nature. Man was created for himself, and society therefore should be ordered not for any ultimate good, but to provide immediate comfort and satisfaction. What human passions desired, so they must receive; humans needed sex and protection; contraception is better than chastity. From his years of hop picking with Fr Sergeant, Trevor had always been intrigued by political radicalism, while remaining theologically conservative; as he grew older, so his religious views became more liberal. But he always believed that he stood apart from many of his liberal friends, who never understood what the demands of chastity and Christianity placed upon their followers.

In Stepney, Trevor was happiest when busy. Apart from his normal duties as a bishop, he would dine with great friends like the millionaire philanthropist Nadir Dinshaw and the less salubrious Tom Driberg. He would attend classical music concerts, the theatre and the opera. He would welcome visitors to Commercial Road, including Julius Nyerere, who popped in on a private visit. He travelled to America and Canada.

Tragedy, meanwhile, was unfurling in his dearest Africa. In Angola, there had been the trial, conviction and execution of men fighting as mercenaries. There had been a series of hijacks and rescues in Entebbe, Uganda, which had involved widespread massacre and death. But most important in Trevor's eyes was the trouble emerging from Soweto, in South Africa. In a seven-month period from June 1976, five hundred young black people were killed in a series of riots against the white government. A new militant wing of the ANC had emerged, happy to fight as part of an armed struggle whilst most of their comrades were arrested and imprisoned and the movement itself banished. Trevor, back in Stepney, was in close contact with leading ANC figures back in South Africa; from them he learnt that apartheid was dissolving at the outskirts, while remaining solid in the centre.

But his faith rendered him hopeful, if not optimistic about the situation in South Africa. He knew that English newspapers presented a caricature of Africa as a dark continent full of bloodshed and disorder; it was as if, he argued, England was the sum of events on the Falls Road. He was delighted when Desmond Tutu, who used to sit on his lap as a child, became the first black Bishop of Lesotho. Speaking at St Paul's Cathedral as Tutu was consecrated at St Mary's Johannesburg in July 1976 – Trevor would have attended, but he had been refused a visa by the South African government – the Bishop called on all Christians to remember John Donne's famous dictum: 'No man is an island, entire of itself . . . any man's death diminishes me, because I am involved in Mankind.' It was right, said Trevor, that Christians should relish the joy of a newly enthroned Desmond Tutu, just as they suffered when a Christian suffered. Trevor, the most English of men in bearing if not temperament, implored his audience to think beyond the cloister and village green and towards the shanty town and white-washed simple church. The Church was international, and in Tutu would welcome into its fellowship a voice that even those in St Paul's needed to hear – the voice of Christian Africa, which neither war or terror had quelled.

Yet, slowly but perceptibly, Trevor tired of Stepney. He was a man who always needed new challenges, and he was keen to move on. He had decided to leave Stepney on his sixty-fifth birthday – 15 June 1978. He wrote to his old friend Gerald Ellison, informing him of his decision. Ellison replied: 'I am sure you will appreciate with what deep regret the news will be received . . . in the Stepney area to which you have made such a profound contribution . . . For the last three-and-a-half years you have been a constant stay and support to me, and your wisdom and loyalty have been of immense help to me.'

The two men remained close friends until the end. Trevor was off, to face a new challenge.

Trevor was leaving England yet again; an overseas posting to the multi-racial Indian Ocean was in the offering. Trevor could look back on real achievements in Stepney, especially with the setting up of team ministries, his attempts to introduce real East End priests into the area and his promotion and welcoming of vulnerable immigrants in his diocese; a tradition, he reminded sceptics, which had begun three centuries before with the French Hugenots, who had made their own way through life by silk weaving (in his house in Commercial Road, he had one of the mulberry trees which were planted by them from all over the East End of London). Stepney had been new for him in one key area: unlike Africa or even Swindon, he had come to an area where the Church was a small minority and needed to be built up; he needed to make the Church more attractive to people who felt disorientated and frozen out by more Western styles of worship. But one thing still remained at the back of Trevor's mind; he remembered those boys he had taught in Sophiatown, and how their futures had been stolen by a pernicious education Act. This burning rage at their plight had not diminished over the years.

26

Mauritius

IT WAS A TRAGEDY which brought Trevor to Mauritius.

In December 1976, the Venerable Ghislain Emmanuel, the Archdeacon of Mauritius, was elected as the twelfth Bishop of Mauritius. He had succeeded an Englishman, the Most Revd Ernest Edwin Curtis, who had stepped down as Bishop, and Archbishop of the Indian Ocean, at the age of 70. Mauritius was granted its independence on 12 March 1968, and now the Mauritian Ghislain Emmanuel was appointed as its first Archbishop. But only three months after his consecration, on 16 March 1977, Ghislain suddenly collapsed and died in Bishop's House, while trying to contact a doctor on a phone which was out of order.

A quick election was held for his successor, which proved indecisive; none of the candidates had gained the necessary amount of votes. If the truth be told, none of the Mauritian candidates had the obvious stature to replace Emmanuel as Archbishop. To complicate matters, nobody could be parachuted from outside; since the new Province had been inaugurated in March 1973, everyone had to stand for election.

After the fiasco of the aborted election, frantic clergy telephoned Alan Rogers, a former Bishop of Mauritius who had been Bishop of Fulham from 1966 to 1970, where he had worked alongside Trevor when he was working in Stepney. Suddenly Bishop Rogers, who was living in innocuous retirement in Northamptonshire, was besieged by telephone calls from clerics seeking advice. The name Trevor Huddleston, who had tired of London, was soon mentioned. A man of Trevor's grit and zest would never look for retirement, but he did believe that a change was as good as a rest. He now knew that he had missed the opportunity to be offered a major Episcopal post, but he did believe that he could offer another five years of service as a bishop somewhere before he retired.

Bishop Rogers's name was still influential in the Indian Ocean. Trevor also had the key support of Gerald Ellison, Bishop of London, and Michael Ramsey, Archbishop of Canterbury. All three men spoke warmly in favour of Trevor.

Trevor was unsure when the possibility of moving to the Indian Ocean came up. His old friend George Briggs, who had worked with him in Tanzania but was now Bishop of the Seychelles, another of the diocese within the province of the Indian Ocean, had doubts whether the area was right to accept a bishop, and possibly an archbishop, from England. Trevor was white and could not speak French; Mauritius was black, and the official language of the Province was French.

But soon he had made up his mind. On 25 October 1977 Trevor was elected Bishop, and he managed a quick visit to Mauritius in the first week of December that year. He was enthroned as Bishop the following April, having resigned from Stepney on 31 March. The enthronement was filmed live on television, and Trevor's cassock became wet with sweat as the temperature increased. The following Sunday, the grand-sounding electoral College of the Province met in St James's Cathedral, Mauritius, and elected Trevor as Archbishop of the Province. The election was a tied vote, but Trevor won because he was senior in Episcopal orders – he had been consecrated Bishop of Masasi in 1960.

Trevor knew his posting in Mauritius was not a sinecure; true, the Archbishop of the Indian Ocean was not a key post, but nor was it a repository for difficult clerics past their sell-by date. His role involved huge responsibility; as Bishop, Trevor would live in and have prime responsibility for the Anglican diocese of Mauritius. As Archbishop of the Indian Ocean, he would need to make regular visits to the diocese of the Seychelles, and the three Anglican dioceses that comprised Madagascar.

Churchgoers in all three dioceses were suspicious of Trevor. They had heard of his life in South Africa and his fame, and parishioners muttered about 'that dreadful man'. Much of the hostility towards Trevor seeped from Madagascar, where people were angry that Trevor had become a bishop and an archbishop; and on top of this he was known to be an archbishop with a fixation with socialism, a dark interest in race relations in South Africa and a strange enthusiasm for

Nyerere's politics in Tanzania. From the East End of London a white man had arrived to take control of their diocese; yet he would live eight hundred miles away in Mauritius and was unable to speak any language spoken in Madagascar. Trevor, though, had one tactic which disarmed his critics; he made it clear that he would only remain Bishop and Archbishop for five years and would retire at 70. So those who loathed the idea of an English bishop realized that they only need to suffer one for a short period of time. For Trevor, it concentrated his mind on the objectives of the diocese and the Province.

But the three areas which he would have control over – Mauritius, the Seychelles and Madagascar – represented very different areas and responsibilities. Mauritius was a small and independent island with a population of just under a million. Some 51 per cent of the people were Hindu, and there were only 7,000 Anglicans. One-third of the island was Christian, and the vast majority were Roman Catholic. The Seychelles consisted of over 60,000 people, who were spread over ninety-two islands, and they were a different breed – Polynesian, Arab, French and British origin – speaking English, French and Creole. Nearly everyone on the island called themselves Christian, but only a small percentage – about one in twenty – were Anglicans. There were fifteen Anglican congregations in the Seychelles, each with a total of about a thousand communicants. Most of the people lived on the largest island of Mahé (with St Paul's Cathedral, Victoria, as the main church), and most of the remainder on the next island, Praslin. George Briggs would be Bishop of the Seychelles for Trevor's first year as Archbishop.

Then there was also Madagascar, which had a population of nine million, three million of whom were Christian. The Anglicans, Lutherans, and Roman Catholics, together with the United Protestant Church, formed the Malagasy Christian Council. The area itself had been divided into three smaller dioceses – Antananarivo, Toamasina and Antsiranana. Antananarivo, based in the central highlands, was the smallest area but had the largest concentration of Anglican clergy and communicants; it was run by the aged and obscurantist Ephraim Randianovona. Toamasina, which ran along the east coast, had about fifteen priests and a total of over 20,000 Anglicans. Its bishop, Samuel Rafanomezana, was old. Antsiranana contained nearly eighty churches and over 13,000 Anglicans. Gabriel Josa was the third of the elderly bishops.

So, the dioceses were complicated, individual and impossible to oversee coherently. Well, this was nothing new for Trevor, who had learnt from his time in Masasi how to deal with truculent clergy and grotesque bureaucracy. But he was also facing a financially precarious period; when, in 1973, the three dioceses of Madagascar, Mauritius and the Seychelles were grouped together to form the one Province, not enough attention had been given to its actual workings. There was little money for Synods and Committees to meet, and the expenses connected with Trevor's election as Bishop and Archbishop had been crippling. Trevor inherited a Province in name only.

He took time to settle. In letters home, he would describe his first fortnight in Mauritius as 'the most fascinating, enthralling, unexpected, tough, happy, sad . . . of my entire life'. He thought that Mauritius was beautiful; he also found the humid conditions – heavy tropical rain followed by hot sun – very difficult to handle. He was living alone in a large house, from where he heard all manners of social calls and briefings. His house, though not as beautifully situated as Masasi, boasted several large rooms and a veranda. He took part in an investiture at Government House and attended two Christian weddings and a Muslim one.

As Archbishop of the Indian Ocean, the demands on Trevor were enormous. Early on in his episcopate, he did a round-robin trip of all three of the dioceses in his Province. The trip, which covered some 3,500 miles, included Auranananivo, whose gorgeous steep narrow streets he compared to Italy. The cathedral was perched at the top of one of the many hills. Trevor wrote excitedly:

In one cathedral the Sunday service took 2 hours 10 minutes and in another 2 hours 40 minutes. And this was not due to anything 'extra' for the Archbishop – and was certainly not due to his long sermons. It's a very poor church in a fairly poor country. In one parish I was told that the parish priest hadn't received his salary for ten months! The distances are so vast and the full-time clergy so few that nearly all the pastoral work in the villages is done by unpaid catechists. Of course the Christian church in Madagascar as a whole has had a very large number of martyrs in its century or so of life. I've now completed my visits to the whole Province (five dioceses) for this year and am almost through with the major parishes in Mauritius.

Trevor had always enjoyed new challenges, but he did find it very hard to settle. He never found it easy to adapt to a decent routine at home and his role involved, for him at least, what he termed 'unnecessary loneliness'. A few months after his arrival, his sense of exclusion was exacerbated by a return trip to London, where he had been attending the 1978 Lambeth Conference. This conference, he believed, had been much better than its predecessor ten years before; in typical Trevor mode, he loved the fact that we 'really did have some religion'. He adored the daily Eucharist, celebrated by a different Province every day that used its own liturgy, and listened attentively to the daily addresses. He also felt that the great clerical issues of the day – human rights, women priests, the future of the Anglican communion – had been dealt with using charity and wisdom. He had, though, suffered his own drama at Lambeth: while concelebrating the Eucharist with all the other bishops of the Indian Ocean – a stressful enough situation for any Archbishop – Trevor collapsed and was carried away from the altar. He had needed insulin, and he recovered sufficiently to attend some evening engagements; nevertheless, Trevor was not a young man and his collapse had shown, in a brutal fashion to a shocked congregation, just how precarious his health could be.

He found Mauritius a very friendly place, while despairing at the languid nature of the people and their desire to put everything off until the next day. He was received with great warmth by most Mauritians, but still he felt very alone. He believed much of his solitude came from the old colonial status of bishop in Mauritius and the fact that their bishops lived in places too remote from the people. It was the bishop, too, who had to provide all the initiatives if anything was ever going to be achieved. It was all very different from Stepney, where Trevor had insisted that the Church Commissioners buy a house in the centre of the diocese.

All three dioceses provided political problems. All three governments were now run on secular grounds. All three were Socialist, as they had been in Tanzania (and this, of course, pleased Trevor); but in all three dioceses schools and hospitals and welfare agencies were now under the control of the government rather than the Church. Relations between Church and state, or Trevor and the ruling President, were cordial in Mauritius and the Seychelles but awful in Madagascar, which was ruled by the gruesome President Didier Ratsiraka, who imitated the 'red book' of his beloved Chairman Mao.

Back in Mauritius, Trevor was getting accustomed to their fabulous summers. He would sit on the veranda and eat his breakfast to the chirping noise of birdsong in the background. Across the veranda, he would stare out towards a large sweep of lawn with a palm tree on one side, a clump of banana on the other and a mixture of tropical and green foliage in the middle. He adored the garden, especially when children would visit him and sip Coca-Cola and run around on the grass.

Trevor was beginning to have a grasp of pidgin French, and paid regular visits to the fourteen parishes in Mauritius, where he would celebrate Mass in French. He would envy Pope John Paul II's command of language, and bemoan the first real sign of age – an inability to retain facts and recite verbs. Trevor was never a natural linguist and found Swahili hard to grasp in his late forties; little wonder that, as he approached his seventies, he found his French verbs an increasing struggle.

Trevor knew that his first responsibility would be inter-faith. In Mauritius, he was faced with all types of communities – French, British, Creole, Chinese and Muslim. He knew that the ordained ministry must be well educated and properly trained and be, above all, Mauritian; they would need to teach the laity what they believed and why they should respect the beliefs of those who believed differently.

Trevor had to take immediate and drastic action. So he visited Mauritius' theological college, which was bizarrely situated some 560 km to the north-east of Mauritius on the island of Rodrigues. On arrival, he informed Fr Donald Smith, the principal of the college, and other assembled ordinands that he had decided to move the college down to Rose Hill, Mauritius. Now the Bishop would be able to keep a close eye on both Principal and students. Every Friday morning, he would say Mass at Rose Hill, have breakfast afterwards in the College and then often lecture or give them devotional addresses. He would make sure that he knew the names of all the ordinands personally, and the risky move appears to have paid off – by 1983, five Mauritian priests and five deacons had been ordained.

Ordinands who had worked under the notoriously abrasive Donald Smith (who was to become a bishop in Madagascar) looked back on their bishop with pleasure. One ordinand, Roger Chung Po Chuen, described Trevor as 'the father of the modern Church in Mauritius'. Trevor, he added, 'prepared me to be an effective priest in a mainly

Moslem area, where there had been race riots between Muslims and Creoles. He taught us to be ecumenical, responsible in our society, open to other faiths. He taught us the centrality of prayer.'

There were also the three bad wolves to deal with, or in particular the bishops of Madagascar: Randrianovona of Antananarivo, Gabriel Josoa of Antsiranana and Rafanomezana of Toamasina. He needed to discuss the training of priests in the three dioceses. When he visited Madagascar at the beginning of June 1978, he found that the morale of the clergy was very low – they seemed emaciated, tired and very old. It was hard to communicate with them; Trevor could not speak a word of Malagasy, his French was very poor, the telephones did not work, the cost of public transport was prohibitive and the postal system was lacklustre.

And there was worse to come. Trevor then made a half a day's journey into the country from Antananarivo, along dirt tracks and dried up river beds to St Paul's College, Ambatoharanana. Here, in the middle of a barren wilderness, he came across the 'cradle of Anglicanism' in Madagascar. This cradle, the theological college of Madagascar, was designed by the Victorian architect William Butterfield and looked like a minor public school – a huge chapel and library, with accommodation provided for staff and students. It was run by Revd Hall Speers, a young and seriously ill Irishman with a wife and young family to support. There was no electricity or running water at the College. Trevor, though inclined to close the College, knew that he could not act as he had in Mauritius: here there were three bishops of Madagascar, and he was only the new Archbishop who had travelled from far away.

There were other problems in Madagascar. It was a Maoist state, with little official regard for institutional Christianity; it was racially mixed, with a combination of animists, Muslims, Hindus, Christians and other faiths. The Church was resistant to any liturgical change; it was wedded to the Book of Common Prayer, translated into French, and would not take kindly to any irritating interference in the name of modernity. Trevor knew that his priority in Madagascar was the same as it had been in Mauritius: to train up a group of ordained and lay men so that they could present a robust and clear defence of Anglicanism in Madagascar, rather than a more muted and rarefied form of Roman Catholicism.

Trevor was based in Mauritius, and needed someone to oversee the renaissance of Anglicanism in parlous Madagascar. He chose Hall Speers, and offered him his full support. Trevor renamed the two theological colleges of Madagascar and Mauritius as 'Provincial' colleges and made them answerable to him; people muttered that he was being high-handed and dictatorial, but Trevor was driven by a sense of urgency and had little time for niceties. He also split the Butterfield college of St Paul's into two, keeping one on its original site and the other in urban Antsiranana, where it would combine its facilities with the local Roman Catholic and Methodist colleges. Of course, the three bishops were furious about this move – during one meeting Bishop Randrianovona cried out 'one cannot pray in a town' – and Trevor's patience wore thin. But he was a man in a hurry; he had committed himself to Mauritius for five years, and he could not stand being delayed by obfuscation and malice. It was never Trevor's nature to go slow, but life in Madagascar was very, very slow indeed.

So, as Archbishop, Trevor tried to reorganize religion and regenerate funds in his Provinces. The island had received a 40 per cent subsidy from the government, which was about to be withdrawn; the Anglican Church now needed to find another £12,000 a year from the 7,000 churchgoers on the island, half of whom had just been recently confirmed. In a bid to raise the profile of the Church on the island, and therefore attract some extra donations, Trevor started the Phoenix Parties from the veranda of his house.

On the last Tuesday of every month, Trevor would give a buffet party at the Bishop's House; after supper, a speaker would deliver a paper and there would then be a question-and-answer session. Fifty people attended the first party, and they were present for many gruelling sessions. The writer Naomi Mitchinson spoke on the Marxist meaning of life. His old South African friend Alan Paton spoke, as did the trade union leader Jack Jones, the Soviet ambassador N. Pavlov and a variety of Muslims and Hindus, who pontificated on suitably general subjects – the religious aspect of peace, say. It was Trevor's intention that people of different religions and cultures would meet; this meeting, he believed, was at the heart of Mauritius.

One of the speakers at the Phoenix Party was Cardinal Jean Margeot, who spoke on authority and became a great friend of Trevor. The Cardinal, who had spent twenty-five years as a bishop in Mauritius, saw Trevor as a very holy man who used to spend a day at their 'Carmel'. The two clerics became close friends at a time when they needed to; since independence in 1968, the government had become increasingly powerful over the Church, to the extent that, at his inaugural service, the Cardinal was asked to submit his sermon to a government official for approval. The Cardinal refused, and relied on Trevor's support when the government proposed new progressive laws on abortion and sterilization. The two men had differing views, but both agreed that such laws made human life banal. The government legislation was withdrawn.

Trevor was used to tetchy relations between the Church of England and the ruling political state. Mauritius was no exception; Britain had been the colonial power for over a century, and the Anglican Church drew its strength from its British connection. Even following independence, and in Trevor's time, the Anglican bishop would sit next to the Prime Minister – unless the Roman Catholic bishop was senior in consecration. Trevor saw the situation as surreal and dangerous: his flock was a tiny minority of 7,000 in a population of one million, and yet his Church had considerable status. It was his responsibility to ensure that the Church lived up to its status – by being a servant church at one with the other churches.

For long gone was the hardened zealot who, like Raynes, had protested against the inclusion of the Church of South India in the Anglican Communion. Trevor had realized, and would appreciate more as time went on, that the island could only hope to be at peace with itself if people learnt to show real respect for other people's faith. From his time in Stepney and Masasi, Trevor had learnt that respect for other faiths was crucial.

But he was not happy to pen sugary platitudes. It was actual events, like the annual pilgrimage in Mauritius to the tomb of the folk hero Père Laval, which gave Trevor the most pleasure. Everyone from whatever faith would walk and honour Laval, who had returned from the Napoleonic War and worked among illiterate Indian labourers. Here, according to eyewitnesses, he lived a life of such saintliness that the love of God shone through all those who he met. In May 1979, Trevor was asked to read at a Mass for his Beatification, which was attended by over 150,000 people, many of whom were Muslim, Hindu and Buddhist. At the sign of peace, twelve young children brought baskets full of white pigeons and released them over the crowd.

Trevor was glad to see his Communion becoming more self-reliant. In July 1979, Trevor made another pastoral visit to the Seychelles, to preside over the consecration of the island's first Seychellois bishop, French Chang Him. The English-trained French-man, who would be Bishop of the Seychelles for over fifteen years and would succeed Trevor as Archbishop of the Indian Ocean, was used to the awkward politics of the area – his brother had been killed in the early years of opposition to the Socialist One-Party State.

Much of his *élan* seemed restored. Trevor's love of and faith in children, which had brought him to the point of collapse in Stepney, had been restored in Mauritius. He would complain that he would feel emotionally deprived if he did not have children playing around him, and he would invite the children of neighbours to play Caromme – snooker played with draughts – on the veranda and football in the garden. After services on Sunday morning, he would take children bathing and buy them food and drink at the beach cafeteria. One child, Gilles, he even adopted, and looked after him through school and university.

Indeed, as in Masasi and Stepney, much of his work was centred around children. With the financial help of the French Government, St Hugh's, a large building for old people, had been established in Mauritius. Trevor felt, though, that the Church had a social responsibility towards young people as well, so a crèche, a nursery school, a dormitory for blind children, and a block for young offenders was set up next to St Hugh's.

Church affairs forced Trevor to make several visits back to England. He was also made many eight-hour flights to Perth, where he became friendly with Howell Witt, the Bishop of Perth and a former Mirfield student. His main priority in Perth had been to lead a series of summer schools, but it also gave him the opportunity to get in touch with many leading figures in the Anti-Apartheid Movement, who were in temporary exile in Australia. In 1981, Trevor succeeded Bishop Ambrose Reeves as President of the Anti-Apartheid Movement and chaired a meeting in London, followed by a freezing march in Trafalgar Square. Back in warmer Perth, he was able to influence Australia's incipient resistance to apartheid. At a rally in Perth's Victorian cathedral, Trevor condemned apartheid, and the British Government's reluctance to support sanctions against South Africa. Alert to the power of language, Trevor described apartheid as heresy; the same word would then be used in resolutions to the Australian General Synod. Trevor's work for the Anti-Apartheid Movement, then not as searingly fashionable as it would become, was winning him accolades, and he was nominated for a Gold Award by the United Nations. He flew first class to New York to address the General Assembly, and then travelled onto London to meet more of his anti-apartheid cronies.

He made a speech to the United Nations General Assembly in which he articulated his beliefs. He said that he had first become aware of the iniquities of the system back when he was a young pastor in the streets of Sophiatown and Orlando, where he was 'confronted with a system so evil that it attacked the very meaning of human life; the very purpose for which, as I believe, Man is created'.

He then added, powerfully: 'Apartheid said (and says) to African children "Your education is an education for servitude."

'Apartheid says to African workers: "We need your labour, black man. We must have your labour, black man, to give white South Africa the power and energy it needs to keep you for ever where you are."

'Apartheid says to African families: "So long as you are here in our white city you can have no security, no permanence, no peace. For you have no citizenship – and you will never have it."

'"Keep over there."'

The death of friends drew near. On the last day of December 1982, his great friend Canon John Collins died. Less than two months later, in a memorial address at St Paul's Cathedral, Trevor again spoke of Canon Collins's visit to South Africa in 1954, shortly before Trevor was recalled, and how he was not deceived that apartheid was a passing phase. Trevor then added:

He was not deceived either by that kind of double talk and hypocrisy which goes greatly to the liking of British, American and European governments to this day: mainly, that the evil of "apartheid" can be overcome by diplomacy, the gentlemanly approach, the patient if time-consuming government to government rapprochements, involving huge investment, secret trade agreements in arms and all the other squalid deals with which we are sadly familiar. John saw 'apartheid' for what it is: a total denial of human rights and human dignity, and an offence to God.

Even during the five years he spent in Mauritius, Trevor's main interest had remained the constant struggle against apartheid; as leader of the Anti-Apartheid Movement he had become a symbol of the world's concern. But in Mauritius he had also learnt how important it was for differing religions to work together, and his final year saw the culmination of this thinking. In January 1983, Trevor held a ten-day conference in his vast house, and invited leaders of major faiths to mull over the purpose of Man. Everyone was there; two Jewish rabbis, a Siberian Muslim, a Christian Arab from the West Bank, three Buddhists, a scattering of Lutherans. He needed allies for his cause. Trevor wanted all the invitees, who were reluctant to worship together, to consider what a future Mauritius would look like. He linked this act of ecumenism with his wider conflict against apartheid, and with anger and force urged co-operation between religions on this subject, when they would have been happier issuing platitudes. As Conference chairman, other multi-faith projects begged for his support. He became Provost of Selly Oak College, Birmingham, a main centre for religions to meet in England. He was now to head both the Anti-Apartheid Movement and the International Defence and Aid Fund for South Africa. His time in Mauritius was over, and he was heading for a restless retirement.

27

A Restless Retirement

SO WHAT WAS TREVOR TO DO, now that he was retired? His anti-apartheid activities would keep him busy, but he needed a base and a place to live.

He could hardly return to Mirfield, a community for whom he felt a tortured love. He found it introverted and conservative, while he was becoming more radical by the day. He could have retired to a cottage and written books, about the race bar and South Africa, but he was an agitated character, and the scholastic life would never have suited him. There was only one thing he really wanted to do – return to South Africa, where he was in a country which he loved and surrounded by people who loved him back. But he would not be able to return there while an increasingly repressive regime took hold; Trevor had always refused to return to South Africa while apartheid was still in place, and would refuse to travel by South African Airways.

Like many men of his class and generation, Trevor had spent little of his adult life in England, and found it mystifying and puzzling. He didn't hate England as such, but there was much of it that he failed to understand. He was now 70, and had bowed out of his bishoprics. Perhaps now was the time to retire, down to Wells perhaps, where he had been a pious and unsure ordinand all those years ago; yet the life of a gentle drowsing towards death amid the roses and rumours of a Cathedral close was never his style. Not for the first time in his life, Trevor was at a loose end. But fortune had played a great role in Trevor's life; he had always found himself in the right place at the right time and the year 1981 was no exception.

Donald Reeves was the vicar of St James, Piccadilly, a church which had built up a reputation over the years as a hotbed of radical thought and religious experimentation. Trevor, who loved to feel that he was in the centre of any action, was happy living in the middle of a great city:

> Trevor had nowhere to live, and a great friend of mine called Nadir Dinshaw recommended that he come and live with me at the rectory. There was a top flat with two bedrooms, a bathroom and sitting room.
>
> He used to tell me that of all the places he had been in this was the best. He was completely independent; there was a group of women who would do his laundry and prepare his meals and mother him a bit.
>
> He would help out at the Eucharist and say Matins and 7.30 and go to sleep. He would be away for three or four months of the year; he was the life of the place. He had an active social life and was great friends with MPs like Harry Greenway. Mark Tweedy, his friend from CR, used to have boozy suppers with him at an Italian restaurant around the corner.

It is never easy for two men, let alone clerics, to live together, but the two men rubbed along well. Donald Reeves was something of an *enfant terrible* in the Church, and Trevor respected that: 'We didn't chat much, but we did bump into each other on the staircase and make conversation. He was in fact deeply shy, but very much on my side. He would ask me why I wasn't made a bishop and he tried to arrange for me to be a chaplain in New York, which he thought would suit me.'

Reeves adds: 'He struck me as someone who was very angry, and depressed. He was a very withdrawn individual; slightly aloof, and certainly not one who would fit into a community. He loved children, and also the controlling aspect of it by being a father figure. He was scathing about the Church of England in the way that bishops sometimes are; he was also very pro the ordination of women, and open to other religions.'

Trevor was now fully retired and intended to devote his remaining years to raising publicity about the situation in South Africa. Based at the rectory at St James, Piccadilly, he could now dash around London and abroad to cajole and bully the powerful into action, and help raise money for the victims of the regime.

He channelled his unusual energy through the Anti-Apartheid Movement. The movement had begun life as a ramshackle outfit, spawned from the Committee of African Organizations (CAO) which was convened by Dr David Pitt and met in a dingy basement in Gower Street in the mid-1950s. In 1958, two years after Trevor had abruptly left South Africa, Dr Pitt was joined by a young student called Abdul Minty. The CAO had also received help from Canon Collins's Christian Action, which had offered financial support to the defendants in the Treason Trials of 1956–61. The CAO enjoyed the support of all kinds of politicians, including the dour David Steel, the mercurial Jeremy Thorpe and the individualistic John Grigg, who had resigned his peerage after making naughty comments about the Royal Family.

Trevor was involved in the movement from the early days, and way back in 1959 had organized a vigil outside South Africa House at which Trevor, along with Julius Nyerere and Michael Scott, spoke. But, despite Trevor's fame and the Movement's clear aims, it had remained largely ignored and unknown until the massacre at Sharpesville in March 1960. The massacre, and the ensuing clamp-down which it provoked, brought a new depth to the cause and placed greater pressure on British governments. As Trevor moved to Masasi in 1960, his commitment to the AAM weakened as Ambrose Reeves took a leading role. But his interest in South Africa, and his call for more sporting boycotts, had never waned. After 1976 and the Soweto uprising, a rebellion provoked by the insistence by the Pretoria government that Afrikaans be the only language of instruction in Bantu secondary schools, the call went up for an immediate arms embargo against South Africa. A year later, Steve Biko died in custody and the 'Black Consciousness' movement was banned; Trevor responded by launching the International Anti-Apartheid Movement to raise the profile of the group.

Even from the tropical outback of Mauritius, Trevor had been informed of the group's progress, and the impact that it was beginning to have. In March 1982, the movement held a three-day conference under the banner: 'South Africa: A Time to Choose'. It ended, predictably enough, with a rally in Trafalgar Square which attracted a crowd of over 200,000. Suddenly Western opinion, which had lain dormant and docile at best, seemed to be moving in Trevor's favour. That same weekend, paramilitaries destroyed the ANC's London offices; it had been believed that Oliver Tambo was in the offices and it was probably an attempt by South African security services to kill him.

From his tiny upstairs flat in Central London, Trevor, who was now 70 years old, masterminded operations. The sofa in his sitting room turned into his bed at night. He was kept in touch with the situation on the ground in Soweto and throughout the country by people from Africa, many of whom were in exile and often had served hefty prison sentences. He took the fight to the British Government and in particular Margaret Thatcher, whose politics he loathed but whose single-mindedness and immunity to charm he admired. He presented the case for sanctions against South Africa, but made very little headway. While his movement was receiving support from the usual suspects – *Guardian* readers, obstinate clergymen, artless students – he had been unable to elicit support for his case from the establishment.

And what was his case? Trevor always saw sanctions as a positive step which would bring down the government; his opponents, many of whom were decent and earnest liberals who agreed with many of his views, believed that they would simply hurt the people they were supposed to help. Trevor believed that sports boycotts had highlighted the scourge of apartheid in the complacent West.

But Trevor was unforgiving towards those who argued for partial sanctions, or no sanctions at all. He claimed that a comprehensive, all-out sanctions policy against South Africa was needed, for it would destroy the double-talk of Western governments. The British Government he held in particular contempt, for he claimed that it was a victim of the English disease in declaring its loathing of apartheid while stymying any effective action against it. He then claimed that the West was turning a blind eye to the South African incursions into Mozambique, Zimbabwe and Botswana and the death in police custody of men like Steve Biko and Neil Aggett. No, he would argue forcefully, sanctions did not work because those who had the power to use them did not have the will to use them; there was just too much at stake.

Trevor could never compromise, and his belligerence even irritated his sympathizers. As he once said: 'A choice against an effective sanctions policy is a choice for apartheid and can be nothing else.' Yet, deep down, Trevor felt that he was losing his battle to convince others of the horrors of apartheid. He believed that the younger generation made the right noises, but had never understood the sheer struggle that was required to make apartheid an issue for the rest of the world. And many remained unconvinced, and Trevor, who always believed in putting on a brave face, knew this. In a sermon delivered on 9 October 1983 at Great St Mary's, Cambridge, he admitted that his 'forty years' of struggle had not made the impact on the Church of England which he would have liked. It was the duty of all Anglicans to be agitators, for 'there is a deep reluctance on the part of many, who claim the name of Catholic, to avoid or evade precisely those challenges by claiming a spirituality and a doctrinal integrity opposed to anything as uncomfortable as the turbulence they create'.

And one of these challenges was Africa. 'Are we, as the Church of England, to be forever diplomatic about the way to compel the South African Government to give freedom and human rights and human dignity to its own citizens? Are we in our diplomacy to condemn what we call terrorism but to condone the spreading institutionalized violence of the state of Africa, in Central America and elsewhere?'

This pounding rhetoric was all very well, but Trevor knew that preaching from the safety of London was never going to be enough, and that he needed to travel to alert other world leaders to his cause. It was important that when he spoke, people knew that he spoke with authority. So he visited leading African states – Zimbabwe, Mozambique and Tanzania, where he paid a visit to his old friend Julius Nyerere. He was well received, particularly in Botswana, where there many exiles from his old Sophiatown days were living. Here, he understood the effect that the South African Government's policies were having on neighbouring states, many of which were poorly run and disastrously dependent on South Africa for trade and business. They were facing attacks by a well-trained South African army and air force, while Western governments continued to pour billions of pounds into South African business and commerce. Trevor's analysis of the situation facing these states was terribly simple – who now would take seriously the words of Mugabe, who had plundered his country and brought a great nation to its knees? But Trevor's blindness, often wilful and often naïve, had the great virtue of simplicity – there could be no compromise or equivocation; there had to be absolute commitment to destroying apartheid in all its forms.

He still felt betrayed by some African states. South Africa and Mozambique signed a treaty – the Accord of Nkomat, ostensibly a sign of peace between warring nations – which Trevor saw as a terrible capitulation of a weaker state to the stronger. Trevor saw any sign of *tendresse* between rival African nations – such as the agreement signed by President Machel of Mozambique and Pieter Botha of South Africa – as a tacit approval of apartheid.

Trevor, ever plausible and direct, was a key public figure for the anti-apartheid movement. From his early days in Sophiatown, he had learnt the value of publicity and the image; he was only too aware that in Catholic circles monasticism had the same appeal that the missionary had in Evangelical circles – and that the appeal of a solitary monk had greater appeal outside ecclesiastical circles. A monk who had spent the best years of his life in the shanty towns of Johannesburg carried a natural authority when he took petitions to Downing Street or appeared on *Any Questions*; there was an authority to him that an earnest politician or *bien-pensant* pop star could never convey.

He was relentless in his criticism of his own government. In a piece in *The Times* written in the mid-1980s, he condemned the West's appeasement of this pariah government:

> Behind all the negotiations and manoeuvrings and deceits of the past few years lies the deliberate policy of 'constructive engagement' with South Africa pursued by the Reagan administration and tacitly supported by the West. It is this which has allowed South Africa to pursue its acts of aggression and destabilization without protest and unhindered.
>
> It is this, too, that has encouraged (if indeed they need encouragement) the Western Powers, and particularly Great Britain, to invest billions in South African industry and commerce.
>
> It is this doubletalk of Western governments who profess abhorrence of apartheid and condemnation of violence but who totally refuse to use the only alternative – an effective sanctions policy – that constitutes their moral depravity and their acceptance of evil.

Yet despite such despondent language, Trevor was beginning to scent victory. In June 1984, President Botha of South Africa made a European tour, and paid a quick visit to Margaret Thatcher. Botha, who was keen to shore up international support, had his visit sabotaged by protestors from the Anti-Apartheid Movement, who followed the President throughout his curtailed visit and then held a mass rally in the centre of the city. More significantly, events were moving fast in South Africa; for the first time, Commonwealth countries were not agonizing over the evils of apartheid, but the practical ways in which they could overthrow it.

Suddenly in South Africa the international community was changing fast; for the first time, the Commonwealth countries were discussing not the evils of apartheid, but the positive and practical steps needed to overthrow it. To Trevor's annoyance, the British Government remained resolutely opposed to sanctions.

So Trevor knew that the movement needed to be better organized, and its aims more vigorously expressed, to keep the conscience of an apathetic public alive. He also knew that the movement needed a central aim; the dismantling of apartheid was too abstract for most people to appreciate. The movement was able to capture the imagination of a sleepy public by demanding the release of Nelson Mandela; a huge rally was held in Clapham Common in favour of his release and the need for sanctions. Mandela was not the crypto-Communist and arbitary terrorist that his enemies would have wished; he was not, as he demonstrated on his release, a cynical or bitter or self-seeking man, but a figure of huge principles and startling integrity who was prepared to be incarcerated for them. Trevor attended a series of bitter meetings at the Home Office, where, according to one official, there was 'blood on the carpet' as the monk berated Malcolm Rifkind and Geoffrey Howe.

Trevor soon appreciated that Foreign Office opinion on the subject of South Africa was shifting fast; most officials appreciated that British interests were not being served by standing up for South Africa. The Prime Minister, who was one of the few individuals capable of holding her own against Trevor, was politically astute enough to realize that she now needed to put pressure on the Government in Pretoria to listen to, and eventually release, Mandela.

Harry Greenway was a Conservative MP and a great friend of Trevor. A letter written to him at the time shows the urgency of Trevor's message, and how frustrated he was at the government's refusal to budge on its line on sanctions and to break off international relations or diplomatic ties or engage in any action which would lose the government potential trade or investment:

The Prime Minister is doing everything in her power to sidestep the Commonwealth Mission and to substitute yet further 'diplomatic' dialogue between the Foreign Secretary and President Botha. Totally ignoring African pleas for effective sanction and – even worse, the appalling suffering of the people under a State of Emergency. Including the torture of political prisoners for which we have ample evidence. I do not believe that the PM cares a damn about the suffering of African people and it is sheer hypocrisy for her to say that she does.

In a further letter, written after Trevor mistakenly thought that Greenway had signed an Early Day Motion rejecting sanctions against South Africa, he wrote:

This issue has been central to all my thinking and commitment since I wrote my book thirty years ago . . . I am deeply troubled that you should find it possible to sign such a motion when in fact you know nothing at first hand about the realities of the South African crisis and the meaning of apartheid and when plenty of other members of your party have not found it necessary to sign the motion.

By 1986, Pretoria was sensing the game was up, as television cameras filmed more examples of oppression and violence which were screened to a worldwide audience. The Commonwealth Secretariat, after a fact-finding mission to South Africa, concluded that there was little point in negotiating with a government and a nation trapped in a cycle of violence and counter-violence. Trevor, however, still feared that the weasel word 'dialogue', which was being used by the governments of Britain, the United States and West Germany, was being offered as their solution to apartheid.

By 1981, Trevor was supposed to have retired. Yet, six years later, in September 1987, he was convening a conference in Harare which highlighted the subject always closest to his heart – the plight of children in South Africa. The conference had been delayed for five months, and had proved to be very difficult to organize, as there were constant threats of attacks against delegates. Trevor gently reminded the delegates that the way a society treats its children is the best way of understanding its character. Academics and church nominees, along with an ailing Trevor and a group of priests, lawyers, social workers, journalists and community organizers from South Africa attended. Glenys Kinnock, the wife of the Labour Party leader, was also present. Victims of child torture, who bore the marks of torture, spoke at the Conference, and delegates read documents which detailed the torture of 9-year-old children. Delegates heard how there was a deliberate policy of terrorizing young people; during the 1986 emergency, nearly half the 22,000 people detained were under the age of 18 and many faced psychological and physical torture. The Afrikaans religious leader and conference organizer Beyers Naude and Oliver Tambo both thanked Huddleston in an address at the conference, the latter thanking 'our old friend and fellow combatant . . . for taking this important initiative. In you the children of our country have always found a protector and a second parent.'

It was at Harare that Huddleston said: 'The thing that sickens me from all these Western politicians I have been talking to all these years is the appalling assumption that it doesn't matter if it takes five, ten, fifteen years to end apartheid, and meanwhile hundreds of thousands of children are destroyed.' But Trevor underestimated the degree to which the US Congress had moved towards comprehensive sanctions by 1986. With this now in place, Pretoria was becoming isolated and, although much blood was needlessly shed between then and 1994, world leaders knew that the end of apartheid was in sight. Trevor, who was suffering from eye infections and general poor health, refused to ease up. In between visits to Moorfields Eye hospital, he attended an International Youth Conference in Delhi against apartheid and celebrated the seventy-fifth anniversary of the ANC. He visited America; received an honorary doctorate; and presented another petition to Downing Street.

Nelson Mandela's seventieth birthday approached, 18 July 1988 was Mandela Day, and a series of events were organized. Another mass rally was held at Hyde Park, at which both Trevor and Desmond Tutu spoke. Then, a huge pop concert was staged at Wembley Stadium, which was screened to over a billion people worldwide. The BBC threw aside its customary caution and filmed the whole ten-hour event live; the Scottish group Simple Minds were among the performers. Trevor was one of the first to arrive at the concert and one of the last to leave. He sat in the front row of the Royal Box, an unknown face to the thousands of teenagers dancing beneath, until his name was called out; suddenly a sea of faces stared at the elderly man, and he returned their interest with a wave. As the music thundered out across the stadium, Trevor kept smiling and tapping his feet, although thanks to his heavy-duty earplugs he was unable to hear a word. The concert was then followed by a rally in Glasgow, attended by 30,000 people who launched a Freedom March from Glasgow to London. Suddenly, the AAM had become as modish as Greenpeace or Amnesty International; membership doubled over the year.

Trevor kept true to his own watchwords: never relax; always press on. Again, he felt that South Africa was regaining the initiative, and took his message to Mauritius (where he spent nearly three weeks), Australia and, again, Nigeria, where he was given the General Commander of the Order of the Niger, for his services to the anti-apartheid movement. He returned to Mirfield, where he attended the requiem Mass for his old friend Mark Tweedy.

Again, he was at loggerheads with the Prime Minister, whom he loathed but also admired. She told him to stop repeating himself over the subject of sanctions; it was now up to South Africans themselves to determine their future. Both characters were resolute and single-minded; Thatcher, though, was an Anglican Tory from Low Church stock while her adversary was a Christian Socialist in the tradition of Charles Gore. Her religion preached self-reliance and discipline; his religion, biblically based on the Sermon on the Mount, was about sharing and a sense of equality. They disagreed with each other's religion and politics; little wonder they were poles apart.

In February 1990, after years of international pressure and some devilish politicking inside South Africa, Nelson Mandela was released. It was just what Trevor had hoped for, but it would force him to make decisions which would leave him desolate and lost.

28

Return to Africa

MANDELA'S RELEASE WAS EXTRAORDINARY, but so too were the events which precipitated it. The decline and eventual death of apartheid were startling and Trevor, even at his most hopeful and exuberant, could not have predicted it.

It was the economy, as much as Trevor's movement and international pressure, which destroyed apartheid. If the first wind of change swept the African continent in the 1950s, then the second occurred thirty years later. Few could have predicted this change; many on the right believed that the South African state would thrive well into the twenty-first century; that First World governments would pay lip service to boycotts and sanctions because they could not afford to make them work; that the South African state would survive Soviet-funded resistance from black guerrillas in Angola and Mozambique; that talk of an armed revolution within South Africa was nothing more than the demented ramblings of old men in Robben Island.

But ultimately apartheid was not destroyed by protest but by itself, for it couldn't deliver. The country's market had been distorted by rioting and the over-promotion of whites and the under-promotion of blacks; despite all these factors, South Africa was still a huge economy, with a Gross Domestic Product three times the size of Portugal's. But its resources had been drained by war in Angola and paranoia over Russian infiltration in Mozambique, and it remained vulnerable to the whims of the world market; gold, its chief export, which earned over half its foreign exchange, had slipped from $800 to $400 per ounce.

So when Trevor in England, and black activists and white radicals all over America, suddenly built up real momentum with their campaign, South Africa looked very vulnerable. Those Western countries whose banks and conglomerates had invested small fortunes questioned what returns they were getting on their stakes. The banks were prepared to anger liberals if their investments were profitable; when their balance sheets suggested otherwise, it was simply not worth the opprobrium heaped upon them.

The climate in Russia had changed, too. By 1989, to the delight of the free West, glasnost had spread like a benign virus through Russia and its government was keen to disentangle itself from Africa. A deal was struck; the Russians would remove both themselves and the Cubans from Africa, and agree not to supply troops and weapons to any front-line states or ANC guerrillas. In return, America would put pressure on the South Africans to stop promoting war in Angola and Mozambique, give Namibia the freedom it deserved and, most importantly, make a fresh start with democracy in South Africa.

So the stage had been set. On 2 February 1990, President F. W. de Klerk delivered an astounding speech, in which he stood up and pronounced, to a mass of white supporters, the end of three centuries of white supremacy in the south of the continent – a supremacy embodied for the last forty-four years in the shape of apartheid – and the birth of the new South Africa. White South Africa, meanwhile, shuddered at de Klerk's proposals as they looked across at a Tanzania governed by incompetence, Uganda ruled by tyranny and Nigeria riddled with corruption.

Trevor had waited for the opportunity to return, but was still not convinced by how deep the changes had been. He saw that the ANC was no longer banned, and that Nelson Mandela was now a free man. But he had been scarred by false dawns – especially in 1985 when a mood of optimism and hope had been quenched by a further wave of repression – and he needed to be persuaded that South Africa had really changed. He wrote to Oliver Tambo asking for his advice. The ANC's National Executive placed huge pressure on Trevor to come, saying: 'The ANC and the people of South Africa have benefited enormously from your selfless and unflinching devotion and contribution to our struggle for freedom, human dignity and justice.' Tambo, in person, said that it was vital that Trevor attend the upcoming ANC conference as a delegate, and he would ensure that he address the hall. All new or reborn countries either lionize or destroy figures from their past; the presence of a silver-haired cleric addressing his comrades in a country from where he had been banned for much of his life was a sign that South Africa had changed for ever. The conference was held from 2–6 July in Durban, and over 2,500 delegates attended it from all regions of South Africa.

Trevor flew out and arrived at Jan Smuts Airport, where he was welcomed by four top ANC leaders: Oliver Tambo, a devout Anglican; Nelson Mandela; Walter Sisulu; and Alfred Nzo. All four had remembered him in his youth, trampling around the dusty back streets of Sophiatown with his cross and black cassock. It was a particular joy for him to meet some of the adults whom he had known as scampering children battling for his affections, and he reflected: 'I have no doubt that, for me, it was my vow of celibacy, depriving me of the possibility of having children of my own, of being the father of a family, which made such love for so many children the most powerful force in my ministry.' In the West, Trevor's love for children could cause suspicion and dark rumours, but Trevor remained candid about his love for them. He believed that there were too many barriers between adults and children in England, and that neurosis about the possibilities of sexual abuse had caused a breakdown in genuine human warmth. In Africa, there was less reserve; people with nothing have less to hide and Trevor could respond to their warmth and directness. Being reunited with some of the children he had once known, Trevor could say without inhibition that he was experiencing 'a love that does no fade or decay or disappear with the years. And a love that was deeply, wildly reciprocated'.

Trevor described his return, and early days back in South Africa, in a sequel to *Naught for Your Comfort*. It was called *Return to South Africa: The Ecstasy and the Agony*. Written under considerable stress in ten days, it lacks the power and lucidity of his masterpiece, and it sold badly. But he knew that it was always going to be hard to follow up *Naught for Your Comfort*. That book was a masterful description of Trevor's thirteen years in Sophiatown, and deserves to rank alongside Alan Paton's *Cry, the Beloved Country* as a classic of South African literature. Trevor's book, though devoured by generations of undergraduates, is less well known than Paton's; but then Trevor was banned, along with his book, from the country in the mid-1950s.

The Sophiatown which Trevor depicts in *Naught for Your Comfort* is a fabled place. He is at the heart of the township, and has a jazz band and a swimming pool named after him. What saves the book from mere polemic or upmarket apologetics is the sense of huge vivacity he conveys – it is a township of jazzmen, swashbuckling journalists and politicians on the make, including a young lawyer called Nelson Mandela. In *Naught for Your Comfort*, the townships stand for a sense of camaraderie among black and white and a spirit of hope. Yet following the election of a Nationalist Government in 1948, and Trevor's departure from South Africa in 1956, the jazzmen and journalists had been exiled, or banned. Mandela was now in jail and Sophiatown was forcibly cleared of its inhabitants and a new white suburb arose called Triomf (Triumph) – a suburb built on a graveyard of dreams.

In the sequel, it is now 1991 and Trevor is an Archbishop who returns to those places which he haunted as a young priest. He sets out his own platform for peace and justice. In his thirty-five-year absence, he finds that much of South Africa has changed very much, yet in other ways it has not changed at all. Mandela is now back, and the jails are more or less emptied of their political prisoners. Television pundits and newspaper columnists talk excitedly about the 'new' South Africa. He also finds that many of the men who had done much of the damage are still in charge.

Trevor was not convinced by President F. W. de Klerk's perestroika, saying that it was as unconvincing as Mikhail Gorbachev's – not so much a revolution as a holding operation. De Klerk, after all, had held senior positions in the ruling National Party since the 1970s and was a product of the party machine. Apartheid, in Trevor's eyes, had not disappeared; it had just gone to a better tailor.

The book is charged with hope and forboding, and is peppered with quotes from the ANC conference. If President de Klerk could be kept to the mark . . . if the ANC could avoid the corruption of power and the 'enticements of western capitalism masquerading as democracy', only then could the new Johannesburg be the new Jerusalem, and its people be 'led in . . . at the golden gate of true fulfilment, peace and liberty'.

Whatever the book's faults, Trevor carried one great advantage which no politician or writer could ever bring to Africa. He wrote with a zeal which was appropriate both for a priest and for the one white man who, alongside Alan Paton, exposed the suffering and humiliation and waste that apartheid entailed for ordinary Africans. He was furious with those who saw apartheid as a 'mistake'. It took a priest with a natural spiritual instinct to see the political system's religious elements. Trevor saw apartheid as a moral crusade, underpinned by divine sanction, enforced by the police, supported by business interests and believed in by the majority of white South Africans. It was a form of armed robbery, carried out ostensibly for the good of the victim.

Trevor, then, had finally returned. After all the fighting, the thirty-five years of absence and struggle, he would finally achieve his dream. When he arrived, he was well received and large crowds came to see and hear him. Typically, Trevor arrived at a time of great carnage in South Africa. There was an uprising of black on black violence and the townships were being engulfed; there was violence between the Inkatha Freedom Party (IFP) and a response from the ANC's militant wing. These were reported in the press, and especially the *Johannesburg Star*. Trevor began to live up to his reputation of four decades ago, when an angry government denounced him as a 'turbulent priest' because of his involvement in anti-apartheid activities. Now 78, and within a day of arriving in South Africa, he was leading a peaceful protest march from the Central Methodist Church to the nearby Supreme Court in the middle of Johannesburg. Trevor was protesting in support of four trade union leaders who had appeared on charges of kidnapping and assaulting a policeman who was discovered by them in August last year while he was spying on them; something which he confessed at a press conference. He was accompanied by an ANC leader and the future President Thabo Mbeki, and leaders and supporters of trade union movements. In front of a national audience on state-controlled television, all South Africa could see was the tall, grey-haired Archbishop criticizing the trial as he talked to journalists on the court steps.

His first return to South Africa was the highlight of his year. He would make several more, culminating in a disastrous attempt to retire and die there in 1995, but there can be little doubt that the release of Mandela and his return to South African soil had brought a level of consolation to this most angry of men. As Chairman of the Anti-Apartheid Movement and the Defence and Aid Fund for South Africa he had toured the world, raised funds and visited political leaders. In effect, he had become the chief white spokesman for black South Africans, and had become angrier and more radical the older he had become. Although by 1991 the political climate had been almost reversed since his first homecoming thirty years before, he was not convinced, and needed to insist that apartheid would die before him. He had seen many false dawns before,

Now, both conservatives and liberals said that they were opposed to apartheid, but even after Mandela's release Western politicians would condemn apartheid without offering any real alternative policy. Trevor's simplicity was his greatest strength; like an Old Testament prophet he was able to see the battle as a clear one between good and evil, and had been exasperated by those who sought any compromise with de Klerk, such as well-meaning friends who said that they had opposed sanctions because of their concern for the welfare of blacks. On a personal level, Trevor also needed to believe that apartheid was still strong when any intelligent onlooker could see that it was disintegrating; his life was given meaning and defined through protest, and without that struggle it would lose all meaning and status. He spent his life furious at injustice; if that injustice disappeared, then he would not want to continue living.

And then his dear friend Oliver Tambo, whom he had known from their days at St Peter's, Rossentville, died. He delivered the eulogy in St Mary's Cathedral, Johannesburg, in April 1993, in which he paid tribute to Tambo's friendship and steadfast involvement with the ANC. On returning home, he lunched with Nelson Mandela, and the two men discussed the prospects of life in post-apartheid South Africa. In April 1993 he celebrated his eightieth birthday, which luckily coincided with an AAM international conference held at Church House, Westminster, on the subject 'Southern Africa: Making Hope a Reality'. Towards the end of the year, he flew to Johannesburg, where he gave the first Oliver Tambo memorial lecture on the prospect of free election in South Africa. Owing to a painful foot ulcer, he was sent to St George's Hospital, Tooting Bec, on 5 November; he was an absolutely impossible hospital patient, and after a rapid recovery at Mirfield and a flat belonging to friends, he returned to St James's Piccadilly on 7 January 1994.

He was desperate to return to die in South Africa, despite the reservations of Nelson Mandela, who believed that he would be happier and more useful back home. Meanwhile, as he prepared for his return to South Africa he continued his work in this country. As the date approached for 'free and fair' elections, he continued to harass the new Major government over its position in South Africa. In April that year he was allowed to enter South Africa House and vote for the

ANC in the General Election; the South African Government, having taken away his South African citizenship forty years before, granted him a passport which allowed him to vote. He travelled down to London, and was cheered by crowds as he entered South Africa House. He spoke of his joy at being allowed to cast a vote in a free election, as diplomats bristled behind him. The following month Trevor, who was under police guard, flew again to South Africa to see Nelson Mandela being inaugurated as the State President. In his hotel, he was confronted by an Afrikaner soldier with a Kalashnikov. The soldier, overwhelmed by the Archbishop's presence, said: 'I would like to touch the Archbishop.' He then added: 'I am an Afrikaner and I represent my people. I also attend the Dutch Reformed Church. I want to say on their behalf how deeply sorry I am for all the terrible things we have done to the black people of this country.' Huddleston calmed him down, explaining that this was now the new South Africa and that it was time to forget. The soldier was not convinced, saying that there was a need for penitence. He placed his gun to one side and removed his cap, asking an emotional Trevor to bless him.

He was becoming old and infirm. He fell in the flat he rented from the Conservative MP Tim Yeo and his wife Diane, and again was admitted to hospital, where he behaved spectacularly badly. He berated the nurses, and walked out of his hospital ward when he was bored and believed that he was well. He recuperated in Mirfield, where he received an award for all his work in Tanzania. He attended the launch of Nelson Mandela's best-selling autobiography *Long Walk to Freedom*, where he made an overlong and incoherent attack on apartheid. A life of intensity and struggle was beginning to leave its mark. In January 1995 he travelled to India, where he received another gong – the Indira Ghandi Award for Peace, Development and Disarmament. In front of a group which included Nelson Mandela, Trevor, who had had an imperial love of India since his father had served out there, paid tribute to the country's anti-apartheid work and, in particular, Mahatama Ghandi's 'unique example of overcoming evil through mortal action [which] touched the hearts and minds of people across the world and transformed the course of anti-apartheid struggle in Asia and Africa'.

Mandela, seeing his friend in the audience, said: 'He lived among people who suffered the atrocity of apartheid, loved them as his own family, wiped their tears and encouraged them to carry on their noble fight. So close a bond did it become that when he was called away to other duties he continued for the next four decades to work, pressing the world to take action on the plight of the South African people.'

Africa beckoned. Trevor knew that he was an ill man, and was determined to die in South Africa now that the country was free. Trevor, true to form, became obsessed with spending the remaining years which God would give him back in Africa, although African friends and sheer common sense suggested that it was a foolish move. He would sit in his room in Mirfield and read brochures about luxury houses to rent in South Africa alongside old copies of the *Christian Socialist Magazine*.

His friends were dubious about the move, but Trevor was stubborn. He said his farewells, and three weeks before his departure he booked into a hotel in Central London, where he held court to streams of supporters and allies. But his friends were right; the move was unrealistic; although he was fiercely independent, he was too old and infirm to live on his own. He wanted to live privately in Soweto with a nurse, but he was too angry and demanding for any nurse to cope with. Flying out to Johannesburg, he stayed in an old people's home where he was looked after by black servants. This situation was abhorrent to him; he railed against the old people's home, claimed that South Africa had not changed at all and returned to England, just three months after he had departed with huge fanfare.

Trevor found his return a crushing blow. Of course, it was naïve of him to think that he could ever have died gracefully in Africa, surrounded by adoring friends and loyal cohorts. He had been driven by guilt; he had always pledged to himself that Africa was his home and the place where he wished to die. There were also many African friends who wanted him out there, although wiser souls like Mandela knew that he would be a more effective friend of South Africa back in England.

But there were other reasons behind Trevor's abrupt return. His sad story highlighted the fact that Africa had changed, and many of the veterans of the anti-apartheid movement had found the change to a post-apartheid Africa more difficult than they imagined. Trevor was never a moderate; he was an absolutist, and in exile had been so close to the ANC and the Communist Party that Alan Paton argued furiously with him over his refusal to let Defence and Aid Fund money go to anti-apartheid liberals.

When Trevor returned to South Africa, to inaugurate the ANC Congress in Durban, he opened with the memorable line: 'Comrades, let us pray.' Trevor saw himself as a militant pastor to a movement, and that was the role he wished to continue when he returned to South Africa. But, despite a glut of media interviews and homecoming parties, Trevor was closeted in an all-white old people's home and was not consulted by the new leaders. The local religious community found him difficult; moral arrogance came naturally to a man who had been on the side of the angels for forty years, and Trevor did little to conceal his hubris. Little wonder that he left in a huff. As he was interviewed at Johannesburg airport on the way back to Britain, his parting shot was bitter: 'Apartheid still lives.' But he was not condemning Nelson Mandela; he was admitting that he needed the struggle and was unable to see life beyond it.

Trevor's crisis was shared by others. For many anti-apartheid campaigners, the crisis came sooner than they realized. Many of them, exiled in Britain for nearly thirty years, had always thought they wanted to return to South Africa; when the opportunity arose, most of them preferred to stay with the lives they had created in Britain. Despite all the noise and protest, only six of the sixty-strong exiles in the Defence and Aid office in London decided to return. And those who stayed in England needed to look closely into themselves; they had seen themselves as victims of a regime, and it was painful to realize that they had freely chosen their exile.

Many of the exiled members of the ANC leadership, who now occupied some of the top positions in government and were fervent supporters of the new 'Rainbow Nation' nationalism, had deeply divided loyalties. Some, including Mendi Msimang, who once headed up the ANC mission in London and was then South African Ambassador to Britain, used their political status to return abroad with renewed status. Others kept hold of illegal foreign bank accounts and passports.

And some of those activists who did bother to return were inexperienced. A lot of activists, especially those from former Communist states, lacked relevant experience, and it showed. A good rhetorician does not make a good manager. Many believed South Africa's participation in the 1992 Olympics was a shambles and most felt that Sam Ramsamy, leader of the sports boycott in exile and now head of the South African Olympic Committee, was hopeless at sports administration.

The ANC was famously divided by vicious internal politics. Daniel Kitson had served twenty years in jail for his role as number two in the ANC's guerrilla movement, but on his release was declared a non-person, expelled from the movement and had his employment and pension ended, for he failed to distance himself from his wife's ideological error in setting up the City of London anti-apartheid movement as a rival to the main movement.

Of course, revolutions destroy the young. Those anti-apartheid activists who returned from exile felt a massive gap between themselves and their more parochial colleagues in South Africa. Those who returned to Africa needed to change their heart as well as mind; Trevor, and many of his generation, were unable to change.

29

The End

SLOWLY, TREVOR WAS FACING THE END. There was only one place where he would be looked after and cared until his death, so he returned to the Community in Mirfield, from where he had set off as a priest. Despite his differences, he had always identified with the Community's ideals, its religious beliefs and its order. Of course, he had many friends outside the religious world, but the Community was his only family – a fact that he would proclaim flamboyantly throughout his life – and it was right that he should stay there.

Up in Yorkshire, he was looked after by some of the younger and more energetic brethren, and most particularly Fr Nicholas Stebbing. He would make brief visits to London; in June 1996 he had breakfast with Nelson Mandela at Buckingham Palace, where he was told by the President that he had done the right thing by staying behind in England. This cheered Trevor up enormously. He would also visit old friends in London, and especially the Ramptons.

But he was an old man, and spent most of his time back in Mirfield. Like many members of the Community who had been bishops, he found it hard to adapt to living amongst his brethren again. He could be moody and depressed as well as energizing and uplifting. He had been away from the Community for thirty-four years and only spent four years at Mirfield. Tension still existed between him and some brethren, who remained suspicious of his fame and argued that he was just one of many missionary priests from the Community who had worked in Africa. Trevor, though, did remain loyal to the Community and its friends.

As he grew more ill, so he became more confined to his room. Like many old people, he loved to be surrounded by objects. Close by his bed lay an alarm clock, a torch, Dextral sugar tablets, painkillers and a glass of water. He would follow world events by reading *The Times* and the *Sunday Telegraph*, and discuss politics with anyone around him. When eating with the Community, he could treat fellow brethren as an audience at a public meeting; he tended to talk at people rather than with them, and even at the end of his life this deeply shy man found it very hard to let go of his public persona. But he loved listening to young people in the evenings, as he chatted to them about politics, music and literature and the arts over a glass of whiskey. With Mirfield students around him, Trevor would show off his appreciation of poetry and music, and enthuse about the latest biographies and novels which he had ordered from Hatchards. Trevor had always adored poetry; his copy of the *New Oxford Book of English Verse* had markers against those poems which were special to him – including Thomas Hardy's 'Midnight on the Great Western', an evocation of a boy leaving home, journeying towards a world unknown. He would read poetry aloud on Sunday mornings with passion and involvement.

The diabetes which he had endured for forty years continued to aggravate him; he also suffered from arthritis and other ailments of old age. He would cry out in pain and berate God when he was being undressed. But he demonstrated the courage which he had shown throughout his life, and was dignified enough to be brave in his continual fight against diabetes and old age and depression. When asked about his 'black dog', he was magnificently insouciant: 'Of course I am not a depressive. It is just the insulin that makes me feel "depressed"'; and still in old age he had the strength to rise above his depressions and be as joyful and charming as possible.

As the night closed in, so Trevor's faults could be magnified. He was always a great name dropper, and had a great sensitivity of being rejected; he would lash out at other members and arrange trips away and give plenty of sermons in which he played the leading role. But to the end he remained a man of real prayer; almost to the last day he said his Offices faithfully and would intercede for friends. And those who gave him Communion found him very collected, and said what a gratifying experience it was. At the same time, he would berate a God in whom he could find it hard to believe.

At the beginning of January 1998, he travelled down to London to unveil a bust of himself in South Africa House. He was in sparkling form, and gave a tremendous speech. But he was becoming physically weaker and his speeches were more obsessive and strange. He was awarded a KCMG in Prime Minister Tony Blair's first New Year's Honours List, which thrilled him; he then returned to Mirfield and berated his delighted brethren for not showing enough appreciation for his award.

But he became calm again towards Holy Week, as he cast off his self-pity and agreed to take painkillers, which made him more euphoric. On Holy Saturday, he asked if the Prior would hear his Confession. The Prior did, and he later described the confession as the single most important thing in his life.

On Easter Monday, after tea, he fell in his room after trying to get to the basin to wash his cup. He fell on the floor in agony and swore. He ripped off his dog collar in disgust as he showed that he was not putting up with a God who would treat him like this. He went to hospital, where it transpired that he had not broken but bruised his shoulders, and he discharged himself the next morning. There was talk of him going to a nearby nursing home, but Trevor could not have borne the presence of strangers. He suffered terrible pain, especially at night. He had a college student with him – Lee Bennett – who nursed Trevor and had to put up with his brutish behaviour. Trevor would harangue him for not giving him enough painkillers and told him he had no right to be a priest. He had cracked ribs and his skin became over-sensitive to the slightest touch. But, yet again, he calmed down as he prepared for death. He kept saying that he wanted to die, but stopped railing at God for not letting him. The following morning he was beyond eating and drinking; by ten o'clock in the morning the colour vanished from his face and he died.

Trevor's obituaries were lengthy and eloquent; all cited him as the radical monk whose anti-apartheid views were defined by his belief in the Incarnation. The *Daily Telegraph* produced the most elegant and sympathetic obituary, which sought to explain to its readers the religious anger which drove Trevor's life. In its most arresting section, the anonymous obituarist noted:

> Huddleston was far removed from the popular image of an agitator. A gentle person, of a deeply religious nature, he exuded warmth, joy and friendship, and was perhaps happiest in the company of children – who adored him.
>
> Yet beneath all this, and often finding dramatic expression, was immense strength and moral courage, and an absolute unwillingness to compromise with what he regarded as evil, especially when this caused suffering to the weak.

The *Guardian*, meanwhile, overcame its lunatic bigotry towards religion and gave Canon Eric James, a putative biographer of Trevor, the opportunity to explain his life from his early childhood in Hampstead to his final years with the Community. James ended, with typical perception: 'If Trevor Huddleston seemed sometimes a man with a cause – to the point of obsession – it was only because he was, first, a man with compassion for individual children of God.'

On the same page, Alan Webster, the former Dean of St Paul's, described him as 'spontaneous, affectionate, steadfast, deeply prayerful. He was perceived by blacks in South Africa as refreshingly unEnglish, partly because he refused to compromise. He succeeded in authenticating God in the real world by living justly with his neighbours.'

In the *Independent*, the pathologically naughty biographer Michael-de-la-Noy dutifully covered the old ground of Trevor's life, before adding at the end:

> It [Canon James's new biography] is expected to explain his sudden translation from Stepney to Mauritius, necessitated in order to hush up a scandal which would raise few eyebrows today, but which the Establishment believed the Church of England would not live with at the time.

The Economist painted a more general picture:

> When Trevor Huddleston spoke, however firmly, he sounded almost the caricature of the kindly, cultivated English vicar who might join you for tea on the lawn after croquet. Tall, pale and sweet-faced, he seemed an unlikely champion of poor, black South Africa against the bully boys of the South African police.

There were other obituaries. Joe Rogaly, writing in the *Financial Times*, described Huddleston as

> [a] man of God, a monk, a socialist possessed of deep faith in Christ and a consistent uplifter of the spirit. He held unwaveringly to his perception of humanity as an expression of the divine. He skilfully manipulated the great and the good in the interests of the wretched . . . He died with the flame of his great crusade, the betterment of the human condition for the love of Christ, held high.

On hearing of his death, Nelson Mandela, the new President of South Africa, said that he was a 'pillar of wisdom, humility and sacrifice to the legions of freedom fighters in the darkest moments of the struggle . . . Fr Huddleston embraced the downtrodden.' Archbishop Tutu said he 'made sure that apartheid got onto the world agenda and stayed there. If you could say that anybody single-handedly made apartheid a world issue, then that person was Trevor Huddleston.' The British Prime Minister, Tony Blair, echoed Mandela's words by saying: 'Trevor Huddleston was a remarkable and a wonderful man. He will be remembered most for the role he played in the fight against apartheid in South Africa, a fight that would not have been won without the courage and commitment . . . Huddleston showed.'

A funeral requiem was sung in the Community's church, which had been Trevor's home for almost sixty years. A solemn Mass was celebrated by the Superior Fr Crispin Harrison and attended by the brothers. Those who attended the drizzly Mass included the Archbishop of York, David Hope, who was the order's official Episcopal visitor; the Bishop of Wakefield Nigel McCulloch, as the local diocesan visitor; and the South African High Commissioner Cheryl Carolus, who was representing the South African government. Among the one hundred relatives and close friends were Lord and Lady Parkinson – Ann Parkinson was Trevor's niece – and Abdul Minty, who had founded the Anti-Apartheid Movement with Trevor in the 1960s.

The requiem was steeped in Anglo-Catholic ceremony. The monks sang Miserere mei, Deus – 'Have mercy upon me, O God' – reciting the 51st Psalm in a chant that, in the words of one journalist, 'seemed not to break the silence of the great monastic church'. And then came the hymn 'Jesu, Son of Mary' with a verse that could have been written for Trevor Huddleston himself:

> Think, O Lord, in mercy
> On the souls of those
> Who, in faith gone from us,
> Now, in death repose.
> Here 'mid stress and conflict
> Toils can never cease;
> There the warfare ended,
> Bid them rest in peace.

In his sermon, Fr Harrison said that Trevor had touched and changed lives as he fought injustice and defended the poor and the oppressed. 'So he belongs not just to us gathered here today but to the whole world,' he said as clouds of incense rose from the thurible and above the altar. The intercessions were for all those who had worked with Trevor Huddleston as monk, priest, Bishop of Masasi, Bishop of Stepney and Archbishop of the Indian Ocean. Surrounded by six tall candles, the coffin was draped in a pall and on top of the pall was the gold mitre of the man who loved Africans and was loved by them.

The weather was filthy, and the Calder Valley seemed desolate and bereft. It rained throughout most of the Mass, but bright sunshine burst out through the clouds as the monks chanted the Contakion of the Dead and carried the coffin to the waiting hearse.

Three months later, on 29 July, a memorial service was held at Westminster Abbey. Two African choirs sang together:

> Farewell good friend
> Until we meet again
> Farewell, sweet friend . . .

Most of all, Africa was there to carry Huddleston's ashes back to Sophiatown, the one-time Jo'burg slum where he started to, in the words of John Ezard in the *Guardian*, 'fight apartheid with a tongue and pen like swords tempered with love'. Nelson Mandela delivered a message to the 2,000-strong congregation, in which he announced that Trevor's ashes would be flown to South Africa that night, and then be interred at the priest's Sophiatown church.

Repeating words first spoken at a South African service honouring Huddleston, Mr Mandela said: 'May we who gather in thanksgiving for his life be as ready as he is to join hands across nations and continents in order to address the need of – especially – the poorest of the poor. May we show the same impatience with empty words which do not translate into action.'

At the memorial service, some one hundred and eighty-three human rights groups were represented, with seventeen overseas ambassadors. A large number of peers and MPs attended, but only one government representative, Peter Mandelson. The rest of the congregation were ordinary black and white people, whom Huddleston had known or won over through four decades of strong argument. The singing at the service was English and African; there were traditional English anthems and jazzed-up village chants from black townships. The abbey choir's tribute was Vaughan Williams's setting of Milton's final lines in *Samson Agonistes*: 'Nothing is here for tears, nothing for wail; nothing but well and fair, and what may quiet us in a death so noble . . .'

A South African quartet gathered around a microphone to sing 'Farewell Good Friend', a song written for Huddleston. They preceded it with a favourite Zulu lullaby, 'Chilon Chilo'. Three members of the quartet were the Manhatten Brothers, formed in the priest's Sophiatown days. They sang with the London South Africa choir. Then Hugh Masakela blew an improvised solo from the pulpit. It was informal, but apt.

The Bishop of Masasi read the lesson and Lady Parkinson, Trevor's niece, read 'The True and Living God', written by Trevor Huddleston in 1964. The South African minister of Foreign Affairs read a message from the President of South Africa, and Abdul Minty, Deputy Director-General of the Multilateral Branch, Department of Foreign Affairs, South Africa, read *The Freedom Charter* (1955).

Lord Hughes of Woodside, Chairman of Action for South Africa, read an extract from *Naught for Your Comfort* and Mike Terry read an excerpt from Trevor Huddleston's *Return to South Africa: The Ecstasy and the Agony*. The Rt Revd Jim Thompson, the Bishop of Bath and Wells, gave an address in which he said: 'Clergymen of my generation were more influenced by Trevor than we were by the Beatles.' It was an appropriate send-off for a religious figure who was more influential than anyone else who had been honoured in the abbey over the decade.

Trevor had promised to haunt Crispin Harrison if his ashes were not interred in the church of Christ the King, Sophiatown, but they languished in the monastery for nine months after his death. There was a dispute over money; the diocese wanted the Community to pay for the restoration of the church, which had just been handed back by a group of Afrikaner Evangelicals to the diocese of Johannesburg. The Community did not believe that this was the right use of funds, and its alternative offer to restore a chapel was accepted. So, an Anglican dispute clouded the death of this most disputatious of Anglicans; Trevor's ashes now lie in that same church which he had entered as a young priest in 1943.

30

Endpiece

A WEEK BEFORE HIS DEATH, Trevor sat in his room at Mirfield and chatted away to old friends. Sipping a glass of malt whisky, he enthused about a new book on the 'Theology of Forgiveness' and then discussed reconciliation and his old enemy President de Klerk, 'who has done so much evil'. Behind his head, on the wall behind, was a framed document of his investiture as a KCMG at Buckingham Palace and a congratulatory telegram from the Duke of Edinburgh, which had thrilled him when it arrived in Yorkshire. Most prominent of all, though, was a picture of President Mandela, leading behind his chair at Buckingham Palace. 'He's a remarkable man', said Trevor with the satisfaction of seeing a lifetime's task complete. This little picture of a dying Trevor at Mirfield encapsulates much of the man – his interest in books, his love of justice, his obsession with the British establishment, his ever sustaining faith and, above all, his love of Africa.

There is little doubt that Trevor's class, and the patrician manner which accompanied it, brought out an authoritarian and dogmatic side to his character. He was the son of a commodore in the Royal Indian Navy and the surity of his background, and the ease with which he carried himself, enabled him to achieve more than a more apologetic and tentative character could ever have. The white public schoolboy and product of Oxford University was suddenly put in charge of a parish of 100,000 black Africans and, later, of an African diocese of 100,000 black Africans – while seeing none of the obvious continuities with the British Raj. And it was as part of a 200-year-old missionary movement that Trevor, while trampling through the streets of Sophiatown, changed history by lifting his hat to a poor washerwoman, while being watched with amazement by her

9-year-old son Desmond Tutu. It was Trevor's natural charm, aligned with a formidable will and natural authority, which enabled him to communicate across racial divides and religious barriers. He would happily chat to elderly dowagers and Swindon railwaymen; he could speak to policemen as well as politicians, and his sure touch was invaluable when he was fighting oppression and hooliganism and striving for better living and employment conditions. His obstinacy and single-mindedness caused unhappiness among his friends, who found his political attitudes hardline and intransigent; yet such attitudes were explained by his loathing of the British policy of gradualism, a view which he hated for its moral corruption.

Everything Trevor ever wrote or said was the product of his experience in Africa. It was the six years he spent at Sophiatown, followed by the seven which he spent at Rossentville as Prior and Provincial, which form the heart of his life. Here he was perceived as unEnglish, because of his unwillingness to compromise. Within days of his arrival in Africa, he was immersed in the onslaught against apartheid, in both the Church and the state – and it was an attack which would eventually be recounted in his bestselling book *Naught for Your Comfort*. With the voice of a visionary and a striking face, he was able to alert not just fellow Christians, but Jews, Hindus, Muslims and agnostics to the horrors of apartheid. As the novelist Nadine Gordimer wrote: 'I have no religious faith, but when I look at that photograph of a profoundly religious man, I see godliness in a way I can understand deeply. I see a man in whom prayer functions . . . as a special form of intelligent concentration.' It was his outstanding gifts of leadership and courage which were brought out in Africa, as he learnt to communicate both as a speaker and as a writer. Of course, this would land him in trouble – with the authorities, with disgruntled Englishmen, and with two furious clerics – Geoffrey Clayton, Archbishop of Cape Town, and Geoffrey Fisher, the Archbishop of Canterbury. It was Fisher who said to him: 'You are entirely wrong in the methods you are using to fight this situation.'

Trevor was unrepentant. He argued with Fisher, as he did throughout the remainder of his life, that since apartheid was fundamentally evil it could not be reformed or collaborated with. This view would lead him to be one of the first to advocate a sports and cultural boycott of South Africa, and demand that economic sanctions be applied by the rest of the world. 'The Christian', he once said, 'is always an agitator if he is true to his calling.' In *Naught for Your Comfort*, he likens apartheid to the racism of Nazi Germany and to slavery. He concludes: 'Hell is not a bad description of South Africa.' As he was about to leave Sophiatown, a government official told him: 'You deserve to be drummed out of the country or strung up from the nearest lamp-post as a renegade.' Many Englishmen would have flinched at such insults; Trevor simply took them a sign of the power of his message.

After his mysterious recall, he spent four unhappy years in England – two as Novice Guardian and then as Prior of the Community House at Notting Hill, London. Here he tried to cope with the bereavement of Africa and with a host of invitations and piles of correspondence dealing with his time in Africa, and more particularly *Naught for Your Comfort*. Masasi followed, thanks to the prompting of Evelyn Baring, and here he became Bishop of a diocese in Tanganyika, just as the fourth poorest country in the world was on the verge of independence under the leadership of Julius Nyerere. They worked as partners – Nyerere, a Roman Catholic, would call him 'our bishop' – and they remained friends, and supporters of African socialism, for life. Back in England in 1968, he spent eight years as the suffragan bishop of Stepney, where he pined for Africa and found the pastoral reorganization and lack of real religion frustrating. He never believed that it was right for him to spend so much time dealing with redundant churches and passing resolutions; he saw himself as a pastor who dealt with victims. It was at Stepney, too, that his theatrical side was indulged through his many appearances on radio and television, where he was renowned as a clear and magnificent broadcaster. When the BBC telephoned for a quote on Africa, he would always make time to do it – and immediately, if necessary. His words on screen were validated by his face. As one viewer noted, he looked as if he was being crucified on behalf of the oppressed: 'What you saw was a black-cassocked, chin-out, fighter-martyr.' But he was a generous martyr; he had a wonderful gift for friendship; and he adopted a wise and open approach to both friends and enemies. He would challenge and cajole others, but however hard he pushed himself, he was endlessly gentle with the troubled.

Despite a personal crisis and much depression, Trevor proved a wise choice to steer the diocese in the face of growing hysteria against the Pakistani population and an increase in the immigrant population.

At the age of 65, it was felt that Trevor needed to be relieved of the responsibilities of a London diocese, while still having it within him to be an excellent bishop overseas. So another overseas appointment beckoned, this time in Mauritius, where for five years he served as both Bishop of Mauritius and Archbishop of the Indian Ocean.

His province was remote, and took in both the Seychelles and the Malagasy Republic. But Trevor was alive to change, even at his age. 'Maybe God can widen the mind of a 70-year-old,' he would say with a chuckle. His experiences in the Indian Ocean, where Christians were very much in the minority in the presence of Muslims and Hindus, deepened his appreciation of non-Christian faiths. Here he became a strong supporter of multi-faith collaboration in the face of much racism and poverty. Shortly after his retirement, at the Oxford Movement's sesquicentenary celebration, he preached in the University Church at Oxford to commemorate Keble's 1833 Assize sermon:

> If we are truly Catholic, then universality – the proclamation of our belief that this is God's world, God's universe – is surely a prior concern to that which would make institutional Christianity our chief objective. It is interfaith ecumenism – the recognition that dialogue between Hindu and Christian, Muslim and Christian, Buddhist and Christian must have priority – that should be the aim of us all at this moment in history.

After Masasi, he returned to London, where he based himself at St James's Piccadilly, a centre for radical thought and experimentation. He would also accept the provostship of the shared Anglican-Nonconformist theological college of Selly Oak, Birmingham. But his cause remained Africa; he became President of the Anti-Apartheid Movement and preached against apartheid just as vehemently as he did against the rest of the world's indifference against it. For him, the Christian church had always been too comfortable and conservative, and his militancy had always been more welcome among political groups than fellow clerics. The Anti-Apartheid Movement was Marxist in tone and its language was left; it spoke in Marxist terms and its support for sanctions and isolation became articles of faith. Could the Anti-Apartheid Movement have been larger and more effective if Trevor had been more pragmatic and willing to seek support from those of the centre and right? Was Trevor simply too blinkered, believing that the end of apartheid would result in massive bloodshed and being pleasantly surprised when the handover was peaceful? Trevor was dogged throughout his life, but perhaps it takes a peculiar type of obsessiveness to speak out against the negotiations and dialogue which would eventually bring democracy to South Africa. Eventually he would be forced to leave Africa behind, and died in Mirfield, surrounded by the love and selfless care of his fellow brethren.

But there is a time to cast aside politics and Africa. For at the heart of Trevor's life lay his Christianity. From childhood he had felt called to the priesthood, and the High Anglican Lancing College was a huge influence. 'I owe everything to the Community,' he would say, and it was only the spartan Christianity within him, structured by the discipline of an Anglo-Catholic monastic community, which gave him the strength to accept his recall from South Africa. It was Donald Mackinnon, a friend from his Oxford days, who noted just how central to his life was the Profession he made on St Mark's Day 1941: 'He has never sought to dissolve the bonds that have bound him to the Community of the Resurrection . . . A deep and costly engagement with the issues of the societies in which he found himself ministering was not the expression of a reckless "trendiness" but rather the inevitable consequence of a persistent religious fidelity.'

And his Christianity was Incarnational. Believing strongly that God has 'made of one blood all nations of men for to dwell on the face of the earth', his own life was transformed as a white person serving, predominantly, black women and children: ministering to them, fighting untiringly for them. And it was his stark, clear Christianity – at heart, Trevor was an old-fashioned Man of God – which gave him an unshakeable belief in the victory of good over evil, a belief which took a simple parish priest in an urban slum and transformed him into an international figure, which Church bodies and governments and oppressors had to take very seriously. He was an indomitable priest who was able to show to an unbelieving, educated West what it could mean to be an Anglican in the twentieth century. On hearing of his death, he was compared by one African journalist to a great baobab tree which stands in the middle of the village. The tree, although ageing and withered, stays upright as a testimony to the village's triumphs and tribulations. Such a tree does not fall.

Afterword

ROWAN WILLIAMS

TREVOR HUDDLESTON'S NAME stands in the forefront of the names of those who have understood that the experience of racial struggle in Africa, and especially in South Africa, is not something different in kind from what goes on in the 'advanced' societies of the West: so much is clear from his work and witness in the UK, as Bishop of Stepney, and as an active and activating presence in so many anti-racist movements for nearly twenty years. It is appropriate, then, to celebrate such a man by attempting a sketch of what it is that unites the various forms of racial injustice, and what exactly it is that the Christian Church's reflection has to bring to bear on what is becoming a more, not less, critical situation in our own society and in the world at large. This means attempting a definition of 'racism' and beginning the task of theological critique. It may be thought that this is both too elementary and too ambitious a project – too elementary because we know what racism means, and it is a waste of time to devote more words to it (rather than getting on with practical responses); too ambitious because it requires a degree of historical and sociological expertise, personal engagement, and innovative theological power that few people – certainly not white academics at Oxford – possess. None the less, the effort seems to be worthwhile, however inadequate its results. I am aware both of a continuing confusion about the word 'racism' itself, and of a rather uncertain quality to some of our theological responses – as if the appeal to a liberal sense of human equality would do the job for us; if this essay can suggest clarifications in both these areas, it will not have been wasted.

1. Defining racism

It is still common enough in Britain to assume that 'racism' is essentially a word that refers to *attitudes*. If we hear statements like 'Britain is a profoundly racist society' or 'the Church is a racist institution', we are inclined ('we' being a large part of the white population – and even the black population – of the United Kingdom) to be baffled or angered. It sounds as if someone is accusing the nation or the Church of racial prejudice, of disliking or despising black people; and it is reasonable enough, in many cases, to reply that we do *not* have such attitudes, that we do not consider black people inferior or treat them differently. This *may* be a self-deceiving response, but it is not always so; and a person in Cornwall or Cumbria or Norfolk may genuinely not know what could possibly be meant by being told that she or he lives in a 'racist' environment. The sense in which it is true that they do so needs careful statement.

Two things compound confusion here, I believe. One is the common radical elision of 'racism' and 'Fascism', manifest in the names of several anti-racist pressure groups, as if racism were simply a function of a particular kind of authoritarian politics, classically represented by the Third Reich and its allies. Several points need to be made about this. German (not Italian) Fascism did indeed rest upon a commitment to the superiority and glorious historical destiny of a particular variety of Caucasian peoples; but if it is suggested that racism entails commitments like this, it is manifest nonsense to say that ours is a racist environment. The running together of racism and Fascism as a single compound iniquity is – you might say – a subtle device of the devil to prevent us grasping the *real* dangers of these phenomena. If we suppose that racism is the crude mythology of the *Herrenvolk*, and if we suppose that Fascism *is* the overt and brutal suppression of non-Caucasians, we are dangerously narrowing our political imagination, making ourselves less capable of seeing and understanding racism in the structures of societies, and Fascism in a pervasive and often elusive trend towards centralized authority, the disenfranchizing (effectually if not openly) of a working population, and the militarization of a national economy. Of course, there are neo-Nazi groups around, which need to be resisted strenuously: the fact that ours is a society that tolerates them, and that our police forces in some areas can give every appearance of luke-warmness in enforcing the law against them, is scandalous. But that is where the heart of the racist problem lies – in those who *know* they are not 'Nazis', but are culpably unaware of the nature of their society as a whole. If racism were simply a problem about the National Front, it would be a good deal easier; as it is, the glib identification of racism and Fascism provides an excellent alibi for the powers that be, because it is so obviously absurd. 'If *this* is racism, of course we're not guilty of it.'

Racism, then, is not the same as overt supremacist ideology. But here the second confusing factor comes into play. Racism is not overt, so it must be hidden; it must be buried deep in our consciousness, needing to be excavated by suitable means. Part of this is rooted in a familiar kind of liberal self-punishment: my good will alone does not secure change, and so perhaps it is impure and in need of challenge and refinement. The popularity of 'racism awareness' as a theme for training events inside and outside the churches, and the development of a whole philosophy of concealed racism, reflect this sort of response. It is not wholly to be dismissed, though it has come in for some fierce criticism from writers both black and white:[1] there are, for most of us, areas of unexamined prejudice and fear that are none the worse for being looked at. But what is there here beyond the inducement of further white guilt exposing itself to further black anger? If 'racism awareness' suggests that the solution lies in improved consciousness of one's own imprisonment in negative attitudes, it risks making the whole issue private, or even seeing it as primarily a question about white people's minds rather than black people's lives.

To a lesser degree, the same thing holds for the pouring of energy into campaigns for the sanitizing of children's reading. There is no doubt that, *given certain cultural circumstances*, a book such as *Little Black Sambo* will reinforce models of black people as alien, mildly comic, or mildly alarming. But since reading is and ought to be – for adults as well as children – an experience in which acceptable and unacceptable images and proposals crowd upon us together, there is never any real possibility of wholly 'safe' literature. There are circumstances in which we ought to be *very* wary of exposing children to certain images; but if we are really interested not in preserving a child's supposedly innocent awareness but in an effective change of relations in society at large, a degree of sceptical detachment about the literature issue will probably do no harm. The banning of a 'racist' book in an area – a country – in which black people are systematically disadvantaged is not going to get us very far (any more than a ban on alcohol advertising at Christmas would reduce the menace of drunken driving in a context in which seasonal alcohol abuse is taken for granted). The priorities should be (and happily often are) the reinforcement in newly written literature of the normality of racial pluralism, and, still more, education in understanding a social history and a social practice which has built racial disadvantage into itself (part of which will, of course, involve the explanation of how literary and narrative and pictorial stereotypes are created).

If these confusions – racism as overt supremacist ideology and racism as secret sin – are set aside or at least put in context, how are we to define the term? The World Council of Churches produced in 1975 a brief report on a consultation dealing with 'Racism in Theology: Theology against Racism', in which they suggested seven marks of the presence of racism;[2] these provide an unusually clear picture of what we are talking about.

Racism is present whenever persons, even before they are born, because of their race, are assigned to a group severely limited in their freedom of movement, their choice of work, their places of residence and so on.

Racism is present whenever groups of people, because of their race, are denied effective participation in the political process, and so are compelled (often by force) to obey the edicts of governments which they were allowed to have no part in choosing.

Racism is present whenever racial groups within a nation are excluded from the normal channels available for gaining economic power, through denial of educational opportunities and entry into occupational groups .

Racism is present whenever the policies of a nation-state ensure benefits for that nation from the labour of racial groups (migrant or otherwise), while at the same time denying to such groups commensurate participation in the affairs of the nation-state.

Racism is present whenever the identity of persons is denigrated through stereotyping of racial and ethnic groups in text books, cinema, mass media, interpersonal relations and other ways.

Racism is present whenever people are denied equal protection of the law, because of race, and when constituted authorities of the state use their powers to protect the interests of the dominant group at the expense of the powerless.

Racism is present whenever groups or nations continue to profit from regional and global structures that are historically related to racist presuppositions and actions.

Racism is here presented with exemplary lucidity and comprehensiveness for what it is, an issue about power, decision and definition. As Ann Dummett points out, in what is still one of the best available studies of racism in the UK, it is in this respect closely akin to other sorts of disadvantage, 'one kind of injustice among many. The very poor in England are insulted for their poverty, bullied by officials, exhaustively interrogated before they can get free school meals or a clothing allowance for their children, placed under intolerable strains and then told they are inadequate when the strains are too much for them';[3] though racism compounds the injustice by assuming the right to tell people (including British citizens) where they can live, the right to deport those deemed undesirable. And it is a simpler matter to identify the victim because of accent or skin colour. But the oppression of the poor and the oppression of the ethnically distinct have in common one central feature picked out by Ann Dummett at the very beginning of her book:[4] the oppressor makes the claim to *tell you who you are*, irrespective of your intention, will, preference, performance. Only certain people have the right to construct an identity for themselves; others have their roles scripted for them. Although all human beings are liable to be drawn into the fantasy lives of others, individual and collective, racism and, in a rather different way, class injustice allow fantasy to be acted out in reality: with these people we really can impose the roles we fantasize because we have the political or economic power to determine the options of the powerless and, in some measure, the very *self*-perception of the powerless. Many of the Victorian poor adopted the images offered them by the wealthy, as even the barest acquaintance with nineteenth-century fiction will show. Many of the disadvantaged in our present society will at some level do the same, accepting the social estimate of their own worthlessness – if not overtly, then in forms of behaviour that express 'worthlessness', violence or extreme passivity or the abuse of the body by alcohol and other drugs. And there are still sections of black communities willing to accept white definition into their own imagining of their humanity.

All the signs of racism identified in the WCC document take for granted this same fundamental privation, the taking away of a right to determine the conditions and possibilities for a specific variety of human living, of the freedom to define oneself, as person or as community, of the freedom to contribute as one wishes and needs to the *public* life, the shared conflict and conversation that shapes the wider community of a state. Ann Dummett comments on the 'Black Power' phenomenon of the late 1960s and 1970s that it makes one central statement: 'I shall tell you what I am. Black Power can mean a hundred different things, but it is always supported by this basic significance.'[5] This statement has commonly been interpreted as implying an unrealistic and destructive separatism: white critics are quick to say that the aspiration to say 'what I am' independently of other communities and persons is a sign of infantile disorder, neurosis, and to talk of 'black racism'. But this is a giveaway. White domination has been built on the assumption that whites may say what they are independently of the needs and *reality* of other groups, who are built into white self-definition. The refusal of that definition is not a bid for an unreal autonomy – though it may need and use violently separatist rhetoric, and some, black as well as white, may be deceived by that rhetoric – but a necessary move in challenging one human group's existing practice of 'saying what they are' in just the infantile and disordered way they are so eager to condemn. And if 'black racism' unquestionably exists, as a matter of structural oppression or discrimination exercised between black groupings, it is *not* to be confused with 'black consciousness' or 'Black Power' movements in their hostility to white culture.

If a dominant culture (linguistic, ethnic, sexual) does in fact work by assuming the right of definition, it is hardly surprising if the reaction is, 'We don't need you to tell us what we are'. Certain kinds of separatism are necessary to highlight the reality of a difference that has been over-ridden by the powerful conscripting the powerless into their story. From being a domesticated curiosity, whose strangeness or otherness is defused by absorption, functionalized by the dominant group, the disadvantaged group must become *real* strangers, with a life manifestly *not* like that of their former masters. They must acquire or re-acquire a kind of shared secret, a distinct human 'dialect' bound up with a distinct group life. Oppressed groups have often done this even in the midst of their very oppression – secret languages, covert religious rituals, a subterranean scheme of authority relations within the group. Liberation has something to do with the presenting and owning in public of this reality of shared life behind and beyond the roles defined by the power-holders; and this means an accentuation, not an erosion, of difference – which is why racial justice and racial equality do not begin with 'treating everyone alike'.

The liberal assumption that 'treating everyone alike' is the answer rests on a view of human nature which is deeply problematic. It assumes that there is a basic 'inner' humanity, beyond flesh and skin pigmentation and history and conflict, which is the same for all people. But human existence is precisely life that is lived in speech and relation, and so in history: what we share as humans is not a human 'essence' outside history, but a common involvement in the limits and relativities of history. The only humanity we have is one that is bound up in difference, in the encounter of physical and linguistic strangers. Of course there is a sense in which we are all *biologically* the same; but the whole point is that properly human life is not confined to biology, to the level of 'species being', as it has been called. It is unavoidably 'cultural', making and remaking its context, and so unavoidably diverse. When great stress is laid upon our oneness 'under the skin', there is always the risk of rendering that as 'this stranger is really the same as *me*' – which subtly reinforces the dominant group's assumption of the right to define. The norm is where I or we stand. This risk is one reason for looking very hard at the goal of 'treating everyone alike'. It represents the worthy and correct commitment to avoid discrimination that overtly disadvantages or distances the stranger; but it can fail to see the prior need to allow them to *be* strangers.

But the liberal's anxieties have some point. Careless talk about proper distances, allowing the independence of another's story and perspective, and so on can be costly, for at least two reasons. The 'licensing' of difference, even the practices of positive discrimination, on the part of a dominant group will fail to move things forward if it is simply a concession that does not alter the basic realities of power in the 'public spaces' shared by dominant and subordinate groups. Or, in plain English, the dominant group's own possibilities have to be affected by this process if there is to be real change. Otherwise, you have the situation classically exemplified in the black 'homelands' of Southern Africa: grants by the dominant group to sustain a fictionally distinct economy, with special opportunities for aspiring black entrepreneurs in their 'own' setting – and a regressive interest in picturesque tribal tradition for its own sake. Nothing substantial has changed.[6] This leads on to the second point. It is actually impossible in any imaginable future world that human groupings should be able to pursue their goals in total mutual independence: 'separate development', by whatever name, is a fantasy in a world of interlocking economy (and ecological crisis). The challenge then is how human beings unashamed of their difference and strangeness are to work with the constraints of this environment – how are they (to use a fashionable term) to discover a common 'human project'? The liberal rightly sees that a world of encapsulated group identities pursuing self-defined goals is a ludicrous and dangerous idea, and insists on some kind of assumption that the human race can acknowledge a shared context and a shared goal – and that at once implies, if it is taken seriously, an effort towards shared 'power' in the world; which in turn involves certain groups facing the potential diminution of the power they actually have.

These remarks are not original or profound: they reflect what has been variously acknowledged by the Brandt Report and explored imaginatively by writers like Schumacher and Capra. However much these explorations may be Utopian dreams, I think it is important that any discussion of racism should carry the recognition that the problem of power and its sharing is a global one. The issue of racism and the combating of racism in this country and its churches, the problems (so wearyingly routine sometimes to those practically involved, black and white) of educational justice, serious attention to even the most elusive forms of disadvantage, vigilance about the methods and assumptions of law enforcement – all this is part of what even the least Utopian must see as the facing of a world-wide crisis about the distribution of power. That it *is* a crisis should be clear enough once we start thinking about the chaotic economies of poorer nations, at the mercy of markets elsewhere, the alarming pressures of drought and famine in Africa, in countries without (or denied) the resources to deal with them, and the way in which East–West conflicts poison and intensify the wars of the Third World (not least through the atrocity of the arms trade). If South Africa dramatizes in its internal life the racial conflict elsewhere, its external relations with Mozambique equally sharply crystallize the far wider problem of First World–Third World relations in all these aspects. Defining racism ought to introduce us to the larger task of defining this human crisis overall.

2. Power and the Gospel

The Christian response to these issues can appear banal. The issue of racism is not much illuminated by the bald statement that all human beings are equally in the image of God and so deserving of 'equal treat-ment'. The belief in equality before God coexisted happily for centuries with all kinds of practical injustice (slavery, the oppression of women, and so on). It is probably right to see *theories* of racial inequality as a product of the post-Renaissance period, as new relations with 'subject peoples' required rationalization – a rationalization commonly provided in the new language of 'primitive' and 'civilized' peoples, further compounded by theories of physiognomically conditioned dif-ferences in levels of intelligence, evolving in the heyday of scientific expansionist confidence in the nineteenth century. The problem, in other words, is not directly with the Christian view of human nature. It is how to prevent that view turning into an impotent abstraction in the face of the development of new power relations and the obstinacy of old ones. And this will involve an attempt to theologize in a way that does not seek to avoid the particularities of human history and yet can act as a point of judgement and hope within that history.

Christianity should have no quarrel – quite the contrary – with what has been said about the unavoidably cultural character of human beings. The Christian faith is, after all, a network of communal rela-tions before it is a theology, and it claims insight into the truth of the universe only by way of engagement in a specific ethnic history (that of the Jewish people) and in the new 'nation' or 'race' of those who come to be in Christ. It is, as is so often pointed out, concrete and narrative in its account of itself and its origins. It is not that we *begin* with a belief in human equality and then try to work it out (or not, as the case may be), but that the inner logic of life shared with others in relation to Jesus of Nazareth pushes the community outwards to 'the ends of the earth' – with all the implications that has for a vision of the common goal or project of the human world as such. *All* may now be invited to share the hope of and the work for the Kingdom; all may find their humanity defined afresh in this project. All therefore can be delivered from the claims to finality of the definitions given them by their social and political context – as Paul suggests in 1 Corinthians 1.26. Those without tangible status are given standing by God, who thereby demonstrates *his* freedom from the social order and the relations it takes for granted. It may be too that those with *anomalous* status in society, those whose actual influence cannot be recognized fully in the terms of the dominant pattern (the freed slave, the independent business woman), are drawn in to such a group.[7] In any case, the point

218

is that the society of the Church in its origins creates considerable tension with the society around because it will not take for granted (even if it will not often challenge head-on) the finality and authority of the socially prevailing accounts of status and power.

The more Christianity ceases to be a distinctive communal life to which adult persons choose to commit themselves, the more this tension is eroded. The more 'natural' it is to be a Christian, the more Christianity will be assimilated to what seems 'natural' in society – a process already visible within the New Testament itself, in the fairly well-established churches to which the letters to Timothy and Titus belong. There is little point in longing romantically for the rediscovery of a purely 'sect-like' Christianity, because that would be to ignore the historical inevitability of second-generation problems, the transmission of belief through upbringing rather than preaching, and so on. But we can ask at least what this definition of human beings in relation to the Kingdom actually means, what it is that gives the Church *some* continuing point of reference beyond what either it or the society around it takes unreflectively for granted. In what is left of this essay, I want to point to two aspects of Christian language that may represent something of this abiding point of reference, and may shed some light on the problems we have been looking at in the first part.

(a) For Paul, the Church as 'body' is a system of *interdependence*: no one part can be reduced to a function of another (defined in terms of another) and no part can claim to subsist in its own right (1 Corinthians 12). And this is not simply a static observation on the underlying structure of the community, but acts as a principle of judgement and direction in its life. In 1 Corinthians, Paul is chiefly concerned with relativizing the claims of the charismatics; but earlier, in 1 Corinthians 10, as in Romans 14, he deploys it also against those who assume the right to set standards of behaviour in disputed matters. There are those who are persuaded (rightly, Paul thinks) that food regulations are of no significance; but such people may see their 'right' to eat anything as a kind of status-conferral, carrying with it the power to prescribe to others the abandonment of their traditions. This is as bad as the tyranny of (presumably Jewish-Christian) conservatives, and is a fertile seed-bed for resentment and division. Paul sharply reminds the anti-traditionalists that Christ died for the Jewish-Christian conservative too (Romans 14.15), and directs all to the central principle of 'building up' (Romans 14.19, 1 Corinthians 10.23). Action in the Church must be regulated not by abstract rule but by the goal of reinforcing and affirming the other believer in such a way that the community overall is affirmed and strengthened and moved on towards the Kingdom. In other words, my act must be a *gift* for the deepening and strengthening of another's faith (and I must be open to receive such a gift likewise); it cannot ever be a manifestation of my status or 'liberty' or 'maturity' as a thing in itself. Paul makes it generally clear in word and practice that one's action can at times be a gift in the form of a challenge (Galatians 2.11 ff.): because it is a particular *kind* of community that is being built up, there are divergences that cannot be tolerated – such as the exclusive and rigorist policy of some of the very Jewish Christians Paul elsewhere defends. Compromise here is *collusion* with what is actually destructive of the other person and of the whole group's integrity.

On the one hand, then, it is foolish and destructive to sneer at the forms of devotion others cling to, however 'weakly' or irrationally. If you want this to change, you must not assume *you* have the right to decide for change, but should ask, How can I come to be *trusted* by the other in such a way that we can both be changed? On the other hand, it is equally foolish and destructive to say, I will tolerate this or that assertion of right and status, whatever the cost to those victimized and bruised by it. That leaves no real opening for change – repentance – at all. Both perspectives take it wholly for granted that change, constant conversion, is central for the Christian community, and that no one group has the right to define unilaterally for others what this is going to mean. There is no alternative to the work of mutual trust – which already implies a certain relinquishing of power. The hope is for a shared and reciprocal *empowering* for growth towards the Kingdom.

This is something like the insight of the desert father who said, 'Our life and our death is with our neighbour'.[8] It is not without each other that we move towards the Kingdom; so that Christian history ought to be the story of continuing and demanding engagement with strangers, abandoning the right to decide who they are. We shall none of us know who we are without each other – which may mean we shan't know who we are until Judgement Day. In the words of the spiritual movingly quoted by Sandra Wilson at the end of a lecture on 'A Black Theology of Liberation', 'Oh nobody knows who I am / Till the judgement morning'.[9] And this should also be related to the great wound and humiliation in Paul's own experience, the growing rift between the Church and the Jews. In Romans 11, he turns on the Gentile Christians with passion: they think Israel has been rejected to make room for them, but in fact their welcome into God's people is only an episode in the greater history of God's reclaiming of all who have been his own. There will be no Gentile salvation without the ultimate reconciliation with the Jews: 'not without each other', once again. The Church's alienation from the Jews is precisely the kind of separation that is necessary for a final unity that is more than trivial. And in the perspective of our own century, these are notions with a sobering immediacy. The Christian must say, 'not without the Jewish victims of the death-camps' – not knowing what imaginable future would find us a common language with them. But it is more important to look unknowingly to such a future than to devise hasty Christian theologies of (definitions of?) the Jewish experience in this century, and to recognize that the Church remains incomplete and in some ways deprived of a fully truthful language for God so long as this wound is open.

That is a matter needing constantly more thought and prayer; but it is not wholly immaterial to what we should say about racism, power, and faith. We have seen a picture of the Church in its beginnings as a community challenging both externally and internally the idea of persons being 'told who they are' by the possessors of a certain kind of status. We are all to find who we are in the light of God in Jesus, and that finding is the process of living in a community struggling to discover means of mutual empowering and affirming, in the conviction that we shall not live or flourish if we consider any person or group dispensable, or merely functional for our own self-definition. And behind the life of such a community stands the event – and the *power* – by which it lives. To understand the Church, we must look at what generates it.

(b) Christian Scripture (which includes Jewish Scripture and is conditioned by it) answers the question of what God it is that Christians worship by relating the stories of communities: this is what a human group that believes itself to be brought into being by God looks like: from this group, you may learn what 'God' means, in its behaviour, its hymns and myths, laws and chronicles, in its social conflicts and resolutions. Above all, you may learn what 'God' means in the ministry and execution of Jesus, and in the re-creation of a faithful community in his name at Easter; you may learn God in this breakage and healing in the story of the community of God's people, 'the tribes of Yahweh',[10] as it becomes the beginning of a community for all nations.

The point is that the pattern of the Christian story shows a God who lets himself be spoken of – defined – in terms of the relation between him and creatures, in terms of the human history he sets in motion and shapes. He chooses to be the God of Israel and of Jesus Christ, chooses not to exist without his creation: he does not merely establish an order other than himself, but engages with it in such a way that we do not and cannot speak of him only as a remote cause, but must 'define' him in and through the lives that struggle to respond to his pressure and presence. Humanity is defined by him; but, for us, God is defined by humanity also – never completely or adequately, because the relation is always a restless and growing one. Yet the most basic point of reference for the Christian believer, which justifies and establishes this possibility and regulates what *kind* of humanity it is that 'carries' the definition of God, is the crucified and glorified human identity of Jesus. Whatever else is to be said, whatever further shifts and developments our language about God undergoes, this at least remains: God is not to be spoken of without humanity, but that humanity is centred not upon a generalized definition of the human, but on Jesus Christ.

In other words, the relations that exist *within* the Church, of mutual gift and reciprocal definition, are founded upon the fact that the Christian God reveals himself, becomes utterable, in a mortal human history. God, so to speak, risks himself in the form of vulnerable humanity – because a particular human life, Jesus, is given to him freely to be a sign and a word. The pattern of mutual definition, the *admirabile commercium* of classical theology, is the ground of the Church's speech and action, so that within its life it seeks to renounce just that kind of unilateral and invulnerable power that God renounces in the history he shares with us as the God of Israel and as Christ. God does not impose his definition and meaning by clear and absolute words of relevation, but perfects his speech to us in and through the contingencies of Israel's and Jesus's history. While in retrospect we may see a logic, even a necessity, in the whole story, it is at each *particular* point a matter of human liberty and risk.

These theological refinements may seem to be a long way from our starting-point; but they may provide a firm basis for a theological critique of racism to the extent that they spell out the nature of Christianity's attitude to power. We are not talking about a repudiation of the whole notion of power, as a hasty reading of the tradition might suggest, but about how the creative and transfiguring power of God actually is seen in our world. God's power 'tells us who we are' only in the risk and reciprocity of God's life with us in Christ, as God displays his identity in the terms of human freedom and human vulnerability. That is the power by which the whole world is given newness of life, humanity itself is given new definition. And because it is *that* kind of power, refusing to functionalize and enslave what it works with, the process of preaching a transfiguring gospel must take place in a community that resists the idea that one human group can ever have licence to define another in terms of its own needs or goals or fantasies. All must be free to find that ultimate self-definition in the encounter with a God who does not use us as tools for his gratification but shares a world of risk and contingency with us to bring us to our fullest liberty in relation with him and each other.

We have seen that this cannot be without conflict and rupture, or without cost to those who claim the power of definition without noticing that this is what they are doing (and yes; it must be said again that the very enterprise of writing as a white academic about racism runs this risk). The Church has been slow to see how and where it is itself trapped in 'telling people who they are'; it is gradually getting used at least to the *idea* that its institution and decision-makers must learn a new tentativeness in listening to those they have assumed they understood – those they have assumed were 'contained' in the categories they work with. But the concrete redefinition of power – as enabling the stranger to be heard, deciding that the stranger has a gift and a challenge that can change you – limps very slowly, in the Church's listening to the voice of women and homosexuals as much as blacks. We are still desperately ill equipped to do what, with daily increasing urgency, presses to be done: to offer our world an effective, a converting, judgement upon a whole culture of exploitative control – the human crisis mentioned earlier in this paper. And we are ill equipped partly because we have so imperfectly heard this judgement as it is passed upon *us* as a Church. What a Church genuinely converted in this respect *can* offer, in judgement and in promise, to the world is something we can, thank God, glimpse in the effect of the lives of those who, like Trevor Huddleston, have responded with integrity to what the Christian gospel has to say about true and false power, who have so let God, and God alone, 'tell them who they are' in Christ that they are free to free others for that encounter. Such lives show us something of what it might be to grow *together* in discovery and definition 'Till the Judgement morning'.

Notes

1. For a particularly savage attack, see A. Sivanandan, 'RAT [Racism Aware-ness Training] and the Degradation of Black Struggle', *Race and Class* 26:4 (1985), 1–33. On some of the cultural difficulties involved in 'selling' white middle-class techniques of group work to the black community, David Moore has some barbed remarks in 'Liberty to the Captives', *Voices from the Urban Wilderness*, ed. P. Barnett (Bristol, 1984), 36.

2. *Racism in Theology: Theology against Racism. Report of a Consultation* (Geneva, 1975), 3–4. For further discussion of the definition of racism, see the entry on the word in F. Ellis Cashmore (ed.), *A Dictionary of Race and Ethnic Relations* (London, 1984), 225–9.

3. Ann Dummett, *A Portrait of English Racism* (London, 1973), 2nd edn. (CARAF Publications, 1984), 150. On the interrelation of race and class dominance, see Philip Mason, *Patterns of Dominance* (Oxford, 1970).

4. Dummett, op cit. 55–8. A recent work which pinpoints the 'intentional' factors in various forms of disadvantage – i.e. the processes of creating roles for the disadvantaged, over and above the economic elements involved in these structures – is Arthur Brittan and Mary Maynard, *Sexism, Racism and Oppression* (Oxford, 1984); see esp. 214–17.

5. Dummett, op. cit. 57. A helpful guide to the evolution of black conscious-ness movements is offered by Chris Mullard, *Race, Power and Resistance* (London, 1985).

6. See David Sheppard, *Built as a City: God and the Urban World Today*, 2nd edn. (London, 1985), 188, on the dangers of replicating white patterns of inequality within the black communities.

7. See, for discussion of these and other possibilities, J. H. Elliott, *A Home for the Homeless* (Philadelphia and London, 1981), and Wayne Meeks, *The First Urban Christians* (New Haven and London, 1983).

8. Attributed to St Antony the Great; B. Ward (trans.), *The Sayings of the Desert Fathers* (London, 1975), 2.

9. *Anglicans and Racism: The Balsall Heath Consultation, 1986* (Board for Social Responsibility, 1986), 15.

10. The title of Norman Gottwald's important study of the meaning of God for ancient Israel in terms of the pattern of their social life (London, 1979).

Index

Index